Behind the Playground Walls
SEXUAL ABUSE IN PRESCHOOLS

Behind the Playground Walls

SEXUAL ABUSE
IN PRESCHOOLS

Jill Waterman, PhD
Robert J. Kelly, PhD
Mary Kay Oliveri, MSW
Jane McCord, PhD

THE GUILFORD PRESS
New York ■ *London*

Printed in the United States of America

This book is printed on acid-free paper.

Last digit is print number: 9 8 7 6 5 4 3 2 1

Library of Congress Cataloging-in-Publication Data

Behind the playground walls: sexual abuse in preschools / Jill
   Waterman . . . [et al.].
       p. cm.
   Includes bibliographical references and index.
   ISBN 0-89862-523-8
   1. Sexually abused children. 2. Sexually abused children—Family
relationships. 3. Preschool children. I. Waterman, Jill, 1945–
   [DNLM: 1. Child Abuse, Sexual. 2. Child, Preschool.   WA 320
B419]
RJ506.C48B44   1993
616.85'83—dc20
DNLM/DLC
for Library of Congress   91-35420
                                                                  CIP

This book is dedicated to the children, families, and therapists struggling with the healing process from their trauma, and in memory of Dr. Sam Basta.

To my parents, Tod and Ada, who taught me honesty and love, and to my children, Justin, Aaron and Ambryn, in hopes that they will experience a better, safer world.

—J.W.

To my parents, Richard and Anne Kelly, for giving me the gifts of love, humor, integrity and self-esteem, and to the children in this study, for whom I wish the same.

—R.J.K.

To my husband, family and friends who provided invaluable love and support throughout this project.

—M.K.O.

To my parents, Pat and Gladys, and my son, Justin, for their support and encouragement throughout this process.

—J.M.

CONTRIBUTORS

Sharon Ben-Meir, PhD, private practice, Los Angeles, California

Martha Cockriel, MSW, Pathways, Manhattan Beach, California

Michele Dugan, PhD, Pathways, Manhattan Beach, California

David Finkelhor, PhD, codirector of the Family Research Laboratory, University of New Hampshire, Durham, New Hampshire

Lauren Shapiro Gonzalez, JD, MA, graduate student in Clinical Psychology PhD program, Department of Psychology, University of California, Los Angeles

Robert Lusk, PhD, Assistant Professor, Department of Psychology, Illinois Wesleyan University, Bloomington, Illinois

Robert J. Kelly, PhD, private practice, Beverly Hills, California; Assistant Clinical Professor, Department of Psychology, University of California, Los Angeles

Kathleen Kendall-Tackett, PhD, Post-Doctoral Fellow, Family Research Laboratory, University of New Hampshire, Durham, New Hampshire

Jane McCord, PhD, Assistant Clinical Professor, Division of Child and Adolescent Psychiatry, Department of Psychiatry, Harbor–UCLA Medical Center, Torrance, California

Mary Kay Oliveri, MSW, Assistant Clinical Professor and Director of Community Response Programs, Division of Child and Adolescent Psychiatry, Department of Psychiatry, Harbor–UCLA Medical Center, Torrance, California

Roland C. Summit, MD, Head Physician, Community Consultation Service, Associate Clinical Professor, Department of Psychiatry, Harbor–UCLA Medical Center, Torrance, California

Jill Waterman, PhD, Adjunct Professor, Department of Psychology, University of California, Los Angeles

PREFACE

The study of sexual and ritualistic abuse reports in preschool–daycare settings on which this book is based was conducted at a time of high visibility, rampant emotion, and significant controversy about the existence of sexual abuse in preschools. In the most well-known case, involving the McMartin Preschool in Manhattan Beach, California, two juries from successive trials became hopelessly deadlocked and failed to agree on a verdict after 7 years of investigation and trial. At the press conference following the first trial, 9 of the 11 jurors who agreed to be interviewed indicated that they believed the children had been molested, but they felt that the evidence presented did not enable them to state beyond a reasonable doubt who had perpetrated the abuse.[1] In contrast to the children from Manhattan Beach, the children from the Reno, Nevada, sample were never subjected to legal proceedings or community controversies because the perpetrator confessed.

In most child abuse research, children are assumed to have been abused if they credibly report being abused. Finkelhor, Williams, and Burns (1988), examining the only national sample of sexual abuse in preschools and day care, utilized their own notion of substantiation: "If at least one of the local investigating agencies had decided that abuse had occurred and that it had happened while the child was at a day-care facility or under its care, then we considered the case substantiated" (p. 13). In 54% of the substantiated cases they studied, an arrest was made; among those arrested, only 56% ever even went to trial, so that only 30% of the substantiated cases even went forward to trial.

In the few published academic studies of ritualistic abuse (Kelley, 1989; Faller, 1988), children were included based on reports of ritualistic abuse made to a law enforcement or child protection agency; in some cases, charges were never proven in or even taken to criminal court (where the need to prove allegations beyond a reasonable doubt makes child sex crimes very hard to prosecute successfully, especially because many cases do not involve penetration). The cases in Manhattan Beach were adjudicated through the appropriate Police and Social Service Departments. There have been convictions in criminal court of ritualistic sexual abuse of children (e.g., Hollingsworth, 1986), and based on our clinical experience, we believe ritualistic sexual abuse does occur.

Because of the emphasis that has been placed on the legal questions, we have chosen to use the acronym "RSA" throughout the book to refer to reported ritualistic sexual abuse in Manhattan Beach cases, acknowledging that the allegations were never proven beyond a reasonable doubt in criminal court. In the Reno case, the need to prove the case in criminal court was averted by the perpetrator's confession. Because no allegations of ritualistic or terrorizing abuse were made in this case, we use the acronym "SA" to refer to sexual abuse occurring in the Reno sample.

The aim of our study is not to utilize our data to prove whether or not the children in the Manhattan Beach group (and particularly those children from the McMartin Preschool) were definitely abused. We have been most concerned with documenting the particular problems that these children have encountered and learning more about what promotes healing. These important issues sometimes seem to have been lost or overlooked because so much attention has been focused on the legal aspects. Our hope is that our information about the psychological and emotional aspects of these cases will help families who face such painful and traumatizing situations, as well as the professionals who seek to help them overcome the trauma.

This book is the product of 6 years of collaboration by four clinician/researchers and our assistants and consultants. During these years we have each experienced a myriad of emotions: anger that child abuse exists; disgust at the accounts of abuse disclosed by the children; helplessness in not being able to take away the children's pain; frustration with bureaucracy; worry that the budget would be overspent; exhaustion from trying to finish the next drafts of our respective chapters while juggling our regular jobs and our personal lives; bafflement upon seeing esoteric bugs in our computer programs; hypervigilance about the possibility that our data would be subpoenaed; fear that our involvement would be scrutinized and misrepresented, as have the actions of others associated with these cases; inspiration from the courage and openness of the children and parents; sadness at the thought of childhood innocence denied; and joy in the making of new friends and colleagues.

This project could not have proceeded without the generous and dedicated help of many people. First and foremost, the cooperation and assistance of the psychotherapists and the families, both in southern California and in Reno, Nevada, provided the backbone of the study. So many worked so hard and gave so generously to share both their time and their painful experiences with us, in order to help other children and families confronted with reported ritualistic and nonritualistic sexual abuse in preschool or day care settings. Our feelings of appreciation to Dr. Sam Basta are mingled with sadness; Sam was responsible for facilitating the inclusion of the Reno families, and with great dedication, he collected data as he was dying of cancer. Kathy Milbeck was also instrumental in serving as a liaison in Reno, and for being an incredible source of support to both Sam and the rest of us during Sam's illness.

We also want to thank several community agencies in both southern California and Reno for absolutely vital assistance in helping us reach potential families for the study. In southern California, Children's Institute International, South Bay Center for Counseling, and Pathways sent out letters about the study to families whose children had received evaluations; in Reno, the Reno Police Department fulfilled a similar essential role. In the recruitment of demographically matched control children who were preschool graduates, we appreciated the efforts of the staffs of Christian Nursery School (especially Corinne Pollard), and Neighborhood Nursery School (especially Mary Klimetz). The Richstone Center, the Manhattan Beach Community Church, and American Martyrs also provided emotional encouragement and places for important meetings at various stages of the project.

Dr. David Finkelhor has been a brilliant and supportive primary research consultant throughout this study. His feedback and his friendship were invaluable and are deeply appreciated. Kee MacFarlane's wisdom, courage, and stamina have been inspirational. This project could not have been undertaken without her originally daring to hear what the children had to say.

Another group of dedicated people who put in time and effort far beyond what was required was the group of psychological testers. These graduate students at UCLA—Robert Lusk, Sharon Ben-Meir, Ginger MacDonald, and Drew Erhardt—had intensive contact with the children and families, and were in turn profoundly affected by the pain and distress experienced by both children and parents in the aftermath of abuse disclosure. Coming to the project later but also intensely involved were Lauren Shapiro Gonzalez and Marcia Rorty, who joined the others in conducting many emotional parent interviews in the follow-up phase of the study.

This study was funded under Grant No. 90-CA-1179 by the National Center on Child Abuse and Neglect (NCCAN). We have deleted some of the statistical details in this book to increase readability, but researchers who are interested in the more in-depth statistical analyses or who want to review the instruments used in our study can request copies of our final report from the NCCAN Clearinghouse, 8201 Greensboro Drive, Suite 600, McLean, VA 22102. We wish to thank our project officers from NCCAN, Cynthia Darling and Jan Kirby-Gell, for their warm support over the years. Barbara Cooke, Yenlin Schweitzer, and Sherry Miranda were stalwarts in our administrative offices. At UCLA, Angelia Dickinson, Marla Law, and Annamarie Maricle provided needed secretarial assistance and computer expertise, while Nanette Aldape gave ongoing clerical assistance at Harbor–UCLA Medical Center, and Marciana Poland provided administrative assistance through the Research and Education Institute. Statistical consultation was provided by Dr. Don Guthrie and Kathy Perham, and Brian Zupan ran innumerable analyses on our huge data set in helping us sort out findings. Additional thanks go to Dr. Steve Hinshaw for his feedback on our Executive Summary, and to Bob Burdick for his help in preparing and formatting the final manuscript.

We complete this project with a feeling of accomplishment and fulfillment. Our sadness at the sight of severe negative emotional effects in many of the children is lifted somewhat by the hopeful finding that most children do heal. We hope that the data and ideas we present will in some way decrease the pain and hasten the healing of future children and families who are forced to endure the horrors involved in child sexual abuse.

Jill Waterman
Robert J. Kelly
Mary Kay Oliveri
Jane McCord

NOTE

1. Los Angeles Times, January 19, 1990, pp. A1 and A22.

REFERENCES

Faller, K.C. (1988). The spectrum of sexual abuse in daycare: An exploratory study. *Journal of Family Violence, 3,* 283–298.

Finkelhor, D., Williams, L., & Burns, N. (1988). *Nursery crimes: Sexual abuse in daycare.* Newbury Park, CA: Sage.

Hollingsworth, J. (1986). *Unspeakable Acts.* New York: Congdon and Weed.

Kelley, S. J. (1990). Parental stress response to sexual abuse and ritualistic abuse of children in day-care centers. *Nursing Research, 39,* 25–29.

CONTENTS

Scope of the Problem of Ritualistic and Nonritualistic Sexual Abuse in Preschools

CHRONOLOGY OF EVENTS
IN THE TWO COMMUNITIES

Reno, Nevada

1983: Spring—A student at the Papoose Palace preschool and kindergarten disclosed sexual abuse. The perpetrator confessed within weeks and was sentenced to four life terms in prison within 2 months.

Manhattan Beach, California

1983: Late summer—a student at the McMartin Preschool disclosed sexual abuse to his mother, who reported it to the local police department.

Fall—The alleged perpetrator at the McMartin Preschool was arrested and subsequently released pending further investigation, which continued until the following spring.

1984: January—The McMartin Preschool closed.

February—A local TV station broke the news about the investigation of McMartin Preschool.

March—Grand jury hearings began and subsequently determined that the evidence was sufficient for proceeding with criminal prosecution.

Summer—Allegations of sexual abuse against teachers at a second school, the Manhattan Ranch Preschool, were reported. The preliminary hearing against seven McMartin teachers began.

1985: Spring—Allegations against several other preschools were investigated but were not filed on. A staff member of the Manhattan Ranch Preschool was brought to trial. The trial lasted 2 months and ended in a hung jury.

1986: January—The McMartin preliminary hearing ended. Two of the original defendants were ultimately bound over for trial.

1987: July—The trial for the McMartin defendants began.

1990: January—The end of the McMartin trial ended. The jury acquitted the defendants on 52 counts and deadlocked on 13 other counts.

May—One of the defendants was bound over for a retrial on eight of the deadlocked counts. This also ended in a hung jury.

CHAPTER 1

A TALE OF TWO COMMUNITIES

Jane McCord

THIS BOOK is based on the stories of two communities where children reported sexual abuse in preschools. The communities are different, the people were dissimilar in many ways, and even the nature of the abuse was different; nevertheless, these communities share the common tragedy of the alleged sexual abuse of many of their children in preschools. This book tells the story of both the tragedy and the triumph of these communities, and of their continuing struggle to heal and to help others who share their pain.

MANHATTAN BEACH, CALIFORNIA

Manhattan Beach, California, is a scenic oceanfront community located on the south side of the Santa Monica Bay in Los Angeles County. Its wide, sandy beaches and picturesque setting make it a popular place to live for affluent Angeleños. One of the established institutions in this town was the McMartin Preschool, which was founded by Virginia McMartin in the mid-1950s. The school was considered one the best in the town, and for many years it had had a waiting list of those who wanted their children to attend. In recent years, Mrs. McMartin's daughter, Peggy Buckey, had become the director of the school. Also employed at the school was Mrs. Buckey's son, 25-year-old Raymond Buckey.

In the summer of 1983, a mother of a 2-year-old boy complained to the Manhattan Beach Police Department that her son had told of being molested by a teacher at the McMartin Preschool. In order to follow up on this, the police department sent a letter to the parents of the children attending the preschool, explaining the situation and requesting that parents question the students about possible abuses at the school, including oral sex and other sex acts. Although the letter requested that the contents be kept confidential, word of mouth spread quickly. An upset parent called Peggy Buckey to ask what was going on; subsequently, the school and homes of the accused were searched after they had been informed of an investigation. Raymond Buckey was arrested, but was soon released because there was as yet no substantial evidence, and the investigation continued.

The reactions of the parents whose children were attending the preschool were mixed. Those families whose children talked of abuse at the preschool found the allegations to be all too real. Those whose children denied that anything had happened displayed a variety of reactions. Certainly no one wanted to think that his or her child had been abused. Some eventually concluded from the stories of their friends' children that there had been abuse at the school, and they began to withdraw their own children from the school. Others came to the defense of the proprietors and kept their children enrolled in the preschool, which remained open several more months.

Although the investigation was being carried out by the local police force, any prosecution would be handled by the Los Angeles County District Attorney's Office. Jean Matusinka, a deputy district attorney and head of the child abuse unit, handled the early phase of the investigation. An experienced prosecutor in child sexual abuse cases, she knew that interviewing small children and preparing a case based their testimony was an extremely difficult task. Ms. Matusinka had met professionals across the country who were involved in forensic child abuse cases. Among those professionals was Kee MacFarlane, a social worker who headed a child sexual abuse diagnostic program at Children's Institute International, a community-based agency that specialized in the assessment and treatment of abused children. For some time, Ms. MacFarlane had been involved with other mental health professionals who were concerned about the welfare of abused children in the criminal justice system. Children were often subjected to multiple interviews with different professionals, as well as having to testify under extremely stressful conditions. She had been involved in a pilot project looking at the possibility of videotaping children's initial interviews, in the hopes that the videotapes could be used instead of subjecting the children to many subsequent interviews, which tended to traumatize them further.

When Jean Matusinka became involved in the Manhattan Beach investigation, she contacted Kee MacFarlane about the possibility of videotaping interviews with children who were thought to have been victimized at the preschool. Ms. Matusinka thought that there would only be a few children, and Ms. MacFarlane agreed to help out. The number of potential victims mushroomed, however; within the next several months, nearly 400 children were interviewed at Children's Institute International.

As the numbers of possible victims began to grow during the fall, community fear began to grow likewise. Parents became impatient with how long the investigation was taking, and it was becoming evident that the media would not hold off on reporting the story much longer. Stories of multiple perpetrators, as well as bizarre tales of children being transported off campus and of ritualistic abuse taking place at local business establishments, other preschools, and various homes, had been reported. As the investigation of these reports was conducted, a polarization of the community between the "believers" and those who thought the investigation was turning into a "witch hunt" began to develop. It was becoming increasingly clear that some type of help was needed in the community to deal with escalating emotions.

Not far from Manhattan Beach is a large county medical center, Harbor–UCLA Medical Center. It was here that Roland Summit, MD, a psychiatrist, acted as a community liaison between the Los Angeles County Department of Mental Health and the communities in his area. One of Dr. Summit's primary involvements was (and is) in the area of child abuse, and he has been a nationally known figure in the area for years. Dr. Summit provided consultation to child abuse agencies in the community, and it was through one such agency to which McMartin children had been referred that he first heard of the Manhattan Beach case. As the local "child abuse expert" in the area, Dr. Summit was soon called upon by parents and professionals who requested help in coping with what was developing in their community, and he was frequently employed for consultation.

Another service frequently used in the community was counseling for the children. After the children were interviewed at Children's Institute International, the families were referred to mental health professionals and child abuse agencies in the area for follow-up. Although the psychotherapists who treated these children were experienced in the area of child sexual abuse, few had much knowledge about or experience with ritualistic abuse or with multiple-perpetrator, multiple-victim cases. These children did not fall into the familiar categories of child abuse cases, and new ways of intervening in this case had to be developed. In this situation, each family was part of a larger and more intricate case. According to the stories that these children told, they had experienced victimization collectively rather than individually. Although such circumstances warranted group treatment by those who had experienced shared trauma, this was not made available to the children initially, nor was it ever made available for children who were to testify. The forensic need to avoid "contaminating" witnesses by exposing them to the stories of other victims led to a clash with the clinical needs of the children and their families. Thus, most children initially received only individual treatment.

The parents of these children, however, began to come together for mutual support soon after they became aware of the alleged abuse. In December 1983, a parent support group began to meet at one of the local child abuse agencies, which was treating some of the children from the McMartin Preschool. This group continued to meet on a weekly basis for the next year. It was through this group that many of the parents who were to become involved in various causes related to child abuse met.

By the beginning of 1984, the potential number of child victims continued to grow, as did the allegations of atrocities that had been perpetrated. During the early phase of the investigation, there was a concerted effort by those involved in the case to keep rumors contained and to avoid public exposure of the investigation. The McMartin Preschool officially closed in January 1984, and the story of the case was first made public on a local television station in February 1984.

Given the immensity of the case, the resources of the community became strained, and professionals in the area began to come together to respond to a community in crisis. The Manhattan Beach City Council set aside $66,000 for a child abuse education and prevention program. Subsequently, a coordinator was hired to administer the program. Dr. Summit, who was increasingly in demand as a consultant on child abuse issues, was released by the Los Angeles Country Department of Mental Health to provide consultation to the Manhattan Beach Schools for one-third of his time. Noreen Noel, a psychiatric nurse who was also an employee of the county department of mental health at Harbor–UCLA Medical Center, was stationed full-time in Manhattan Beach to coordinate mental health information and referrals.

As the case continued to grow, and allegations of abuse at other preschools began to emerge, the resources of the Manhattan Beach Police Department also became overburdened. The Los Angeles County Sheriff's Task Force on Child Abuse was called in by the district attorney's office to assist in the investigation. During the second half of the year and into 1985, six more preschools in the South Bay area closed because of sexual abuse allegations.

Early in 1984, mental health professionals involved in the case began meeting to discuss the needs of the families and issues relevant to the mental health field. One point that emerged from these meetings was the importance of documenting and researching this type of case. Mental health professionals from various agencies began meeting regularly to discuss research issues and procedures for this population. Funding was sought with help through the California Community Foundation. A research proposal was submitted and funding was obtained through the

National Center on Child Abuse and Neglect. The study that comprises the backbone of this book was the result.

It was also during the spring of 1984 that a group of McMartin parents organized to lobby through the Children's Civil Rights Fund for providing closed-circuit television in the court, so that a child could be cross-examined without having to face the alleged perpetrator. This legislation eventually was passed. During the preliminary hearing, one child witness in the McMartin case did testify over closed-circuit television.

In the meantime, the legal proceedings were continuing. The preliminary hearing for the seven McMartin defendants began in the late summer of 1984, with a prosecution team consisting of deputy district attorneys Lael Rubin, Christine Johnston, and Glenn Stevens. The defense team consisted of seven different attorneys representing each of the seven defendants. The preliminary hearing, characterized by some as a "circus" in which each child witness was cross-examined by each of the seven different defense attorneys, took 17 months to conclude. In January 1986, Judge Aviva Bobb found the evidence sufficiently compelling to bind all seven defendants over for trial. However, a new district attorney, Ira Reiner, had been elected during the hearing; after reviewing the evidence, he dismissed the charges against all of the defendants except for Peggy and Raymond Buckey, who were the only two who ultimately went to trial.

After the conclusion of the preliminary hearing, two of the prosecutors left the case. Christine Johnston asked to be reassigned, and Glenn Stevens lost his job with the district attorney's office after making public statements concerning his doubts about the case. He subsequently collaborated with film producer Abby Mann; Mr. Mann and his wife, Myra, recorded approximately 30 hours of interviews with Mr. Stevens concerning the McMartin case. Transcripts of these interviews were later made available to the court.

During 1985, the investigation into other preschools continued. Although allegations of abuse at each of the other preschools involved multiple perpetrators, only one employee of one of these preschools was ever charged. A teacher's aide at the Manhattan Ranch Preschool was brought to trial in the spring of 1985. The trial lasted approximately 2 months and ended with the jury deadlocked. The case was not retried.

A support group consisting of parents whose children had attended the Manhattan Ranch Preschool formed at one of the mental health agencies in the fall of 1984 and continued to meet for 2 to 3 years. It was from this group that Clout, a legislative action group, was formed. These parents were involved in lobbying the California legislature on child advocacy issues, and this group succeeded in getting three pieces of legislation passed. This legislation guaranteed the following: (1) A prosecutor has the right to object to cross-examination questions that are not appropriate to a child's developmental level; (2) defense subpoenas must be submitted to the parents of child victims no less than 14 days in advance; and (3) judges must instruct juries that a child's testimony, although different from an adult's, is no less credible.

Another organization to emerge from the South Bay preschool cases was a networking and education group that came to be known as Believe the Children. A group of parents whose children had attended the preschools gave a presentation on ritualistic child sexual abuse at the First National Conference on Child Victimization in New Orleans in May 1986. There they met parents and professionals who were dealing with other cases of reported sexual abuse in preschools across the country, some of which showed remarkable similarity to the cases in the South Bay. From this forum, an organization consisting of chapters across the nation was formed. This organization serves as a clearinghouse on ritualistic child sexual abuse, has a speaker's bureau, and acts as a referral service to psychotherapists experienced in treating ritualistic abuse.

As time passed, those who had been involved with the preschool cases also went their various ways. Some of the parents became actively involved in child abuse issues such as those that have been discussed. Others felt the need to put the trauma behind them and focus on other matters. Some of the families "got on with their lives" in the community, whereas others decided to move away and make a fresh start for themselves and their children. To this day, there is considerable variation in how families have adjusted to and integrated this overwhelming experience.

The prevailing mood in the South Bay community has also had its vicissitudes. Initially, the community seemed to rally around the children and to believe that they had been abused. Media coverage was generally supportive of the notion that the abuse had taken place. However, as the legal proceedings dragged on and the stories of incredible atrocities came to light, doubt began to creep into the community's consciousness. Media coverage in support of the defendants became more prevalent, and the community became more obviously divided. Without a doubt, no issue ever created as much controversy in this beach community as did the child abuse preschool cases.

Because the legal proceedings truly seemed interminable, the community was not able to put the issue to rest. The trial of Peggy McMartin Buckey and Raymond Buckey finally began in July 1987, 4 years after the investigation began. It was to become the longest and most costly trial in U.S. history. After their experience with the preliminary hearing, many of the parents refused to allow their children to be subjected to the rigors of testifying, and only nine children testified during the trial. The focus of the defense, however, was to attack the interviewing technique used by Kee MacFarlane and her associates at Children's Institute International. They contended that the children had been led to believe that they were abused, but that this was the result of mass hysteria in the community. In the final analysis, the jury did not find the evidence presented by the prosecution sufficient to convict the defendants. After $2^1/2$ years, the trial ended in January 1990 with the jury acquitting Peggy and Raymond Buckey on 52 counts. They deadlocked on 13 counts against Mr. Buckey. In the posttrial press conference, many jurors stated that they believed the children had been abused, but that the evidence presented could not permit them to state without a reasonable doubt who the perpetrators were. Raymond Buckey was subsequently retried on eight of those counts. That trial began in May 1990, and also ended in a hung jury.

As of the spring of 1991, $7^1/2$ years had passed since the McMartin saga began. The community was still divided, and people were still asking, "What really happened at those preschools?" The criminal justice system was not able to put the issue to rest, and the community was still not healed. Most of the families involved were trying to put the past behind them and get on with their lives. A few were still putting their effort into influencing the political process and helping victimized children in various ways.

In the aftermath of this long and controversial case, there appear to be no winners and many, many losers. The children who alleged abuse have spent most of their young lives with controversy, disbelief, and ongoing uncertainty. The families have been unable to put the reported abuse behind them because of the lengthy legal proceedings and media coverage. One of the defendants spent 5 years in jail, while others lost their life savings, their homes, and even their children. The McMartin case will remain infamous, and in the end, it certainly raised more questions than it ever answered.

RENO, NEVADA

Far to the north and east of Los Angeles lies the bustling town of Reno, Nevada. It is a working-class town that is best known for its casinos and night life. Here, in the spring of 1983, a school-age boy told his mother that he had been molested when he was in preschool. He had attended Papoose Palace, a child care center that functioned as a preschool and kindergarten, and also provided before- and after-school care for older children. Because of these services, it was a popular facility with working parents, particularly single parents. The school had originally been located in one of the less affluent sections of town, but had moved near the University of Nevada during the early 1980s.

The mother contacted the Reno Police Department about her son's allegations, and Detective Lucky Birch, an experienced investigator in sexual abuse cases, was assigned to the case. He interviewed the first boy who disclosed abuse, and subsequently interviewed other children who were identified as involved in the molestations. Many of these children were 10 to 11 years old when they were interviewed and provided evidence that the abuse had been going on for 5 or 6 years.

The alleged perpetrator, Steven Boatwright, was the 28-year-old son of the proprietor of the preschool. Over the years, he had taught in the preschool and in the kindergarten classes. His classroom was in the basement of the preschool, away from the rest of the classes. No other teachers were implicated in the abuse. However, some of the other teachers had suspected something and had reported their suspicions to the Nevada Department of Social Services. The state had never followed up on these reports, however.

Although Detective Birch interviewed approximately 50 children, he filed on the case after the initial interviews with the first few children. Steven Boatwright was arrested and within 2 to 3 weeks pled guilty to the charges. Within 2 months, he was sentenced to four life sentences and is presently in prison.

The parents of the children sued the school, and a multimillion-dollar settlement was made out of court. Some of the parents also sued the Nevada Department of Social Services; at trial, the families of the children won the case. The children were referred for psychological evaluations early in the investigation, and because there were no legal constraints, treatment was able to proceed according to the recommendations of the professionals with the agreement of the parents.

Clearly, this case contrasts markedly with the Southern California cases. There were no lengthy legal proceedings. The children's allegations were validated, and healing was able to progress. Restitution was made, at least in the form of financial compensation to some of the families involved. Although the scars will remain with these children and families, there was some justice rendered from their point of view; this was not the case with the South Bay preschools. Both the differences and the similarities in these cases intrigued us. We suspected that not only the trauma of abuse, but how it is played out, matters in the long run. Six years have been devoted to exploring this issue. In the chapters that follow, we present findings from our study, with special emphasis on issues such as how children disclosed abuse in psychotherapy; how children, families, and therapists were affected by their experience; and what factors promoted healing.

BACKGROUND LITERATURE

Jill Waterman
Sharon Ben-Meir

V ERY LITTLE has been written about sexual abuse of very young children or about sexual abuse in preschool settings, and almost no empirical studies have been completed. However, a review of what is known about relevant aspects of sexual abuse can set the stage and provide a conceptual and empirical backdrop for the findings of our study.

DYNAMICS OF SEXUAL ABUSE

Previously, the stereotype of a molested child was that of a preadolescent girl molested either by her father or by a stranger bearing candy. Current research, however, calls into question every aspect of that stereotype. It appears that many more boys are sexually abused than ever suspected, with estimates ranging from 2.5% to 24% of men in the general population having experienced sexual victimization in childhood (Finkelhor, 1984; Kercher & McShane, 1984; Siegel, Sorenson, Golding, Burnam, & Stein, 1987). Furthermore, the only existing study of child molesters who were not in jail (Abel et al., 1987) suggests that sexual assaults against boys are more likely to go unreported, probably because of the double stigma associated with same-sex child molestation. From confidential clinical interviews with 561 child molesters, the investigators discovered that these men molested boys five times as often as they molested girls. In fact, of the different forms of molestation included in that survey, offenders targeting young boys outside their homes committed the largest number of crimes; the mean number of crimes for these offenders was an alarming 281, compared with 23 crimes per offender of nonincestuous assault on girls.

Similarly, new findings are calling into question the long-held assumption that school-age children are the most frequently abused age group. Specifically, younger children may be abused with much greater frequency than previously thought. The percentage of children sexually abused in younger age groups has been greatly underestimated because of a variety of factors (Waterman & Lusk, 1986): (1) Preschoolers frequently lack the cognitive and communication skills necessary to disclose sexual abuse; (2) the credibility of young children is questionable, and they almost never are able to testify in court; (3) the age at disclosure is usually higher than the true age of abuse onset, because of the dynamics of sexual abuse; and (4) children's recall of the onset of early sexual abuse is severely hampered by their lack of accurate time sense in the preschool and early school years. Estimates suggest that somewhere between 18% and 33% of reported victims of child sexual abuse are under the age of 6 years (Waterman & Lusk, 1986; Mannarino & Cohen, 1986; DeJong, Hervada, & Emmett, 1983). Given the reasons for underreporting of abuse in this age group listed above, the percentage of children whose molestation begins in the preschool years is probably even higher.

The third part of the stereotype—that the molester is either the girl's father or an unknown stranger in a trenchcoat offering candy—is also being disputed by recent findings. Certainly, it has become abundantly clear that strangers constitute only a small proportion of the molesters of children. Most sexual abuse is perpetrated by someone from a child's closest, most trusted circle of adults; studies suggest that from 60% to 80% of sexual abusers are family members, teachers, babysitters, or friends of the child victims. In the only national study of sexual abuse in day care and preschool facilities, Finkelhor, Williams, and Burns (1988) estimated that 5.5 children per 10,000 are abused in day care, compared with 8.9 children per 10,000 under age 6 who are abused in their own homes. Although they conclude that day care for preschoolers does not pose a high risk for sexual abuse, the authors note that the multiple-perpetrator cases (17% of the sample) "were clearly the most serious ones, involving the most children, the youngest children, the most serious sexual activities, and the highest likelihood of pornography production and ritualistic abuse" (Finkelhor et al., 1988, p. 250).

THEORETICAL MODELS OF ABUSE IMPACT

The two most frequently cited conceptual frameworks (Finkelhor, 1987) for explaining how an experience of childhood molestation contributes to an individual's psychosocial adaptation are the "post-traumatic stress disorder (PTSD) model" and Finkelhor and Browne's (1986) "traumagenic dynamics model." In the former, sexual abuse is equated with other traumatic experiences, and a victim's response to child sexual abuse is understood as a variant of the PTSD syndrome. By contrast, Finkelhor and Browne focus on the unique aspects of sexual abuse encounters, postulating four "traumagenic dynamics" that coexist exclusively in childhood molestation experiences. At the current time, a more specific variant of PTSD is being proposed to cover symptoms of abuse of children, known as "disorders of extreme stress not otherwise specified" (DESNOS).

The Post-Traumatic Stress Disorder Model

Some writers in the child sexual abuse field (e.g., Berliner & Wheeler, 1987; Briere & Runtz, 1987; Courtois, 1986) advocate the adoption of the diagnosis of PTSD for children for whom psychological treatment following sexual abuse is sought. According to Finkelhor (1987), the factors supporting this point of view include the following: (1) the opportunity to treat children without affixing a stigmatizing label, since PTSD, with its emphasis on an external stressor, is a relatively stigma-free condition; (2) the finding that work with child survivors of other traumas, such as kidnapping, produced some overlap in psychological outcomes (e.g., Terr, 1985; Pynoos & Eth, 1985); and (3) the close resemblance between the symptom picture of PTSD and children's initial reactions to sexual victimization, which is frequently dominated by anxiety-related symptoms.

However, Finkelhor (1987) argues that the PTSD model adequately describes only a subset of symptoms seen in only a subsample of abuse survivors. Specifically, the self-blame, suicidality, revictimization, substance abuse, and sexual problems found among abuse survivors are not neatly subsumed within the PTSD conceptualization. Perhaps most important, however, is the recognition that a diagnostic condition does not in itself constitute a theoretical *model*, because it lacks clear etiological mechanisms.

The Traumagenic Dynamics Model

Finkelhor and his associates (Finkelhor & Browne, 1985, 1986; Finkelhor, 1987) have developed a conceptual model that traces the dysfunctional sequelae of child sexual abuse to four central traumagenic dynamics: traumatic sexualization, stigmatization, betrayal, and powerlessness. Although some combination of these dynamics occur in other traumatic experiences, Finkelhor and Browne (1986) contend that the convergence of all these dynamics is what distinguishes an experience of childhood molestation from all other childhood traumas. Despite this claim, it appears that the only factor unique to sexual victimization is traumatic sexualization.

"Traumatic sexualization" refers to the conditions in sexual abuse under which a child's sexuality is shaped in developmentally inappropriate and interpersonally dysfunctional ways (Finkelhor, 1987). Since experiences of sexual abuse vary considerably in severity, in the use of coercion or violence, and in the developmental level of the child (among other dimensions), this model is useful in that it predicts differential outcomes stemming directly from the specifics of an individual's molestation experience. Within this model, what all sexual abuse experiences have in common is distortion in the meaning and function of sexual activity, so that for some victims sex becomes a way to satisfy interpersonal needs, while for others sex evokes terror, humiliation, pain, or guilt. Finkelhor and Browne (1986) mention poor sexual self-esteem; sexual preoccupations, aversions, or compulsions; promiscuity; prostitution; and intergenerational patterns of sexual abuse as possible correlates of this dynamic of traumatic sexualization.

A second dynamic, "stigmatization," refers to the negative messages about the self—evilness, worthlessness, shamefulness, and guilt—that are communicated to a child through the experience of sexual abuse. Finkelhor and Browne (1986) suggest that children incorporate these negative attributions into their self-images when they are blamed or denigrated by an abuser, involved in furtive activities and pressured to maintain the secret of abuse, or exposed to the moral judgments and upset of others when abuse is disclosed. Possible effects linked to stigmatization are low self-esteem, isolation, guilt and shame, substance abuse and suicide.

"Betrayal," the third dynamic, involves a child's realization that an individual whom he or she trusted and depended upon has allowed the child to come to harm. Finkelhor asserts that betrayal is experienced in all types of sexual abuse because of the inherent dependency of children on adults, as well as their expectation of parental omnipotence. So, although betrayal may be exacerbated or ameliorated by the response of caretakers to disclosure, the child experiences a fundamental betrayal, regardless of the circumstances under which the abuse occurs. Symptoms traced to this dynamic include depression, excessive dependency, problems in managing anger and hostility, mistrust of both women and men, difficulties in intimate relationships, and vulnerability to subsequent exploitation and mistreatment.

The final dynamic is "powerlessness," in which (1) a child's will, wishes, and sense of efficacy are repeatedly overruled and frustrated; and (2) a child experiences the threat of injury or annihilation. Powerlessness is believed to be further intensified by violent or coercive sexual abuse; by frustrated attempts to terminate the abuse; or by postdisclosure experiences (such as separation from the family or court prosecution) in which the child is excluded from decision-making processes, yet profoundly affected by them. Finkelhor (1987) claims that powerlessness is the organizing principle in the PTSD conceptualization of abuse impact. Effects attributed to the powerlessness factor include pervasive anxiety and fear, diminished self-efficacy, attempts to dominate others, nightmares, phobias, depression, dissociation, school problems, and delinquency.

Finkelhor and Browne (1986) argue that for different children involved in different kinds of abuse, different inter-relationships of traumagenic dynamics are represented, and different psychosocial outcomes may be predicted. For example, a child who has colluded with incestuous abuse based on manipulation of familial authority rather than use of force may, on disclosure, experience profound betrayal, with significant traumatic sexualization and stigmatization, but a lesser degree of powerlessness. By contrast, Satanic abuse by a stranger may be experienced primarily through the dynamic of powerlessness, with extreme terrorization dominating the child's reaction and subsequent symptomatology, above all other factors. Unfortunately, to date, few studies have been designed with the goal of testing such theory-driven hypotheses.

EFFECTS OF CHILD SEXUAL ABUSE

Much effort in the past decade has been devoted to examining the personality characteristics and psychological dynamics associated with victims of child sexual abuse. Presently, reviewers of the literature (Alter-Reid, Gibbs, Lachanmeyer, Sigal, & Massoth, 1986; Browne & Finkelhor, 1986; Conte, 1985; Waterman & Lusk, 1986) agree that most published studies provide evidence that sexual abuse in childhood is harmful, both in the immediate aftermath and in adulthood.

Although much of what is known about the effects of child sexual abuse has been drawn from studies focusing primarily on intrafamilial sexual abuse, the long-held clinical assumption that incest is associated with the most severe damage to child victims has been questioned by recent clinical and empirical observations. Unfortunately, many of the studies on effects of sexual abuse on children did not separate out or even detail whether the abuse occurred with family members or nonrelatives. In this review of effects of sexual abuse, general effects are presented first, with more detail given in later sections on extrafamilial sexual abuse, abuse of young children, and sexual abuse in day care.

Global Symptomatology

A number of studies of children, using steadily improving methodologies, have begun to examine the overall emotional adjustment after disclosure of abuse. Browne and Finkelhor (1986), in their extensive review, asserted that there is growing evidence for initial reactions of depression, fear, anxiety, anger, and hostility in a subset of children who have been sexually abused. Many studies of global symptomatology (e.g., Friedrich, Beilke, & Urquiza, 1987) have utilized the Child Behavior Checklist (CBCL; Achenbach & Edelbrock, 1983). In general, these studies indicate that parents rate their children as more disturbed than nonclinical children, but no more pathological than clinical comparison groups. Not surprisingly, sexual problems are often rated as worse for sexually abused children than for any other groups. Sexually abused children have been rated as showing both Internalizing symptoms (e.g., fearfulness, inhibition, depression, and excessive self-control) and Externalizing symptoms (e.g., aggressive, antisocial, and undercontrolled behaviors). Other behavior checklists besides the CBCL filled out by parents have yielded similar results: sexually abused children are rated as more symptomatic and distressed than are normative and control groups (Adams-Tucker, 1981; Gomes-Schwartz, Horowitz, & Cardarelli, 1990; Basta & Peterson, 1990; Conte & Schuerman, 1987).

Self-Concept

Distortions in self-esteem and self-perceptions have consistently been identified as core deficits by many clinicians working with victims of sexual abuse (deYoung, 1982; Gelinas, 1983; Herman, 1981; Knittle & Tuana, 1980; Meiselman, 1978). Nevertheless, the bulk of the evidence comes from clinical case descriptions or from studies of adults molested as children (e.g., Briere, 1984). Despite the limitations of such retrospective data, recent improvements in studies with adult survivors led Browne and Finkelhor (1986) to conclude that poor self-esteem has been established as a long-term effect of abuse (see also Gold, 1986; Bagley & Ramsey, 1985, 1986; Urquiza & Crowley, 1986).

Unfortunately, information from child victims has remained contradictory and inconclusive. Whereas Conte and Schuerman's (1987) study found significant differences between abused and nonabused children on self-esteem, such differences have not been discovered in other investigations (Cohen & Mannarino, 1988; Mannarino, Cohen, & Gregor, 1989; Gomes-Schwartz et al., 1990). In fact, sexually abused children have sometimes been found to exhibit a *higher* self-concept than nonabused normal children (Gomes-Schwartz, Horowitz, & Sauzier, 1985, with preschoolers; DiPietro, 1987, with adolescents).

The self-concept difficulties consistently found among adult survivors may be a consequence of other problems (e.g., impaired relationships), which cause survivors of sexual abuse to form a negative self-image over time. Alternatively, it appears likely that results on self-esteem depend on the aspect of self-concept being measured, as well as the type of measure employed. Investigators (e.g., Briere & Runtz, 1986) have called for a shift from questionnaires currently used to more subtle and differentiated measures of self-perception; they believe that such approaches might find the early precursors of the damaged self-concept that has been clearly documented in adult survivors of childhood molestation.

Anxiety

Anxiety and related symptoms have long been noted as prevalent in molestation victims of all age groups, including preschool and school-age children (Adams-Tucker, 1981, 1982; Brandt & Tisza, 1978) and adolescents or adults (Brassard, Tyler, & Kehle, 1983; Gelinas, 1983; Meiselman, 1978). Sexual abuse in childhood has been linked to severe anxiety symptoms in adulthood, including panic episodes and phobias (Briere, 1984; Sgroi, 1982) and dissociative disorders (Kluft, 1987; Putnam, Guroff, & Silberman, 1986). Unfortunately, few studies have been conducted with child victims; moreover, those that exist have frequently failed to distinguish between anxiety and fearfulness, utilizing the presence of a variety of symptoms (e.g., nightmares) as indicators of both. Fear has been described as an initial response to molestation in as few as 13% (Gomes-Schwartz et al., 1990) and as many as 83% (DeFrancis, 1969) of victims.

One recent study has presented data on fear and anxiety as distinct responses. Researchers in New England (Gomes-Schwartz et al., 1990) measured anxiety and fearfulness for their three age groups of children who had recently disclosed sexual abuse. The preschool-age children showed little evidence of overall significant impairment, with only 17% meeting criteria for clinically meaningful psychopathology. The preschoolers showed more symptomatology than the normative group, but less than the clinical nonabused comparison group. The exception was inappropriate sexual behavior, where the sexually abused group showed significantly higher levels. Although fear was among the preschoolers' most common symptoms, only 13% demonstrated severe fears (as noted above), and the sexually abused children obtained manifest anxiety levels that were actually *lower* than the norms for the general population.

Preadolescent children (aged 7–13) showed more overall disturbance than preschoolers, with 40% scoring as "seriously disturbed" in one or more clinical areas. Severe fears were evident in 45% of the abused children tested during latency. Interestingly, while only 11% of these children were significantly elevated on manifest anxiety, 41% were elevated on "ambivalent hostility," a scale designed to measure the fear of being harmed by others, and this scale significantly differentiated abused from nonabused children in this age group. Finally, among the adolescents (aged 14–18 years), anxiety, obsessiveness, and depression constituted the most common cluster of symptoms among the sexually abused group. High levels of manifest anxiety were again quite rare (5%), although ambivalent hostility (the fear of being harmed by others) was also elevated above the norms for 36% of the sexually abused adolescents.

Although these results could be interpreted as showing that younger children are less traumatized by abuse, Gomes-Schwartz et al. (1990) suggest that it may be the age when evaluated, rather than the age at the time of abuse, that explains the low levels of symptomatic disturbance in the preschool group. Children abused as preschoolers may become symptomatic when they are faced with subsequent developmental tasks (e.g., dating and forming intimate relationships) that tap into their abuse-related issues. Alternatively, abuse dimensions may account for the relatively low rate of distress in Gomes-Schwartz et al.'s sample of young children. The preschoolers in their study were characterized by the briefest duration of abuse (with many preschoolers disclosing abuse after a single episode of molestation) and less invasive types of abuse (with intercourse less frequent among this age group). Preliminary evidence from studies of young children exposed to more invasive sexual acts, which occur more typically in extrafamilial abuse situations (e.g., Finkelhor et al., 1988; Kelley, 1989; Valliere, Bybee, & Mowbray, 1988), suggests that young children do react with fear and anxiety following more severe sexual maltreatment.

Post-Traumatic Stress Disorder

Reports of PTSD symptoms in abuse survivors have begun to emerge (e.g., Blake-White & Kline, 1984; Goodwin, 1984; Lindberg & Distad, 1985a). Eth and Pynoos (1985) have outlined children's reactions to traumatic experiences as a function of their developmental stage. These authors argue that the limited cognitive abilities and the developmentally normative dependency of preschool-age children exacerbate their powerlessness in the face of trauma. Numerous clinical reports (Gislason & Call, 1982; Schetky, 1978; Terr, 1979, 1981, 1983a, 1983b, 1983c, 1984, 1985) have described symptoms consistent with a diagnosis of PTSD in children who have been traumatized. The extent and severity of PTSD symptoms would be predicted to vary with dimensions of the abuse experience: More violent abuse would appear to be most likely to produce this type of symptomatology, while other types of abuse may produce qualitatively different symptom clusters.

Depression

After anxiety, the second most frequently cited emotional response following childhood sexual abuse is depression (Browne & Finkelhor, 1986; Kent, 1988; Meiselman, 1978; Tsai & Wagner, 1978; Yates, 1982). A pattern of chronic anhedonia with periodic episodes of clinical depression is commonly mentioned by clinicians (e.g., Friedrich & Reams, 1986) as characteristic of adult women molested as children. Support for this assertion comes from methodologically sound research comparing nonclinical samples of women who report having been molested as children with women who claim no such history; this research has utilized both college student populations (Briere & Runtz, 1985; Sedney & Brooks, 1984; Urquiza & Crowley, 1986) and community surveys (Bagley & Ramsey, 1986; Peters, 1985). Each of these studies has demonstrated a consistent relationship between childhood sexual abuse and subsequent depression.

Studies of sexually abused children have rarely focused on depression per se. However, several studies (Friedrich et al., 1987; Friedrich, Beilke, & Urquiza, 1988; Adams-Tucker, 1982) have documented that a subset of abused children do become depressed. Some findings indicate that this reaction may be limited to children abused at later ages (Gomes-Schwartz et al., 1990). Alternatively, it may be that early sexual abuse also contributes to depression, but that this depression does not become evident until a child faces subsequent developmental tasks.

Anger Management

Survivors of child sexual abuse have been described as exhibiting different forms of difficulties in the modulation and appropriate management of anger. It can be argued that these problems with anger parallel the two extremes found for sexual problems. That is, abuse victims exhibit symptoms consistent with excessive denial or suppression of anger (paralleling inhibited sexuality) as well as inadequate control of anger (equivalent to hypersexuality).

In general, adult abuse victims report more problems with anger than do nonabused adults (Briere, 1984; Briere & Runtz, 1987; Murphy et al., 1988). For example, in their study of college students, Urquiza and Crowley (1986) found that students of both sexes who had been molested as children reported a "desire to hurt others" more frequently than did nonmolested controls.

In recently abused children, a dual pattern—excessive suppression of anger, along with aggressive acting out—has begun to emerge from the research. A coexistence of inhibition of aggression with impulsive aggression was noted by Conte and Schuerman (1987); 19% of their large clinical sample showed "repressed hostility" on social workers' ratings, and aggressive behavior was one of seven factors that significantly differentiated abused from nonabused children. Similarly, Gomes-Schwartz et al. (1990) found aggression to be a clinically significant problem for 25%–35% of the children in different age ranges.

EXTRAFAMILIAL ABUSE

One major controversy in the field is whether it is sexual abuse per se, or the dysfunctional family context (which appears to be a necessary precondition for incestuous abuse to occur), that is responsible for the maladaptive outcomes seen in some abused children. Browne and Finkelhor (1986) contend that the relative impact of abuse within the family, as opposed to extrafamilial sexual abuse, has not yet received adequate research attention; they speculate that abuse perpetrated outside the family may be characterized by dynamics differing from, but just as traumatizing as, the dynamics characteristic of intrafamilial abuse. For example, factors that co-occur with extrafamilial abuse, such as increased fear or more violent, forceful approaches to obtain compliance, may cause substantially different patterns of outcome from those typical for children molested within their families.

Thus far, very few studies have focused upon the impact of sexual abuse occurring exclusively outside the family. Furthermore, intrafamilial abuse and extrafamilial abuse represent such broad categories that they may well be conceptually meaningless, since there is large variability in the types of relationships falling within each of these dimensions.

Some preliminary studies concentrating on the sequelae of extrafamilial abuse have been completed. Burgess and her associates (Burgess, Groth, & McCausland, 1981; Burgess, Hartman, McCausland, & Powers, 1984) reported the first studies of personality formation of children abused exclusively by individuals outside their families. They examined 62 children who had been sexually exploited in "child sex rings," and reported a variety of symptoms consistent with a diagnosis of PTSD among these children at the time of disclosure: 72.5% of the children related reexperiencing memories and flashbacks of threats made by their abuser(s). Moreover, 79% developed *new* symptoms (including hyperalertness, guilt, crying spells, sleep disturbance, moodiness, and somaticizing) at the follow-up stage.

In addition, four "response patterns" were identified at the 2-year follow-up point. Only 26% were judged to have "integrated" the experience of sexual exploitation and made a successful psychosocial adaptation. The remaining children were characterized as showing one of three maladaptive outcomes. The first was "avoiding the event" (27%), a pattern in which "the anxiety about the exploitation remains sealed off. . . . So long as the child is not under stress, life is managed as if nothing has happened" (Burgess et al., 1984, p. 658). These children were thought to remain vulnerable to stress and to show chronic low-level symptoms of strained interpersonal relating and school difficulties.

A second dysfunctional outcome pattern, involving 26% of the children, was marked by "repetition of symptoms" in which "the acute post-traumatic stress disorder becomes chronic" (p. 659). The authors described this chronic symptom pattern as being characterized by depression, hopelessness, an orientation to the past, and a pattern of being repeatedly revictimized. Interestingly, this response pattern closely resembles the clinical presentation discussed by Gelinas (1983) as common in adult survivors of sexual abuse who were never in psychological treatment prior to adulthood.

A final pattern, characteristic of 21% of the children, involved "identification with the exploiter." "In this response pattern the child has introjected some characteristic of the anxiety by impersonating the aggressor. . . . The child masters the anxiety by exploiting others and adopting an antisocial position towards peers, school and family" (Burgess et al., 1984, p. 659). Here, serious antisocial acts were typical; five children perpetrated sexual abuse against younger children and six were convicted of felony crimes, with three functioning as pimps during their adolescence. As the authors have acknowledged, the problems of retrospective assessment of symptoms, global descriptions without specific statistics, and the absence of nonabused comparison groups limit the generalizability of these findings.

A report by Frederick (1986) on 15 male victims of abuse by a medical professional, and one by Krentz-Johnson (1979) on girls molested outside the family, give converging evidence of significant distress and dysfunction in survivors of extrafamilial sexual abuse. However, the small sample sizes, the reliance on unspecified scoring systems, and the absence of control groups render the findings of both investigations speculative.

Two more recent studies have addressed emotional and personality development among extrafamilially abused children. Tong, Oates, and McDowell (1987) studied 34 children abused by nonrelatives and 15 incest victims. On the CBCL, both parents and teachers reported significantly more Internalizing and Externalizing behavior problems for the abused groups than for controls. Abused children scored significantly lower on the Piers–Harris Self-Concept Scale than nonabused children; however, the scores for abused females (the lowest-scoring group) fell in the lower limit of the normal range of scores on this measure. In contrast to the child data, 76% of the parents of abused children reported in interviews that their children showed diminished self-confidence following sexual abuse. Most importantly, teachers (unaware of abuse history), though not specifically rating self-esteem, described these children as lacking a host of adaptive skills; such deficits would be expected to correlate with a poor self-concept.

Thus far, only one study has been reported that explicitly compared the impact of intrafamilial sexual abuse with molestation occurring outside the context of the family. Basta and Peterson (1990) gathered data on a small ($n = 16$), homogeneous sample of children molested by an after-school program teacher, and compared them with children reporting incestuous abuse and with nonabused controls. Results of this study indicated that sexually molested children, when grouped together, showed significantly more impairment than nonmolested children on all personality measures.

Most relevant to the present discussion, however, is the absence of differences found between incestuously abused and extrafamilially abused children. As rated by their parents, there were *no* significant differences in personality between the two molested groups. Furthermore, only two child-completed scales, measuring tension and anxiety, showed higher levels of disturbance for intrafamilially abused children than for extrafamilial victims. Taken together, the results are suggestive of significant personality and mood disturbance in the aftermath of extrafamilial abuse, with these children appearing to have immediate outcomes almost indistinguishable from those of intrafamilially abused children.

A note of caution must be added with respect to the comparisons between the molested and nonmolested children. Basta and Peterson (1990) reported that the abused groups had significantly lower Verbal IQ scores than the nonabused controls, and that their mothers were more limited intellectually, socioeconomically, and emotionally than the nonabused children's mothers; these differences could account for the differences obtained in the children's mental health outcomes.

Thus, it can be seen that the existing literature on the effects of extrafamilial sexual abuse consists almost exclusively of uncontrolled clinical case reports on small, unrepresentative samples. Therefore, it is perhaps not surprising that little has been learned about the impact of sexual abuse occurring outside the context of the nuclear family.

SEXUAL ABUSE OF YOUNG CHILDREN

Another significant controversy in the field concerns the ways in which age of the victim influences the sequelae of sexual abuse. One aspect of this controversy is the question of whether young children suffer trauma similar to that of older children, who are more aware of social proscriptions against such early sexual experiences. Writers within a social learning perspective have suggested that young age is a protective factor, whereas psychodynamic theorists contend that earlier abuse is more disruptive to future personality development. Research to date has not resolved the debate regarding which age group is associated with greater disturbance (Browne & Finkelhor, 1986). However, as the average age of reported abuse onset continues to decline (Waterman & Lusk, 1986), interest in victims abused at the younger end of the spectrum has grown.

Presently, only a handful of studies have examined the reactions of children to sexual abuse in the preschool years. Several clinical reports (Friedrich & Reams, 1986; Leaman, 1980; Lewis & Sarrel, 1969; Pascoe & Duterte, 1981) suggest that preschoolers exhibit regressive behaviors in response to sexual abuse, including a reemergence of baby talk, bedwetting, and hyperactivity; they also show inappropriately sexualized behavior. In addition, excessive anxiety, fear, nightmares, and difficulties with separation have been noted by clinicians (Adams-Tucker, 1982; Rosenfeld, Nadelson, & Krieger, 1979).

A longitudinal prospective study of high-risk mother–child pairs (Erickson, 1986) identified a small ($n = 11$) group of children molested prior to age 6 and compared them with 67 nonabused children in the high-risk sample. Followed into first grade, the sexually abused children were rated on the CBCL as more anxious, unpopular, overactive, and aggressive, and as exhibiting more Externalizing symptoms than their nonabused peers. Teacher ratings indicated a marked inability in these children to work independently, partly because of low frustration tolerance and constant demands for teachers' approval and reassurance.

Confirmation of Friedrich and colleagues' (Friedrich, Urquiza, & Beilke, 1986; Friedrich et al., 1987) findings that internalizing symptoms, particularly anxiety-related symptoms, are characteristic of young children's reaction to molestation comes from several studies. Specifically,

Mian, Wehrspann, Klajner-Diamond, LeBaron, and Winder (1986) found that symptomatic reactions were exhibited by 66% of abused children under 6 years of age, with anxiety and somatic complaints especially elevated, and Mannarino and Cohen (1986) reported that over two-thirds of abused preschool children were rated as showing one or more serious psychological problems, with the most common symptoms being nightmares (56%) and anxiety, while sadness and clinging behavior were each seen in 22% of the abused children. Both sets of authors argue that these studies challenge the contention that young children are not damaged by early sexual experiences, and their findings converge with those of the methodologically more sound Friedrich et al. (1986, 1987) studies.

Although it shares with other studies the limitation of a small sexual abuse group (n = 17), a study by White, Halpin, Strom, and Santilli (1986) did utilize outcome instruments specifically developed to assess the theorized effects of sexual abuse, and compared the abused children to both neglected and nonreferred peers. The only symptom that differentiated both sexually abused males and females from the comparison groups was sexualized behavior; sexually abused children masturbated more in public when stressed, and made more comments regarding adults' genitalia, than did either neglected or nonreferred children. On factors such as somaticization, risk behaviors, and problems with self-esteem and parent–child relationships, sexually abused males but not females appeared impaired. Overall, sexually abused females showed similar problems to those of neglected females, appearing generally developmentally delayed and overly anxious for adult approval, and exhibiting regressive symptoms.

To examine the hypothesis that abuse at different developmental levels would be associated with qualitatively distinct patterns of disturbance, Zivney, Nash, and Hulsey (1988) utilized the Rorschach Inkblot Test to examine the adjustment of recently abused children. These investigators found greater psychological disturbance to be associated with an early age of abuse onset (prior to age 7), and identified a specific pattern of a damaged self-concept, disturbed cognition, and primitive object relations that differentiated children abused at an early age from late-onset abuse victims.

SEXUAL ABUSE IN PRESCHOOL AND DAY CARE

The increased use of day care facilities, and the highly publicized reports of sexual abuse within some day care centers (e.g., Timnick, 1985a, 1985b), have prompted examination of abuse in these settings. Since the majority of these studies have focused on preschool settings, this work represents the intersection of work on extrafamilial abuse and on the abuse of very young children. In addition, the sparse data available on the impact of "Satanic" or ritualistic abuse has been gathered in day care studies.

The only national study (Finkelhor et al., 1988) to examine the incidence and impact of sexual abuse in day care facilities reported data on 270 substantiated cases of preschool sexual abuse, involving 1,639 victims. As noted earlier in this chapter, Finkelhor and his associates contend that day care is not a high-risk situation for young children, since their estimated rate of 5.5 children per 10,000 abused in day care is lower than the estimated 8.9 children (under age 6) per 10,000 who are sexually abused in their own homes. Nevertheless, this study suggests that sexual abuse is disturbingly common in the preschool years and occurs in day care centers in a wide variety of patterns, some of which appear to be particularly traumatizing to children. The vast majority of cases (83%) involved a single perpetrator, but those cases involving multiple perpetrators (17%) had the most severe sexual abuse, the youngest children, and the highest likelihood of ritualistic sexual abuse. In this study, 66% of the multiple-perpetrator cases (as opposed to 5% of the single-perpetrator cases) included allegations of ritualistic abuse, defined as "abuse that occurs in a context linked to some symbols or group activity that have a religious, magical, or supernatural connotation, and where the invocation of these symbols or activities, repeated over time, is used to frighten and intimidate the children" (Finkelhor et al., 1988, p. 59), in conjunction with the sexual abuse.

Common sequelae of abuse in day care included physical injury (in 62% of cases, involving at least one child), fears, sleep difficulties, regressive behavior, and age-inappropriate sexual behavior. Importantly, the poorest outcomes (i.e., the most postabuse symptomatology) were associated with abuse by trusted care providers and with abuse including force or ritualistic aspects.

Strikingly similar findings were reported in another study of 48 victims of sexual abuse in day care settings, conducted by Faller (1987). Her data match those of Finkelhor et al. (1988) in both the patterns of abuse noted and the unusual severity of abusive acts occurring in the day care context. Faller reports that in addition to the usual high rates of fondling for preschool-age children (72.4%), 73.9% of the children were involved in group sex activities, 18.8% experienced oral sex, and 12.5% were subjected to acts involving Satanic rituals.

Not surprisingly, the children abused by multiple perpetrators showed an average of 5.7 symptoms per child, as opposed to an average of 2.1 symptoms in single-perpetrator cases. The most common symptoms seen in this population were (1) sexual acting out (23.3%); (2) "emotional difficulties," including depression, anxiety, suicidal ideation, clinginess, and regressive behavior (18.8%); (3) phobias (15.9%), particularly of bugs and of being without their parents; and (4) behavioral problems, including aggression and firesetting (14.8%). Faller has acknowledged that the study has significant methodological limitations, including failing to include comparison groups and leaving outcome indices unspecified.

A recent study (Valliere et al., 1988) utilized the CBCL to examine the impact of sexual abuse occurring in day care. Sexually abused children showed significantly more behavioral dysfunction on the CBCL than their nonabused peers. Two years after disclosure, the abused children scored significantly higher on *all* subscales of the CBCL than the nonabused children, with elevations as high as the clinical norms for most scales. It is noteworthy that in this study, abuse at an early age occurring outside the context of children's families produced symptoms consistent with the literature on intrafamilially abused children, indicating significant behavioral and emotional impairment.

RITUALISTIC SEXUAL ABUSE

Thus far, only one study (Kelley, 1989) has compared the impact of ritualistic abuse to sexual abuse without such features, and has compared abused children to nonabused controls. Kelley defined ritualistic abuse as "repetitive and systematic sexual, physical and psychological abuse of children by adults as part of cult or satanic worship" (p. 503). In addition to sexual abuse, the child victims might have been involved in any of the following acts: "ingestion of human excrement, semen, or blood; ceremonial killing of animals; threats of harm from supernatural powers; ingestion of drugs or magic potions; and use of satanic rituals, songs, chants, or symbols" (p. 503). Kelley obtained data on 32 children involved in day care sexual abuse without ritualistic elements and 35 children involved in day care ritualistic sexual abuse. These children were compared with 67 nonabused controls, matched on age, sex, socioeconomic status, and a history of day care attendance. Questionnaires were filled out by parents an average of 2.2 years after disclosure of abuse.

The results of this study indicated that ritualistic abuse was associated with significantly more victims, abused by a significantly greater number of offenders per child. Not surprisingly, the factors defining ritualistic abuse, such as the use of drugs and involvement in rituals invoking supernatural powers, were significantly more common in the ritualistic abuse group. In addition, ritualistically abused children experienced more incidents of abuse, more types of abuse, more severe and intrusive sexual acts (i.e., more vaginal, rectal and oral penetration), more involvement in sexual activity with other children and pornography, more co-occurring physical abuse, and more terrorizing verbal abuse than did the children who were sexually abused without ritualistic elements. Verbal abuse was characterized by highly concrete, violent death threats against the victims (86%) and/or their parents (94%) linked to disclosure of abuse. Thus, this study is in agreement with clinical presentations (Crewdson, 1988; Gould, 1987; Kagy, 1986; Strieff, 1988) and previously discussed studies (Faller, 1987; Finkelhor et al., 1988) in documenting ritualistic and Satanic abuse cases as being marked by a disturbingly high level of the most traumatizing forms of child maltreatment.

Consistent with this picture are Kelly's (1989) findings demonstrating the severity of impact of sexual abuse in day care, and the particularly negative outcomes associated with ritualistic abuse. On the CBCL, both the total number of behavior problems and the tendency to show Internalizing symptoms were significantly higher for abused children than for controls, and the most impaired on these scales were the ritualistically abused children. For Total Behavior Problems, 48% of the ritualistically abused children were in the clinical range, as opposed to 32% of the nonritualistically sexually abused group. By contrast, the tendency to exhibit Externalizing symptoms and Social Competence difficulties were more common in both sexually abused groups, and the type of sexual abuse was not linked to these outcome indices. The severity of effects is surprisingly similar to that found in comparable studies of intrafamilially abused children (e.g., Friedrich et al., 1986).

These results suggest that extrafamilial sexual abuse occurring in day care facilities is frequently highly traumatizing, and may in fact be as disruptive to adjustment as intrafamilial sexual abuse. Children of both sexes were found to be equally affected by sexual abuse of this type, and the atypically young age of onset of abuse ($\bar{X} = 2.8$ years) in this and other day care samples did not serve to prevent significant emotional trauma. In Kelley's samples, sexual abuse involving ritualistic components was associated with increased negative impact, including excessive anxiety and fearfulness, as well as acting-out behaviors.

However, while this study provides an important source of data on the impact of ritualistic abuse, its exclusive reliance upon parent-completed questionnaires introduces the possibility of bias stemming from parental expectations of harm, especially when children endured Satanic abuse. In addition, parent ratings of effects of sexual abuse are generally higher than measures of effects gathered from the children themselves (Waterman & Lusk, 1993).

A study with adult survivors of various forms of child sexual abuse provides some basis for arguing that Kelley's (1989) parent data may accurately reflect true psychosocial outcomes. Briere (1988) compared sexually victimized female outpatients to female outpatients with no history of abuse. Among this clinical sample, 17% of the sexually abused women experienced at least one incident of "bizarre abuse, which included reports of ritualistic sexual contact, the use of animals, insertion of foreign objects, and/or sexual torture" (p. 4). Briere found that longer duration of abuse, bizarre sexual abuse, co-occurring physical abuse, and the involvement of multiple perpetrators were all significantly associated with sexual problems, alcoholism, drug addiction, suicidality, and revictimization in adulthood. In addition, abuse involving sexual intercourse was linked to greater suicidality and dissociation. Thus, the evidence from victims in this long-term outcome study suggests that ritualistic abuse may be particularly traumagenic.

SUMMARY

Although the many methodological limitations of the studies cited here clearly reflect the preliminary status of research on child sexual abuse, some fundamental conclusions do seem to be emerging. Child sexual abuse is an unexpectedly common problem, affecting children of both sexes and spanning all age groups. The weight of the evidence suggests that the impact of sexual abuse is characteristically negative, with both immediate and long-term ill effects.

In the realm of emotional sequelae, adult survivors of abuse have consistently been found to show (1) negative self-concept, (2) pervasive anxiety, (3) depression and self-destructive behaviors, (4) impairments in trust and intimacy, (5) interpersonal hostility, and (6) sexual problems. Consistently, more sophisticated studies have shown that child sexual abuse appears to be associated with increased risk of emotional and social problems, but it is not inevitably linked with dysfunction.

Because of the paucity of adequate studies, conclusions regarding child victims remain much more tentative. Sexualized behavior has thus far been the only symptom cluster to consistently distinguish children who have been molested from nonmolested clinical populations. Existing studies of children suggest that responses of fear and anxiety are frequent following the disclosure of abuse, and are found even among abuse victims younger than 6 years. By contrast, depression appears more typical of older abuse victims. From studies of internalizing and externalizing behaviors, it appears that sexual abuse victims may be globally symptomatic, displaying a variety of emotional reactions rather than any discrete mood disturbance. Results of self-concept studies have been contradictory, with parents typically describing their children as showing diminished self-confidence, while child self-esteem scales frequently fail to find direct evidence for this.

In general, as studies of abuse correlates in children have begun to utilize standardized measures, they have relied exclusively upon parent-completed questionnaires, often neglecting to collect any data on the children themselves. Although this approach is a marked improvement over the use of case studies to study abuse impact, it is impossible to determine the contribution of parental expectations and perceptions to such ratings of outcome. Clearly, studies utilizing multiple data sources, preferably including observers who are unaware of the abuse history of the children (such as teachers or independent raters), will be needed before more substantive conclusions can be drawn. In addition, areas that have received scant attention (such as young child victims, extrafamilial abuse, and ritualistic abuse) need to be examined empirically, with the increasing methodological sophistication that is developing in investigations of child sexual abuse. Finally, if studies in this area are to inform our clinical work meaningfully, it is essential for research to test hypotheses that are theoretically derived, with longitudinal designs. It is only when we begin to understand the process by which sexual victimization in childhood contributes to the formation of psychological problems that we can intervene more effectively and compassionately with child and adult survivors of abuse.

STUDY METHODS AND PROCEDURES

Robert J. Kelly

T HE RESEARCH METHODOLOGY for the study to be described in this book is perhaps best discussed in four sections: (1) a description of the three samples included in the study; (2) an overview of the procedures used in the four phases of data collection; (3) a delineation of the instruments used in our collection of data from parents, therapists, children, and examiners; and (4) an outline of the overall data analysis plan.

THE SAMPLES

The study was originally planned to include just two groups of subjects. The first group comprised children who had reported experiencing ritualistic sexual abuse (RSA) in preschools in the South Bay area of southern California, in or near Manhattan Beach (the RSA group). These initial disclosures occurred in 1983 and 1984. The second group was a demographically similar control group of children who had also attended preschools in southern California but who had experienced no abuse (the NA group). Two years into the study, we obtained funding to include another comparison group made up of children from Reno, Nevada, who had reported experiencing sexual abuse but not ritualistic abuse in a school setting (the SA group). All children, parents, and therapists in each of the three groups signed informed consent or assent forms that were approved by both the UCLA and Harbor–UCLA Medical Center Research and Education Institute Human Subjects Protection Committees.

Group 1: The Sample Reporting Ritualistic Sexual Abuse

The biggest question mark in our minds during the first year of the study was whether we would be able to obtain a large enough number of subjects for the RSA sample. Given the trauma that the families from Manhattan Beach had experienced, combined with the general feelings of mistrust pervading the community (see Chapter 1), we wondered whether families would allow relative strangers into their worlds. Contact letters describing the study were sent to subjects from three of the diagnostic agencies that had evaluated many of the children from the RSA cases. Since the letters were sent from the agencies, the names and addresses of families involved in these cases remained protected and unknown to us, until and unless parents who received the letter returned a portion of the letter in the enclosed stamped envelope indicating that they wished to be contacted to learn more about the study.

A total of 201 letters were sent from the first diagnostic agency, Children's Institute International. Over 100 additional letters were sent from the other two diagnostic agencies, Pathways and the South Bay Center for Counseling. A total of 88 children from 70 families agreed to participate in the study. Six children were eventually dropped from this sample because, according to therapist data, they had never directly disclosed having been abused.

Thus the final RSA sample was comprised of 82 children from 64 families (see Table 3.1). These children ranged in age from 4 to 14, with a mean age of 8.2 years and 66% of the sample between 7 and 12 years of age. Ninety-one percent of the children were white, 1% were of Asian-American descent, and 7% were from mixed or other unspecified backgrounds. Most of the children were being raised Catholic (36%) or Protestant (29%). Six percent were being raised in the Jewish faith, 3% were being brought up in another unspecified religion, and 26% had no religious affiliation. Seventy-nine percent of the parents were married at the time of this study.

The children had attended one or more of six preschools at which there had been allegations of ritualistic sexual abuse. The majority of the children (62%) had attended the McMartin Preschool at some time. Twelve percent of the children had attended more than one of these preschools.

The sample consisted of 45 girls (55%) and 37 boys (45%), all of whom had undergone some degree of psychotherapy. Our attempts to include children who did not attend therapy were unsuccessful. Therapist data were collected from 19 therapists. Five therapists had at least five participating children as clients. The highest number of subjects seen by

TABLE 3.1. Demographic Data on Reportedly Ritualistically

Item	RSA (n = 82)	NA (n = 37)
Mean age (years)	8.2	8.7
Gender: (% girls)	55	64
Hollingshead SES (mean score)	50	57*
Hollingshead categories		
1. Major business and professional (%)	43	62
2. Medium business, minor professional, technical (%)	39	38
3. Skilled crafts, clerical, sales (%)	17	0
4. Machine operators, semiskilled workers (%)	1	0
5. Unskilled laborers (%)	0	0
Marital status		
Married (%)	79	88
Separated (%)	3	6
Divorced (%)	17	6
Never Married (%)	1	0
Child's race		
White (%)	91	82
Asian-American (%)	1	0
Other or mixed (%)	7	18
Child's religion		
Catholic (%)	36	15
Protestant (%)	29	46
Jewish (%)	6	18
Other religion (%)	3	3
No religion (%)	26	18

*$p < .05$

any one therapist was 18, or 22% of the sample. The average number of weeks of therapy was 69.1, or about 1 1/4 years.

Group 2: The Nonabused Control Sample

We originally considered recruiting a control group from other preschools in Manhattan Beach at which there had been no allegations of sexual abuse. We quickly abandoned this idea when we realized that the allegations of abuse had permeated the entire community, to the point that we could not be sure which preschools were not involved. Moreover, when we did find a preschool with no allegations of abuse, that preschool chose not to respond to our request. (Allegations did indeed surface against this preschool a few years into the study.) It became evident that families in the Manhattan Beach area would not be the best choice for a control group, since their lives were affected by the tumult in the community even if their own children had not been abused.

We then examined census data in the library to determine which communities in southern California best matched the demographic characteristics of our Manhattan Beach sample. Once we had chosen the targeted communities, we began our search to find a well-respected preschool that had been in existence for many years and had no allegations of any form of child abuse. We spent a few months discussing the project and procedures with the director of a preschool in Sherman Oaks, but unrelated circumstances caused this preschool to pull out of the study before actual recruitment began. We eventually learned from a colleague in the child abuse field that a preschool in the Studio City/North Hollywood section of Los Angeles seemed to match our demographic criteria and had a board of directors that was interested in helping children and families in the battle against child abuse in any way it could. We contacted the director of the First Christian Nursery School, Corinne Pollard, who invited us to meet with the board to discuss our project. The board approved our study, and has been extremely supportive of our efforts throughout the project.

We adopted a recruitment strategy for the control sample that was similar to that used for the Manhattan Beach sample. First Christian Nursery School sent our recruitment letter to parents of children who were approximately the same age as those in Manhattan Beach, along with a cover letter from the school. Once again, names and addresses were protected and were not available to us unless parents sent back a portion of the letter in the enclosed stamped envelope requesting more information about the study. Unlike the families in the Manhattan Beach sample, families in the control sample were told that each child would be given $20 for participating in the study. In both samples, parents were told that they would receive verbal feedback about their children's scores on the psychological tests that were to be administered, if they desired such feedback.

Twenty-six of the 61 families receiving the letter agreed to participate in the study, with a total of 35 children being involved. Two of the children had attended a different preschool, at which there had also been no allegations of child abuse. These two were siblings of children who had gone to First Christian Nursery School.

In order to increase the size of our control sample, we contacted Mary Klimetz, the director of the Neighborhood Nursery School in Westwood. This preschool also had been in existence for many years, had an excellent reputation, had no allegations of child abuse, and served families with demographic characteristics similar to those of the Manhattan Beach sample. Ms. Klimetz approved the study and was an invaluable ally in helping us recruit subjects. Of the 38 families who received this letter, 8 families with 13 children eventually agreed to participate in the study.

In recruiting the control sample, we attempted to screen out any child who may have been sexually abused. We did this in three ways. First, our recruitment letter indicated that we specifically were seeking children who had never been abused. Second, in our phone conversations with parents who expressed interest in the study, we reiterated the need to have only children without abuse histories in the control sample, and we requested that the parents not join the study if they had any suspicion that their child might have been abused. Third, in the informed consent form that parents signed we again stated that "we are interested in your participation as a family with a child who attended preschool but has not been molested in any setting." The consent form also informed parents that "if instances of child abuse are discovered, they will need to be reported, as required by law."

Overall, 34 families with 48 children originally agreed to participate as the control (NA) sample. Six boys eventually dropped out of the study before their first testing session, and one other dropped out after his first session. One family with a boy and a girl were dropped from the study because the family income was much higher than that of other subjects. Another family with a boy and a girl were excluded because their babysitter's husband had been accused of molesting another child, and there was some question as to whether these children had ever been abused. The final control sample included 37 children from 28 families. Because of the unusually large number of boys who withdrew from the study, the control sample was made up of 24 girls (65%) and 13 boys (35%). This proportion of girls to boys did not differ significantly from that of the RSA sample, however.

The children in the control sample ranged in age from 5 to 14, with a mean age of 8.7 years and 68% of the sample between the ages of 7 and 12. Eighty-two percent of the children were white, with 18% being of mixed or unspecified other backgrounds. We had originally been concerned that our control group, based on census data estimates, would have a lower socioeconomic status (SES) than the RSA sample. The result was the opposite, in that the NA sample was actually higher in SES. On the Hollingshead four-factor index (1975), the NA sample had a mean SES score of 56.9, compared with a mean SES score of 50.1 for the RSA sample. Although both samples fell in the upper-middle-class range, the difference in SES score was statistically significant, and needed to be controlled for in our statistical analyses. Whenever SES correlated with an outcome variable, we utilized analysis-of-covariance techniques.

As in the RSA sample, most of the families were either Protestant (46%) or Catholic (15%). Eighteen percent were Jewish, 3% were of an unspecified religion, and 18% indicated no religious affiliation. Eighty-eight percent of the parents were married at the time of this study. Unlike the RSA children, almost none of the children in the NA group had ever received psychotherapy.

Group 3: The Sample Reporting Sexual Abuse Only

Approximately 2 years into the study, we obtained funding to include another comparison group, comprised of children who had been sexually but not ritualistically abused in a school setting. We had been in contact with Sam Basta, PhD, and Kathy Milbeck, MA, who had been the primary diagnosticians in a highly publicized case in Reno, Nevada, involving a school named Papoose Palace (see Chapter 1). This case involved a single perpetrator, Steven Boatwright, who confessed to having molested over 50 children.

We were not able to send our recruitment letter through Dr. Basta or Ms. Milbeck, since they had also been the primary therapists for many of the children. These therapists suggested that the letter be sent through Detective Lucky Birch, who had conducted the initial police evaluations and was trusted and respected by the parents in the case. This also seemed to be the best way to parallel our recruitment procedure with the RSA group, where the letters were sent through diagnostic agencies. Fifty letters were sent by Detective Birch. Sixteen families with 17 children originally agreed to be in the study. One girl later refused to participate, and a second girl was dropped from the study because she had also been abused by her mother.

The final comparison (SA) group consisted of 15 children from 14 families (see Chapter 12, Table 12.1). The 9 girls (60%) and 6 boys (40%) ranged in age from 11 to 14, with a mean age of 13.1 years and a median age of 13.1 years. Although these children had reported being abused at about the same age as children in the RSA sample, they were now significantly older than many of the children from Manhattan Beach. In order to make meaningful comparisons, a matched subsample of 15 children was chosen from the RSA sample, using the propensity score method developed by Rosenbaum and Rubin (1985). This matching procedure was conducted as part of a master's thesis by Kathy Perham, a UCLA graduate student. We attempted to minimize differences in age, gender, SES, and IQ, but we were only able to eliminate differences in gender. Thus, analyses of covariance were conducted whenever age, SES, or IQ significantly correlated with our outcome measures.

Ninety percent of the children in the SA sample with complete ethnicity data were white, with 10% being of Hispanic descent. Only 33% of the parents were married at the time their children disclosed the abuse; 42% were currently married at the time of the study. One-third of the children in the SA sample were being raised without a religious affiliation. Twenty-five percent were Catholic, 8% Protestant, and 33% were of some unspecified religion.

PROCEDURES

The procedures used for data collection can best be described in terms of four phases. Phases I, II, and III actually overlapped during the first 3 years of the study. Phase IV was conducted in the fourth year.

Phase I

Since the study did not begin until 3 years after children began disclosing their abuse experiences, we needed to rely on the diagnostic agencies for data collected at the time of disclosure. One instrument that we incorporated into the study had been collected from RSA parents on the day of each child's initial diagnostic evaluation. Before the parents knew the outcome of the child's evaluation, they had been asked to report whether their child had exhibited certain behaviors, such as problems related to sleeping, eating, being around people, or going to school, as well as any inappropriate sex play. We also requested results from the medical evaluations conducted at this time. Both the behavioral and medical records were only requested for those children whose parents had signed separate consent forms permitting us to collect these data.

Phase II

Phase II involved data collection from three sources. First, each child's therapist conducted a 1-hour assessment session with the child, which included some easily administered psychological tests and drawings. If a child could not be tested by his or her therapist, this first testing session was conducted by a trained advanced graduate student from the UCLA Department of Psychology. These examiners conducted all first sessions on the NA group, since these children did not have therapists participating in the study.

Second, each child's therapist was asked to complete an extensive packet of questionnaires describing the child's symptoms, behaviors, coping mechanisms, family environment, and disclosures about the abuse. In order to spare children and parents the ordeal of repeating the disclosures, we did not ask them any questions about what abuse acts the children reported. Instead, we relied on the therapist's completion of a detailed Sexual Abuse Grid to document the types of acts each child disclosed. Therapists were paid $50 for conducting the initial testing session, and $100 for completing each therapist packet.

Third, each child's parents were asked to complete a separate packet of questionnaires describing the child's behavior at various time periods, including the first month after the diagnostic interview, the period of most distress since the abuse disclosure, and currently (i.e., approximately 3 years after the abuse was disclosed). Questionnaires also examined stressful life events and family coping styles. Data were collected from both mothers and fathers whenever possible.

Phase III

Most of the children also underwent two additional sessions of more in-depth psychological assessment. These sessions were conducted almost exclusively by the trained examiners, although a few children were tested by the principal investigators of the study. As described in the next section, these assessments included a combination of projective and nonprojective tests of cognitive, emotional, and behavioral functioning. The testers also completed a brief psychiatric rating scale to describe the children's functioning at the time of the testing.

Phase IV

Parents in the RSA and SA samples were asked whether they wished to participate in a structured interview to discuss the impact that the abuse disclosures had had on their lives. These interviews took place as part of a follow-up process approximately 5 years after the children's initial abuse disclosures. In the interviews, we asked parents about the impact of the experiences on their children, their marriages, their relationships with the children in the study and any other siblings, their relationships with friends and extended family, and their views on various institutions (such as the police, lawyers, doctors, therapists, and people in the mass media). We also asked parents about the coping mechanisms they used in dealing with their traumatic experiences, as well as any advice they would give to parents faced with a similar tragedy. Each child's parents were asked to complete a final packet of questionnaires assessing the family environment and the child's functioning 5 years after the initial abuse disclosures.

INSTRUMENTS

Following the recommendations of sociologist and research consultant David Finkelhor and other researchers in the field, we included a combination of standardized instruments, which had proven validity and reliability but not much specificity in terms of symptoms pertinent to child sexual abuse, and nonstandardized instruments, which focused more on pertinent symptoms but had no formal scale development. The study involved over 40 instruments, each of which is briefly described. The instruments are discussed in relation to the phase of data collection when they were used. The reader may find it helpful to refer to Tables 3.2, 3.3, and 3.4 for summaries of these measures.

Phase I Instruments

Only two instruments were used in Phase I. The first was a nonstandardized behavioral questionnaire developed by the staff of Children's Institute International and utilized in their diagnostic evaluations. Parents were asked to indicate on this questionnaire whether their children had recently been exhibiting any of the following types of behavior: withdrawal, sleep problems, regressive behavior, eating problems, bathing problems, school problems, inappropriate sex play, violence, or secretive behavior.

The second Phase I instrument was a medical examination summary sheet, on which physicians who had examined the children were asked to summarize their findings and to state whether they had observed medical findings indicating sexual abuse.

Phase II Instruments

Phase II instruments were collected from parents, therapists, and children.

Parent Instruments

Eight parent instruments were used in Phase II.

1. *Parent Information Questionnaire (PIQ)*. This nonstandardized instrument asked for demographic information, such as a child's age, gender, and ethnicity; parent's education and occupations; family constellation; religious involvement; parents' own abuse history; parental marital status; and parental beliefs about the occurrence and effects of their child's abuse.

TABLE 3.2. Parent Instruments

Phase	Instrument
I	1. Children's Institute International's original survey of child symptoms
II	1. Parent Information Questionnaire: demographic survey 2. Behaviors After Diagnostic Interview (BADI): checklist of behavior symptoms 3. Child Behavior Checklist (CBCL) 4. Louisville Fear Survey: list of children's fears 5. Family Crisis Oriented Personal Evaluation Scales (F-COPES): family coping styles 6. Coping with Sexual Abuse (CSA): ratings of the usefulness of specific coping behaviors 7. Family Adaptability and Cohesion Evaluation Scales (FACES-III): measure of family adaptability and cohesion 8. Family Inventory of Life Events (FILE): life stress scale
III	None
IV	1. Parent Reaction Questionnaire: ratings paralleling follow-up interview 2. CBCL 3. Parent Perception Inventory (PPI)—Parent Version: parents' perception of parent–child dyads 4. Family Environment Scale (FES) 5. FILE

2. Behaviors after Diagnostic Interview (BADI). This nonstandardized instrument was designed to measure changes in children's functioning from the period before the diagnostic interview to 1 month after the interview, and again 3 years later. The measure was a modified version of the above-mentioned form used in Phase I by Children's Institute International, which had assessed certain behaviors before the diagnostic interview. The BADI asked parents to indicate which behaviors the children exhibited during the month following the interview, and which behaviors the children were currently exhibiting approximately 3 years later.

3. Child Behavior Checklist (CBCL). Perhaps the most widely used standardized measure of children's behavior, the CBCL was used by parents to rate their children's behavior during the period of most distress (Achenbach & Edelbrock, 1983). We appended some additional behaviors characteristic of traumatized children to the end of the measure.

4. Louisville Fear Survey. This standardized instrument lists 81 fears taken from the clinical literature (Miller, 1972, 1974, 1976). Parents were asked to rate whether their children were currently exhibiting no fear of each item, a reasonable amount of fear, or an excessive or unreasonable amount of fear.

5. *Family Crisis-Oriented Personal Evaluation Scales (F-COPES)*. This standardized instrument features 30 coping behaviors that families might use in times of difficulty (McCubbin, Larsen, & Olson, 1982).

6. *Coping with Sexual Abuse (CSA)*. This nonstandardized instrument was created to assess additional coping strategies that parents might have used, such as seeking help from professionals, seeking help from others, seeking help from inner resources, or taking social action. Parents were asked to indicate which strategies they used, and whether the strategy made things better, made things worse, or neither helped nor hurt.

7. *Family Adaptability and Cohesion Evaluation Scales (FACES-III)*. FACES-III is a standardized 20-item measure designed to assess a family's level of cohesion and adaptability (Olson, Portner, & Lavee, 1985).

8. *Family Inventory of Life Events (FILE)*. This standardized 71-item measure assesses the degree of life stress being experienced by a family, and includes a variety of marital and intrafamily strains (McCubbin, Patterson, & Wilson, 1981).

Therapist Instruments

Twelve instruments were completed by the therapists during Phase II.

1. *Therapist Demographic Survey*. This nonstandardized instrument was used to gather demographic information about the therapists, including their age, gender, theoretical orientation, professional license, and experience in treating abused children.

2. *Children's Therapy Questionnaire*. This nonstandardized measure asked factual questions about the type and extent of therapy given to each child.

3. *DSM-III categorization*. This sheet simply asked a therapist who used the *Diagnostic and Statistical Manual of Mental Disorders*, third edition (DSM-III; American Psychiatric Association, 1980) to document the diagnosis given to each child at the start of therapy and at the end of therapy (or currently, for a child still in therapy).

4. *Sexual Abuse Grid*. This nonstandardized instrument lists 32 sexual, ·terrorizing, and ritualistic acts. Each child's therapist indicated which acts, if any, the child had disclosed. For each act, the therapist could also specify the gender of the adult(s) alleged to be involved, as well as the degree of the child's reported involvement (e.g., whether the child was forced to perform an act on an adult vs. being forced to observe an act occurring).

TABLE 3.3. Therapist Instruments

Phase	Instrument
I	None
II	1. Therapist Demographic Survey: demographic and professional information
	2. Children's Therapy Questionnaire: specific facts about child's therapy
	3. DSM-III categorization: psychodiagnostic information
	4. Sexual Abuse Grid: checklist of specific abuse acts reported by child
	5. Brief Psychiatric Rating Scale for Children (BPRS-C): ratings of child's psychiatric symptoms
	6. CBCL, therapist version: ratings of child's behavior problems
	7. Children's Global Assessment Scale (CGAS): global rating of child's functioning
	8. Child Symptom Pattern (CSP): child's symptoms for each month of therapy
	9. Child Disclosure and Recantation Pattern: child's pattern of disclosing and/or recanting abuse allegations
	10. Therapist's Rating of Parental Reaction to Sexual Abuse (TRPRSA): ratings of parents' reactions to child's abuse allegations
	11. Clinical Rating Scale for the Circumplex Model of Marital and Family Systems (Family Profile): ratings of family cohesion, adaptability, and communication
	12. Child Coping and Defense Strategies: description of child's use of coping and defense strategies
III	None
IV	1. Therapist Reaction Questionnaire (TRQ): therapist's ratings of his or her own reactions throughout 5-year ordeal

5. *Brief Psychiatric Rating Scale for Children (BPRS-C)*. The BPRS-C is a 21-item measure comprised of seven relatively independent factors of psychopathology: Behavior Problems, Depression, Thinking Disturbance, Psychomotor Excitation, Withdrawal, Anxiety, and Organicity (Overall & Pfefferbaum, 1982). We added one additional item assessing inappropriate sexual behavior. Each child's therapist completed the BPRS-C twice—first rating the child's functioning during the period of most distress, then rating the child's functioning at the end of therapy (or currently, for a child still in therapy).

6. *Therapist's CBCL*. This measure incorporated the standardized 113-item Teacher Report Form of the CBCL (Achenbach & Edelbrock, 1986) with additional items assessing post-traumatic stress disorder and other symptoms commonly experienced by abuse victims. Therapists rated children on this instrument according to their behavior during the period of most distress.

7. *Children's Global Assessment Scale (CGAS)*. This descriptive measure asks therapists to give a global rating of each child's overall functioning on a 100 point scale (Shaffer et al., 1985). As with the BPRS-C, each child's therapist rated each child for two time periods: the period of most distress and the end of therapy (or currently, for a child still in therapy).

8. *Child Symptom Pattern*. This nonstandardized instrument assessed a child's overall symptomatology during each month of therapy, thus allowing us to chart each child's pattern of healing.

9. *Child Disclosure and Recantation Pattern*. We developed this nonstandardized measure to ascertain the number, types, and pattern of disclosures made by each child, as well as those times a child might have "taken back" or recanted a previous disclosure. Coding systems were developed by Jane McCord and Lauren Shapiro Gonzalez.

10. *Therapist's Rating of Parental Reaction to Sexual Abuse (TRPRSA)*. On this nonstandardized measure, we listed 16 ways a child's parents might react to reports that the child had been sexually abused. Items included the use of denial, self-blame, or depression, as well as the presence of supportive behaviors toward the child. Therapists rated the reactions of both mothers and fathers whenever possible.

11. *Clinical Rating Scale for the Circumplex Model of Marital and Family Systems (Family Profile)*. This standardized measure documents a therapist's assessment of the degree of family cohesion, adaptability, and communication (Olson & Killorin, 1985).

12. *Child Coping and Defense Strategies*. This nonstandardized instrument, developed primarily by Mary Kay Oliveri, was used to gather therapist ratings of the types of defense mechanisms and coping strategies used by each child at times of general stress (in this or any child's life) and at times of stress related to specific abuse events reported by the child.

Child Instruments

Seven measures were given to each child during the Phase II initial testing session.

1. *Draw-A-Person (DAP)*. Children were instructed to draw a picture of a person, and then to name the person and state what the person was doing, thinking, and feeling. Later in the same testing session, children were then asked to draw a person of the opposite sex and to answer the same questions. Drawings were scored by raters unaware of group membership, using criteria developed by Koppitz (1968, 1984) for scoring emotional indicators, as well as an additional scoring method for nonverbal ability developed by Naglieri (1988).

TABLE 3.4. Child Instruments

Phase	Instrument
I	None
II	1. Draw-A-Person (DAP): semiprojective child drawings
	2. Pictorial Scale of Perceived Competence and Social Acceptance for Young Children, or Self-Perception Profile for Children: age appropriate self-concept measures
	3. Parent Perception Inventory (PPI): child's perception of parent–child dyads
	4. Incomplete Sentence Test: open-ended attitudes toward self, school, peers, adults, family, and affection/touch
	5. Draw Your Preschool: semiprojective drawing of preschool
	6. Preschool and Primary Nowicki–Strickland Internal–External Locus of Control Scale, or Why Things Happen: age-appropriate locus of control measure
	7. Kinetic Family Drawing (KFD): semiprojective family drawing
III	1. Developmental Test of Visual–Motor Integration (VMI): neuropsychiatric screening for visual–motor deficits
	2. Wechsler Intelligence Scale for Children—Revised (WISC-R): estimates of verbal and performance intelligence
	3. Roberts Apperception Test for Children (RATC): projective measure of clinical symptoms and problem-solving skills
	4. Rorschach Inkblot Test: projective measure of cognitive and emotional functioning
	5. Peabody Individual Achievement Test (PIAT): achievement levels in spelling, math, reading, and general information
IV	None

2. *Self-concept scale*. Each child completed one of three standardized self-concept scales, depending upon his or her age. Children who had not yet reached third grade were given either the preschool–kindergarten or the first-grade–second-grade version of the Pictorial Scale of Perceived Competence and Social Acceptance for Young Children (Harter & Pike, 1984). Children who were in third grade or higher completed the Self-Perception Profile for Children (Harter, 1985).

3. *Parent Perception Inventory (PPI)*. The PPI is a measure of a child's perception of his or her parents' behavior at home (Hazzard, Christensen, & Margolin, 1983). Children rated the degree to which they perceived their mothers and fathers as exhibiting positive behaviors, such as saying "Thank you," and negative behaviors, such as criticizing.

4. *Incomplete Sentence Test*. We developed a nonstandardized list of incomplete sentences that each child was asked to complete. The

sentences were chosen to tap attitudes toward self, school, peers, adults, family, and affection/touch, and were rated for positive, negative, or neutral content by raters unaware of group status.

5. *Draw Your Preschool.* Children were asked simply to draw a picture of their preschool.

6. *Locus of control scale.* Children completed one of two locus of control scales, depending on their age. These standardized scales are designed to measure the extent to which children see themselves as having power in their environment, as opposed to seeing external forces or powerful others as having more control. Children who had not yet completed second grade were given the Preschool and Primary Nowicki-Strickland Internal–External Locus of Control Scale (Nowicki & Duke, 1974). Older children completed the Why Things Happen scale (Connell, 1985).

7. *Kinetic Family Drawing.* Using the traditional version of this instrument, testers instructed children to draw a picture of their family doing something. Children were then asked what each person in the picture was feeling. A special coding system was adapted from Burns and Kaufman (1975) by graduate student Marcia Rorty, and drawings were scored by raters unaware of group membership.

Phase III Instruments

Two additional child testing sessions were conducted in Phase III.

Child Instruments—Session 2

1. *Developmental Test of Visual–Motor Integration (VMI).* This standardized screening measure was used to assess gross abnormalities in visual–motor skills (Beery, 1982). It also served as an "ice breaker" since it was the first instrument given in what was typically a child's first meeting with the tester.

2. *Wechsler Intelligence Scale for Children—Revised (WISC-R).* Children completed four subscales of this widely used measure of intellectual functioning: Similarities, Block Design, Vocabulary, and Object Assembly (Wechsler, 1974). We calculated deviation quotients based on the extrapolation procedures of Sattler (1988) to obtain estimates of Full Scale, Performance, and Verbal IQ.

3. *Roberts Apperception Test for Children (RATC).* This standardized projective test asks children to look at 16 pictures and compose a story with a beginning, middle, and end, and to state what the characters are doing, feeling, and thinking (McArthur & Roberts, 1982). The test is

designed to assess a child's level of anxiety, depression, aggression, and feelings of rejection, as well as his or her ability to identify and resolve problems, and the extent to which he or she relies on self or others when faced with problems.

Child Instruments—Session 3

1. *Rorschach Inkblot Test.* This widely used projective test asks children to describe what they see in 10 cards containing inkblots. We scored children's answers using the standardized Comprehensive System (Exner & Weiner, 1982).

2. *Peabody Individual Achievement Test (PIAT).* Children completed all subtests of this standardized test, which assesses several areas of academic achievement: Spelling, Mathematics, Reading Recognition, Reading Comprehension, and General Information (Dunn & Markwardt, 1970).

Examiner Instrument

Examiners completed the BPRS-C, described above, at the completion of the child's third testing session.

Phase IV

Parents who participated in the parent interview phase of data collection completed one questionnaire based on the interview itself, along with four other instruments.

Parent Interview Instruments

1. *Parent Reaction Questionnaire.* We developed this instrument to parallel the parent interview, so that we could obtain quantifiable answers to questions that were open-ended in the interview.

2. *CBCL.* Parents were asked to fill out another version of this previously described checklist (Achenbach & Edelbrock, 1983), this time rating their children's behavior during the past 6 months. In addition to the extra items attached to the previous CBCL, we incorporated items designed to assess the presence of post-traumatic stress disorder.

3. *PPI—Parent Version.* On this standardized measure parallel to the child version of the PPI, parents rated the extent to which they and their spouses exhibited positive and negative behaviors toward their children (Christensen & Shenk, 1988).

4. *Family Environment Scale (FES)*. This more detailed, standardized measure of family environment was completed by parents. The scale factors into 10 subscales assessing relationship, personal growth, and system maintenance dimensions (Moos & Moos, 1981).

5. *FILE*. We obtained a second version of this life stress scale to measure the degree and types of stressors experienced by families in the fourth year following the abuse disclosure (McCubbin et al., 1981).

Therapist Instrument

Therapists completed the Therapist Reaction Questionnaire, a nonstandardized survey of how they themselves were affected by their involvement in these cases.

DATA ANALYSIS PLAN

We developed a data analysis plan that would allow us to answer a series of questions relating to the psychological functioning of children reporting ritualistic and nonritualistic sexual abuse. To accomplish this task, we used a combination of between-group and within-group comparisons.

Between-Group Comparisons

Many of our analyses focused on the question of how children in the RSA sample had functioned since their abuse, as compared with children who had never been abused (the NA group). The entire RSA and NA samples were used for these analyses. Parent and child data from Phase II and child data from Phase III were utilized, since these data were collected from both groups. We conducted one-way analyses of variance and χ^2 procedures to compare the two groups. Since the NA sample had a higher SES than the RSA sample, we employed analyses of covariance to partial out the effects of SES whenever SES correlated significantly with a target variable. In addition, we conducted discriminant-function analyses to examine how well we could distinguish between RSA and NA children, based upon their scores on various psychological tests.

We also wanted to answer the question of how the RSA children compare with the SA children. As mentioned previously, we used Rosenbaum and Rubin's (1985) propensity score matching method to select an RSA match subsample in which demographic differences would be minimized. Once again, we conducted one-way analyses of variance and χ^2 procedures to compare the two groups, and utilized analyses of covariance whenever key demographic variables correlated with our outcome measures. The small sample sizes in these matched groups prohibited us from conducting additional discriminant-function analyses.

Within-Group Comparisons

In addition to investigating how the RSA children were functioning relative to the SA and NA children, we were very interested in examining how the RSA children functioned over the past 5 years relative to themselves. We wanted to know whether they were getting better, and if so, what factors contributed to the healing process. Thus, we conducted a series of repeated-measures analyses to compare the functioning of children in the Manhattan Beach sample at different time periods: the time just before the initial diagnostic evaluation, the month after this evaluation, the period of most distress, the time 3 years after the evaluation, and (for children whose parents participated in the parent interview) the period 5 years after the evaluation. We also used multiple-regression procedures to determine the extent to which a child's functioning could be accounted for by such variables as type of abuse, demographics, psychotherapy factors, parent activism, and family environment and coping styles.

LIMITATIONS
OF THE STUDY

Robert J. Kelly

A S WITH ALL RESEARCH STUDIES, there are limits on the degree to which we can justifiably generalize our results as being representative of all cases involving reports of ritualistic sexual abuse. In our study, there are five primary areas one must keep in mind when attempting to make any conclusions or generalizations: (1) the complicated community atmosphere; (2) lack of certain knowledge about the specifics of abuse incidents; (3) sampling limitations; (4) instrument and measurement limitations; and (5) issues related to time and developmental maturation.

It would be a gross oversight to discuss abuse effects without acknowledging the powerful effects of the broader community conflict that arose following the first allegations of sexual abuse in Manhattan Beach preschools. By the time we assessed the children reporting ritualistic sexual abuse (the RSA sample) and their families, several years had passed, during which the children were repeatedly questioned by parents, police, diagnostic evaluators, therapists, and (in some cases) numerous lawyers. Parents had been forced to cope not only with the thought that their children had been sexually abused, but with a very emotionally charged community that had become polarized over the issue of whether a large group of Satanic child abusers had infiltrated their preschools. The divisive, sensationalistic media reports, from local papers to 60 *Minutes*, added to an unprecedented degree of public scrutiny surrounding this extremely personal ordeal. Young children were placed in the sadly ironic, confusing, and ultimately damaging position of being celebrities. Furthermore, the courtroom dramas in the most publicized case led to the longest and most expensive court case in U.S. criminal history. The sheer length of this litigation prolonged families' inability to gain any type of closure on their nightmarish experience, thus hindering their attempts to move forward in the healing process. In short, the effects of the reported abuse acts cannot be clearly distinguished from the effects of this unusual community atmosphere.

Often in the field of child sexual abuse, researchers cannot be absolutely certain about the specific acts children have experienced. This study was clearly no exception. To begin with, we agreed with the UCLA Human Subjects Protection Committee that it would not be in the children's best interest for us to ask them or their parents about specific acts, since they had already been repeatedly questioned, and they did not have an ongoing, secure relationship with our psychological examiners. Thus, our data about specific acts came from a secondary source, the therapists, to whom the children had disclosed abuse during the preceding years of therapy. We do not consider this a major limitation of the study, however, since therapists are often the source of this information in other child abuse studies, and they would be expected to have the most complete knowledge of what children had disclosed. We also attempted to collect the results of medical examinations the children had undergone, even though we were aware that often there are no conclusive medical findings in cases of child sexual abuse. Although most of the parents in our study agreed to allow us to collect these data from the medical evaluators and signed a release-of-information form, some physicians refused to provide this information, in part because they feared future legal liability. Thus, although a large proportion of parents told us that their children did have positive medical findings, we were able to systematically review and present the official medical results only for a small subsample, and we could not assess whether children with medical findings differed in their emotional and behavioral functioning from those without medical findings.

In addition to the limitations related to the community atmosphere and the lack of certainty about specific acts, this study also had its share of limitations related to sampling restrictions. Almost all of the children in the RSA sample received psychotherapy, which made it impossible to determine what the effects would be for children who were not in therapy. We also do not know whether these children were placed in therapy because they were having more problems than those children who were not in therapy. However, we do not think that was the case, since therapy was routinely recommended to parents by the initial diagnostic evaluators. In fact, the placement of children in therapy may be more reflective of parents' attempts at supporting their children.

Fortunately, the time between the reports of abuse and our psychological assessments of the children were approximately the same in the RSA sample and the sample of children reporting sexual abuse only (the SA sample). But there were other differences between the samples.

Although some of these differences could be controlled for statistically, such as differences in age, socioeconomic status, and intelligence, other differences could not be eliminated. Most important, perhaps, is the fact that the SA case involved a single perpetrator who confessed (to even more acts than the children disclosed), was convicted, and is currently serving four consecutive life sentences behind bars. The families in this case did not experience the same degree of public doubt about their children's allegations; they were able to gain "legal closure" relatively rapidly; and some even gained a measure of financial retribution. It was impossible to partial out the effects of these sociopolitical events from the effects of the presence or absence of reported ritualistic and terrorizing abuse acts.

Many of our analyses focused on differences between the RSA and nonabused (NA) samples, both of which were composed primarily of white, upper-middle-class children with above-average intelligence. Furthermore, the RSA children reported being abused in a group preschool setting. Thus, we must be cautious in making any generalizations to children of other races, socioeconomic classes, and intelligence levels, as well as to children who are abused in other environments. As in most studies, the control group consisted of children whose parents volunteered to be in this study. This can sometimes lead to the formation of a "supercontrol group," since parents whose children are functioning at a high level may be more likely to volunteer. However, we were initially concerned about the opposite problem. Since our study involved free psychological assessments by testers from a major university, we were concerned that parents who were more distressed by their children's lower functioning might be more likely to volunteer. In fact, some of the parents in the control group specifically stated that they were worried about their children's behavior and thus joined the study to have their children evaluated. However, we were relieved to see that the children in the NA sample scored very similarly to the normative groups on our standardized instruments, and thus seemed to be an appropriate control group.

There were also limitations related to instrumentation and measurement. We followed the advice of Finkelhor (1986) in combining traditional, well-standardized psychological instruments with other measures designed to assess abuse-specific effects that traditional measures do not assess. We also wanted to combine instruments that would provide quantitative data with those that would increase our knowledge of the qualitative aspects of these experiences, such as the parents' descriptions in the interviews of how the experience affected their lives. In doing so, we realized that the results from these nonstandardized instruments must be considered exploratory, since the instruments themselves have not undergone formal scale development. Furthermore, since many of these analyses were exploratory, we conducted a large number of analyses, which increased the likelihood that some findings were due to chance. In many cases, we tried to reduce the likelihood of this type of experiment-wide error problem by presenting our primary, hypothesized analyses first and then labeling secondary analyses as exploratory. We also tried to acknowledge when multiple analyses resulted in only one or two significant results, and were thus more likely to represent false-positive findings.

The fifth area of potential limitations is related to the problems associated with the timing of our assessments. Once the children in the RSA sample made their disclosures of abuse, many of us in the community met together under the auspices of the Research Advisory Group in order to put together a comprehensive research study. By the time our study was conceived, proposed, and funded by the National Center on Child Abuse and Neglect, 2 years had already elapsed. We then needed to wait an additional 5 months before receiving final approval from the UCLA Human Subjects Protection Committee, which was understandably concerned with the volatility of these cases. Thus, since we did not begin assessing children and families until 2 to 3 years after their initial disclosures, some of the measures asked parents and therapists to rate the children retrospectively. As with all retrospective measures, we can never be sure that the raters' assessments were as accurate as they would have been if the ratings were contemporaneous. Since we are particularly interested in longitudinal and developmental effects of child sexual abuse, we have attempted to present some data based on different time periods: just prior to the initial disclosure (based on patient records); just after the initial disclosure; during the period of most distress; 2 to 3 years after the initial disclosure; and 5 years after the initial disclosure. However, only our data from just prior to, 2 to 3 years after, and 5 years after initial disclosure were collected at those specific times, as opposed to the other data, which were based on retrospective ratings.

One other time-related limitation involves the fact that although children generally disclosed their alleged preschool abuse at approximately the same time, and they were approximately the same age during the times they were in those preschools, children were of different ages by the time the initial evaluations were conducted. Moreover, it had been several years since some of the older children had attended preschool, and therefore the time since the reported abuse differed between some of the children. In general, however, our analyses showed that time since reported abuse did not seem to be related to our outcome measures. The findings based on child age that we did report seem related to actual developmental differences, which are important for our understanding of how reported abuse affects children as they mature. For those analyses that did not directly focus on developmental differences, we controlled for the confounding effects of child age through the use of analysis-of-covariance techniques.

In conclusion, despite the fact that this study produced a plethora of valuable data, we must keep in mind the above-described limitations and must not overgeneralize from these results. Moreover, we should look at these results in combination with results of future studies on ritualistic child sexual abuse, so that we can draw our conclusions from a broad data base obtained at several sites across the country.

As a final note, we would like to comment upon the manner in which our findings may be received. Since the inception of this study, many people, including some members of the media, have been most concerned with whether our data prove that the children in the RSA sample were definitely abused. Given the fact that the related legal cases were indeterminate, we can appreciate the public's desire for solid, definitive evidence. However, we have never intended our study to be used in this way. We have been most concerned with documenting the particular problems that these children have encountered, and learning more about what promotes healing. These are important questions, which sometimes seem to have been lost or overlooked because so much attention has focused on the legal aspects. Our hope is that our information about the psychological and emotional aspects of these cases will help the families in our study, as well as other families who face similarly painful and traumatizing crisis situations, and the professionals who seek to help them overcome this trauma.

Content
and Process
of Disclosures
# of Sexual Abuse
in Preschools

PERSPECTIVES ON WHAT HAPPENED TO THE CHILDREN

Jill Waterman

Amidst the never-ending controversy surrounding the McMartin Preschool case and other cases of alleged molestation in preschools in the South Bay area of Los Angeles, the question of what happened to the children is neither a clear nor a straightforward one. Nine years later, many questions still exist as to what exactly took place in the preschools of these idyllic beach towns.

In our study, we did not ask either children or parents directly about what abusive experiences allegedly befell the children, for three reasons. First, we felt that they had been badgered and questioned enough already, and that further questioning could be upsetting to the children and parents. It seemed more humane to gather this information in other ways. Second, not gathering information about the alleged abuse directly from the children diminished the possibility of our having to fight subpoenas for the data in ongoing court cases; although the data were protected by a Certificate of Confidentiality from the federal government, we did not want to risk the confidentiality of children and families if the certificate were challenged in court.[1] In fact, our data *were* subpoenaed by the defense in the McMartin trial, but the defense attorneys decided to quash

---

[1]The Certificate of Confidentiality is obtainable from the National Institute of Mental Health. It is designed to protect the identity of research subjects from subpoena in any court proceeding. However, the validity of the certificate has never been tested in court, and we needed to let our research subjects know that in our consent form.

the subpoena when they discovered that testing the Certificate of Confidentiality in court might add another year to the already lengthy proceedings. Third, we believed that the potential for the children's distress to color the information we were gathering on how they were functioning would be lessened if we did not ask them about the upsetting experiences involved in the reported abuse.

Therefore, our understanding of what happened to the children comes primarily from detailed reports filled out by therapists on the children in the allegedly abused groups, and from medical reports filled out by physicians who examined a subsample of our group in Manhattan Beach. Data were also obtained from parents on their general degree of belief in what their children disclosed.

THE SEXUAL ABUSE GRID

The Sexual Abuse Grid was filled out by 18 psychotherapists in regard to the disclosures of 65 children in the group reporting ritualistic sexual abuse (the RSA group), as well as by 6 psychotherapists who documented the disclosures of the 15 children in the group reporting sexual abuse only (the SA group). Each therapist was asked to check on the Sexual Abuse Grid which of 32 sexual, terrorizing, and ritualistic acts were disclosed by a child. A total Sexual Abuse Grid score was calculated by adding all items checked. The grid was also divided into three categories of sexual abuse for purposes of description and analysis, according to Russell's (1983) criteria based on seriousness: "less intrusive," "intrusive," and "highly intrusive" sexual abuse.

As can be seen from Table 5.1, less intrusive sexual acts included exhibitionism and kissing; intrusive sexual acts included fondling, ejaculation, and intercrural intercourse ("dry humping"); and very intrusive sexual acts included penetration of various kinds and oral–genital contact. In addition, terrorizing acts were grouped, as were ritualistic acts, making a total of five categories. Items within each category were summed to yield five category scores for each child, in addition to the total score. Items included in each category, as well as the percentage of children disclosing each type of act in the RSA and SA groups, are listed in Table 5.1.

There were no significant differences between groups on the three major sexual categories. Both the RSA and the SA groups disclosed many less intrusive, intrusive, and highly intrusive sexual acts. In the RSA group, there were significantly more reports of sex games and stories, ejaculation, anal intercourse, and foreign object penetration. It appeared that the single perpetrator in the SA group was mostly involved in

TABLE 5.1. Percentage of Children Reporting Specific Acts on the
Sexual Abuse Grid

Type of act	RSA	SA
Less intrusive sexual acts	90.8	92.9
Exposure of genitalia	87.7	92.9
Kissing	44.6	42.9
Shown pornography	38.5	28.6
Sex games/stories	72.3	21.4****
Intrusive sexual acts	86.2	100.0
Ejaculation	46.2	7.1*
Fondling of genitals or breasts, masturbation	86.2	100.0
Intercrural intercourse	18.5	42.9
Highly intrusive sexual acts	81.5	71.4
Vaginal intercourse[a]	48.6	0.0*
Anal intercourse	40.0	0.0**
Oral–genital contact	63.1	71.4
Foreign object penetration	63.1	0.0****
Terrorizing acts	98.5	0.0***
Abuse of animals	80.0	0.0****
Sadistic acts (physical abuse, biting, burning, whipping, bondage)	78.5	0.0****
Drugs taken	58.5	0.0***
Acts involving use of weapons	78.5	0.0****
Acts involving use of blood	63.1	0.0****
Acts involving feces or urine	55.4	0.0***
Acts involving monsters or ghosts	46.2	0.0**
Threats to use magic powers	66.2	0.0****
Threats of death to child	80.0	0.0****
Acts involving dead bodies	36.9	0.0*
Acts involving killing of babies	33.8	0.0*
Acts involving killing of children	21.5	0.0
Acts involving killing of adults	10.8	0.0
Ritualistic acts	87.7	7.1***
Satanic rituals	58.5	0.0***
Acts involving churches	50.8	0.0**
Acts involving singing or chanting	49.2	7.1**
Acts involving circus or zoo	20.0	0.0
Acts involving symbols	40.0	0.0**
Acts involving fire	32.3	0.0*
Acts involving magic	67.7	0.0****

[a]Only girls could be included in this category.
*$p < .05$; **$p < .01$; ***$p < .001$; ****$p < .0001$.

fondling and oral–genital contact, while the alleged multiple perpetrators in the RSA group were involved in several types of penetration (vaginal and anal penetration, as well as penetration with a foreign object).

The RSA group reported a variety of terrorizing, physically abusive, and ritualistic acts, whereas the SA children reported no terrorizing acts and only one ritualistic act: one child in the SA group reported "acts involving singing or chanting." Summary data for the total Sexual Abuse Grid score for the RSA and SA groups are given in Table 5.2. It is evident that children in the RSA group reported more total types of abuse, as well as a wider range of abusive acts, than those in the SA group.

The degree of terrorization felt by some RSA children is exemplified by the statement of a mother:

> The things my daughter disclosed are very awful. . . . Sometimes I feel like she's like a survivor of a concentration camp or a survivor of torture. You read about Amnesty International and these clinics they've set up for people who have experienced torture, and I see a lot of similarities with their way of coping with life and the way she is. The whole way she looks at the world . . . I don't think she thinks of it as a safe place.

The acts reported by children in the RSA group are very similar to those obtained by Susan Kelley (1989) from parents of 67 children who reported being ritualistically sexually abused in day care in different centers across the country. In her group, 51% reported vaginal intercourse, 49% alleged rectal intercourse, and 74% reported oral–genital contact. The vast majority of the children in her sample reported being told that they or their families would be killed if they disclosed the abuse; 81% of our RSA children reported such threats. As an example, one mother in our study reported at the 5-year follow-up:

> My daughter was really afraid to tell us about the abuse because they told her they'd murder us and set our house on fire. Even now, she's constantly in fear that something's going to happen to us. If I'm 5

TABLE 5.2. Means, Range, and Standard Deviation for Total Sexual Abuse Grid Score

	RSA	SA
Range	3–30	1–9
Mean	17.91	4.21
Standard deviation	7.63	2.05

Note. Possible scores: 0–32.

minutes late picking her up, she'll run to a teacher, she'll call my sister, she's in a state of panic.

In their national study of sexual abuse in day care, Finkelhor, Williams, and Burns (1988) found that more severe sexual abuse, a higher likelihood of ritualistic abuse and pornography, and younger victims seemed to be more characteristic of cases involving multiple perpetrators than of those with a single perpetrator. The findings in our RSA and SA groups parallel the results of Finkelhor et al.

What can we conclude about some of the more bizarre acts reported by the RSA children? Many of the acts reported by children involved in ritualistic sexual abuse are so outrageous and reprehensible that it is hard to believe that they could have occurred. Examples of such acts, which have been reported across several research samples (e.g., Kelley, 1989; Finkelhor et al., 1988; Faller, 1987), include foreign object penetration, sadistic physical abuse, administration of drugs, Satanic rituals, and acts involving urine and feces.

Several factors can be considered. First, many of the worst types of acts reported are so gruesome and antithetical to our personal belief systems that we want to reject the possibility of their occurrence. How could anyone insert a stick into the vagina of a 3-year-old girl? What kind of monster could force preschool children to eat or play in feces? These notions are so unbelievable that often we decide the children reporting them must be making them up. They are too fantastic to have really occurred. When children in several day care cases from different parts of the country report very similar acts, we are confronted with incompatible information: These outrageous acts could not have occurred, but children from a variety of locations are reporting similar phenomena. Along the same lines, adult survivors of ritualistic abuse in childhood are beginning to tell their stories, and many are remarkably similar to those reported by the RSA children in our sample.

A second factor involves trying to make sense in other than literal ways of some of the more fantastic things reported. For example, in our RSA sample, 33.8% of the children reported to their therapists that they had witnessed acts involving killing of babies. No dead babies were ever found, to our knowledge. How can this be? It is possible that babies were killed and the evidence destroyed. But it is also possible that the perpetrators might have staged an act that appeared to be a murder of a baby in order to frighten children into silence, but that such an act involved a doll, or involved a baby who was not really killed, or was staged in some other way.

Another example of the importance of examining such stories from the perspective of the child can be illustrated by case material. One RSA child had extreme difficulty with eating any meat products, declaring that meat had the Devil in it. Over the course of treatment, he was able to tell his therapist that the alleged perpetrators had killed an animal, stating that the blood was the blood of Satan. The child had become terrified that any meat where blood might be visible after cooking (e.g., steak, hamburger) had the Devil in it, and that if the child ate the meat he would be swallowing the Devil, who would always be inside him.

A third factor to be considered involves the possibility of contamination of information reported by children, parents, and therapists. The issue of influence of one child's or family's reports on the reports of other children or families is a very complex one. Since the reports of abuse all occurred in preschools, some families certainly *did* talk with one another. They were neighbors and friends trying to deal with a crisis of overwhelming proportions occurring with regard to their children. Certainly conversations with other parents may have influenced what parents believed happened to their children; for example, if one child identified a friend as being present during an abusive incident, the parents might have queried the child about whether he or she remembered being in that situation. It is possible that this sharing would lead to false beliefs on the part of a parent if the initial allegations were wrong; on the other hand, it might cut through the denial of some parents and help them accept the trauma to their own children.

Issues of credibility are common in the whole field of child sexual abuse, where denial rather than admission is the rule on the part of perpetrators and sometimes on the part of victims as well (Summit, 1983), and where most evidence involves the words of a child against the words of an adult. Empirical research has shown that false reports of child sexual abuse are the exception, rather than the rule (e.g., Jones & McGraw, 1987), and that children are unlikely to comply with attempts by adults to mislead them into making false statements about what happened to them (Saywitz, Goodman, Nicholas, & Moan, 1991).

As researchers, we tried as much as possible to avoid the maelstrom of controversy surrounding the issues of disclosure and credibility. We wanted to remain objective, and therefore utilized therapists' reports of children's disclosures, rather than reports from children or parents.

MEDICAL REPORTS

In order to gain a further understanding of what happened to children in our groups, we sent requests for medical information to examining physicians in all cases where the children's parents signed consents to request such information. Physicians were asked to state what the medical findings were and to give an opinion with degree of certainty in each case about whether or not a child had been sexually abused. Although medical findings are often used as "proof" that sexual abuse occurred, it should be kept in mind that in the majority of cases the most common sexual act is fondling, which is unlikely to produce medical findings. Similarly, if a child is involved in oral–genital sex, there will not be positive medical findings (unless the perpetrator has a sexually transmitted disease, such as gonorrhea). Generally, only in cases involving vaginal or anal penetration (and sometimes digital penetration) are medical findings likely. Even in cases where perpetrators have confessed to penetration, physical findings are not always evident (Muram, 1989). Since there were many allegations involving vaginal and anal penetration in the RSA group, positive medical findings were expected for this group. For the SA group, where the main penetration was oral–genital, fewer medical findings were predicted.

A great deal of difficulty ensued in gathering the medical data. The pediatrician who examined many of the RSA children, and the lawyers for the agency through which many of the examinations were conducted, were reluctant to release the medical information in view of ongoing legal proceedings, despite the existence of the Certificate of Confidentiality exempting the data from subpoena.

At this writing we have received medical findings forms on 10 children in the RSA group, filled out by five different physicians. Not enough data are available to make statistical analysis possible; however, of the 10 children on whom we have data, positive medical findings were reported for 8 (80%). These findings included infections in one child (monilial vulvitis); hymenal findings in three children (abnormal hymenal anatomy and scar in fourchette area; 6 o'clock hymenal thickening and scar tissue, extending under posterior fourchette, diffuse adhesions; hymenal scarring); and anal findings in four children (abnormal anal exam on basis of relaxation and presence of anal scar; anal scar at 9 o'clock; changes in anal area—loss of adiposity and slight funneling, loss of five folds and increased prominence of remaining folds, absent anal wink; thickened prominent rugal folds, anal discoloration). One child had both anal and hymenal findings, while the physician for one child reported "evidence of old sexual misuse" without further specification. Interestingly, the medical records indicated that monilial vulvitis and vaginitis for one child, and erythema and irritation of vulvar area for another child had been diagnosed 1 or 2 years previous to the disclosure of sexual abuse while the child was attending preschool, but there was no mention in the records of possible sexual abuse.

At the time of the in-depth parent interviews 5 years after initial disclosure, parents were also asked whether their children were evaluated medically and what (if any) findings there were. In the RSA group at follow-up, 27 of 40 children were reported to have received medical evaluations. For 18 of the 27 children, mothers reported positive medical findings (67%). Similar information was obtained for the SA group at the time of the parent interview. In this group, 7 of the 11 children whose mothers participated in the parent interviews received medical evaluations. According to the mothers, 2 had positive medical findings (28.5%).

The contrast between the high percentage of positive medical findings in the RSA group (where allegations of vaginal and anal penetration and of penetration with a foreign object were frequent) and the low percentage of positive medical findings in the SA group (where the main invasive sexual abuse was oral–genital contact) again demonstrates the importance of placing medical findings in suspected sexual abuse in perspective. In the SA group, where the perpetrator confessed, only about one-fourth of the children had positive medical findings; in contrast, in the RSA group, where the alleged perpetrators were acquitted of most charges, two-thirds to four-fifths of the children had positive medical findings. Moreover, the pediatrician who examined a great many of the RSA children has said that this group exhibited the most severe anal findings of any children she has ever examined.

The minimal medical findings in the SA group, where sexual abuse was clearly substantiated by a detailed confession, again remind us that lack of medical evidence is certainly not definitive proof that sexual abuse has not occurred. The reader is referred to articles by McCann, Voris, Simon, and Wells (1989), Hobbs and Wynne (1989), White, Ingram, and Lyna (1989), and Paradise (1989) for findings and discussions of medical evidence in child sexual abuse.

PARENTAL BELIEF IN
CHILDREN'S DISCLOSURES

Information on parental belief was available from two sources. First, parents were asked several questions on the Parent Information Questionnaire about their belief in whether their child had been abused. These questionnaires were typically filled out by the child's mother. Therapists also gave information about their opinion of the parents' belief in the abuse on a questionnaire entitled Therapist's Rating of Parental Reaction to Sexual Abuse. Therapists' opinions are discussed in Chapter 16 and are not described in detail here.

Each child's parents were asked what their current degree of certainty was about whether their child was abused, and how much they believed of what the child disclosed. Results are presented in Table 5.3. As might be

TABLE 5.3. Percentage of Parents Endorsing Belief Statements

	RSA	SA
Current certainty that abuse took place		
Don't know	2.8	0.0
Probably abused	8.3	9.1
Definitely abused	88.9	90.9
Amount of child's disclosure believed[a]		
Half of what child disclosed	1.4	—
Most of what child disclosed	11.1	—
All of what child disclosed	12.5	—
More happened than child disclosed	69.5	—

[a]These statements were not applicable to SA parents, since the perpetrator confessed in this case.

expected, parents who participated in the study showed very high degrees of belief that their children had been sexually abused. There were no significant differences between the RSA and SA groups in parental belief in the abuse. It is interesting to note that the majority of RSA parents believed that their children had experienced more abuse than the children reported. Reasons for this may have included the following: A child may have had positive medical findings but never disclosed abuse consistent with the findings; a child may have been identified by other children as having participated in particular acts, but the child did not report these acts; or a child may have shown certain symptoms consistent with particular acts but never reported such acts. An example of the last-mentioned possibility is a case in which a child became freeway-phobic during preschool, but had no recollection of having been taken places away from the school, although other children placed him at other locations where abuse was reported. Some of what the children disclosed was not believed by 12.5% of the RSA parents. This probably reflects parents' difficulty in believing some of the disclosures that were implausible or probably physically impossible; for example, several children reported being taken for plane trips or watching babies being killed, as discussed earlier. In the SA group, the perpetrator made detailed confessions about each child; when his confessions were compared with the children's reports, it became clear that he had performed more abusive acts and types of acts than the child victims had reported (Terry, 1990).

SUMMARY

In summary, it appears that both the ritualistic sexual abuse group and the sexual abuse only group reported intrusive and highly intrusive sexual abuse in preschool/day care settings. In addition, the RSA group, but not the SA group, reported terrorizing acts that included killing of animals, death threats to the children or their families, sadistic acts and physical abuse, and ritualistic acts that included Satanic activities. Parents and physicians reported that many of the RSA children had positive medical findings; legal problems have impeded the gathering of more specific medical information on RSA children in the sample.

Parents generally believed their children's reports of sexual abuse; in fact, many believed that more happened to their children than the children reported. In conclusion, children's reports to therapists, medical evidence, and parental beliefs are generally convergent for both the RSA and SA groups.

DISCLOSURE PATTERNS IN PSYCHOTHERAPY

Jane McCord
Lauren Shapiro Gonzalez

ONE OF THE MOST CONTROVERSIAL ISSUES in the field of sexual abuse is how to make sense of the ways children talk about being victimized. As those who work with children suspected of having been abused can attest, children often initially deny abuse and then disclose weeks or months later. When they do begin talking about their molestation experiences, they tend not to give clear accounts, and their stories may change over time. Sometimes children recant allegations altogether. The "child sexual abuse accommodation syndrome" (Summit, 1983) provides theoretical insight into these dynamics of disclosure and retraction.

According to Summit (1983), child sexual abuse invariably takes place in an atmosphere of secrecy. A child is dependent on trusted adults and if not divulging abuse is a condition of his or her continued well-being, then the child is essentially entrapped in a situation from which there is no escape. The child, for survival, accommodates in silence, and the abuse continues. Since revealing the abuse carries grave consequences, when and if a disclosure is made, it is probably conflicted and often unconvincing. After disclosure (particularly if family support is lacking), the potential threat to the child's welfare can become too overwhelming, and the child may retract. Although Summit's model is limited by the lack of empirical basis and the sole focus on father–daughter incest, it provides a valuable theoretical springboard for further study of the processes surrounding disclosures of abuse.

In a first attempt to address the need for empirical study in this area, we examined children's disclosures and retractions over the course of psychotherapy. We investigated delays in disclosure, the order in which specific types of abuse were disclosed, and the presence of retractions. We also explored events in the children's worlds that might be associated with the timing of their disclosures and retractions.

Seventeen therapists provided information about the disclosure patterns of 61 of the children who reported ritualistic sexual abuse (the RSA sample). The same data were obtained from four different therapists on 13 of the children who reported sexual abuse only (the SA sample). At the time these data were gathered, the average length of time the RSA children had spent in therapy was approximately 14 months, with a range of 2 months to a little over 2¹/2 years. The RSA children ranged in age from 2 years, 11 months to 12 years, 10 months when they entered treatment, with a mean of 6¹/2 years. Most of the 13 SA children had been in therapy between 1 and 2 years, but this ranged from one evaluation to 5 years.

Therapists completed the Child Disclosure and Recantation Pattern, an open-ended questionnaire that we created for the specific purpose of obtaining qualitative descriptions of the sequence of children's disclosures and retractions in the therapy context. From case notes, each child's therapist provided brief descriptions of abuse that was disclosed or recanted, the approximate time after the child began treatment when each disclosure or recantation was made, and any event that the therapist suspected might be related to the timing of a particular disclosure or retraction.

Disclosures were categorized into types of events the children witnessed or experienced at the preschools. We coded the time (since the start of therapy) of the initial disclosure of each different category of abuse. Then initial disclosures were charted over time, in order to investigate specific patterns and to see whether these patterns were associated with other events in the children's lives.

TYPES OF ABUSIVE EXPERIENCES DISCLOSED

Table 6.1 contains the categories of abuse used for the purposes of analyzing the patterns of disclosure in the RSA sample. The second column identifies the number of children who disclosed each type of abuse. In the RSA sample, these categories consisted of vague references to abuse, sexual acts, threats, physically violent or terrorizing acts, and ritualistic acts. The therapists in the SA sample were generally not specific about the details of the abuse disclosed. However, fondling, oral

TABLE 6.1. Percentage of Children Making Initial Disclosures of Different
Types of Abuse by Number of Months in Psychotherapy: RSA Sample (n = 61)

Type of abuse	(n)	Percentage of initial disclosures by months in therapy					
		1	2–3	4–5	6–8	9–11	12+
Vague reference	(14)	71	14	0	7	2	0
Sexualized games	(13)	85	8	8	0	0	0
Fondling	(16)	69	25	6	0	0	0
Oral copulation/intercourse	(27)	37	30	19	7	4	4
Observed abuse of others	(16)	69	6	13	13	0	0
Molested others	(17)	6	47	18	18	12	0
Threats against self/parent	(39)	51	18	15	13	3	0
Acts involving urine/feces	(19)	0	26	21	26	11	11
Torture/killing of animals	(48)	40	40	4	10	2	4
Torture/killing of humans	(16)	0	38	25	6	25	6
Satanic rituals	(34)	12	41	21	18	6	3
Transported to other sites	(39)	21	46	18	10	3	3
Photographed	(16)	27	35	15	12	8	4

copulation, and observing another child's abuse were specified for one child, and two children reported having to molest other children. There were no allegations of ritualistic abuse in the SA sample.

The reader is referred to the description of the Sexual Abuse Grid (see Chapter 5) for the most accurate information concerning percentages of children who reported the range of different types of abuse in the overall samples, and for more details about the reported experiences. The data described here were derived from a content analysis of open-ended responses from therapists; they are much less complete than the data obtained with the Sexual Abuse Grid, but they provide interesting qualitative descriptions. Furthermore, the focus of this chapter is on the timing of disclosures and recantations in therapy, and on which types of abuse were revealed earlier or later in the course of treatment.

DELAYED DISCLOSURE

Research has documented that victims of child sexual abuse may never disclose their abuse to others; even if they do, it may be revealed long after the abuse has occurred (see Haugaard, 1988; Russell, 1983). We questioned whether children would also demonstrate "delayed" disclosure in therapy. Our data revealed that within the first month of therapy, approximately 84% of the RSA sample and 62% of the SA sample made an initial disclosure of some type of abuse. Overall in the RSA sample, the mean week of first disclosure was week 4 and the median was week 2. There were no significant sex differences between children who disclosed in the first month and those who did not.

Although the children tended to disclose early in the course of treatment, it is critical to note that most children in our samples had already broken their silence by disclosing abuse to a professional evaluator prior to beginning therapy. Our findings only highlight the lack of a significant delay in disclosure in this very specific treatment context. They certainly do not imply that children who do not immediately reveal abuse, inside or outside the therapy realm, should be disbelieved. Furthermore, the high percentage of early disclosure in therapy is in no way indicative of how children deal with issues of disclosure before the abuse is externally identified and a safe environment for talking about the abuse is made available. For many of the children, the alleged abuse had actually occurred months or years before they disclosed it to anyone. Our results do suggest that children provided with an appropriate supportive environment are able to put abusive experiences into words.

DISCLOSURE PATTERNS

A phenomenon noted by these clinicians was that the children tended to report less frightening or severe aspects of abuse experiences first and then to proceed to the more traumatic aspects. We utilized two different methods to explore the existence of particular patterns of disclosure in the RSA sample. First, we calculated the percentage of children who made initial disclosures of several categories of abuse by the number of months they had been in treatment (see Table 6.1). "Initial disclosure" in this context refers to the first time a child talked about a type of abuse. These data provide relative time frames of initial disclosures in the overall sample. Second, we examined different subsamples of children in the RSA sample who disclosed the same two types of abuse. To identify specific sequential preferences, the percentages of children in each particular subsample who disclosed one type of abuse before the other, who disclosed in the reverse order, and who disclosed the two types simultaneously (in the same week) were calculated. The information available on the SA sample was not detailed enough to permit us to explore specific patterns for this group.

Clinical reports in the literature suggest that children seize every opportunity to be vague during disclosure (Burgess & Grant, 1988) and begin by providing small bits of information as initial tests (Damon, Todd, & MacFarlane, 1987). Consistent with these observations was the finding that, as shown in Table 6.1, the majority (71%) of initial disclosures of vague references to abuse (e.g., "bad things" happening at the school) were made during the first month of therapy. We also looked at subsamples of children who had made a vague disclosure and had disclosed another specific type of abuse. In most instances, a greater percentage of children made vague disclosures before reporting other types of abuse. For example, of the 18 children who both made vague disclosures and disclosed sexual acts, 78% made vague references to abuse before reporting sexual acts. These findings support the idea that some children go through a process of "testing the waters" before they feel safe enough to disclose more specifics about abuse.

We also looked at patterns related to the children's disclosures of threats and terrorizing acts in the RSA sample. Jones (1986) has suggested that violence and threats may be more difficult for children to disclose than sexual aspects of abuse may be. However, when we examined a subsample of 55 children who had disclosed both terrorizing and sexual acts, we found that 40% disclosed the sexual abuse first, and that approximately the same percentage of children reversed the order and disclosed the terrorizing acts first (18% disclosed both in the same session). No specific pattern emerged to suggest which aspect of abuse, sexual or violent, was likely to be disclosed first. Still, a further breakdown of the "terrorizing acts" category revealed interesting findings.

As shown in Table 6.1, 51% of the disclosures about threats of harm to the children or their parents were made in the first month. It can be hypothesized that for a certain percentage of the children, threats served as barriers to revealing more specifics. Many of these children truly believed that if they told, something would happen to them or harm would come to their parents. Therefore, it seemed necessary to address their fears and help them develop a belief in their families' safety to facilitate disclosure of other aspects of abuse.

Also as indicated in Table 6.1, 80% of the children who made references to animals being tortured or killed did so in the first few months of therapy. The relatively early disclosure of this type of terrorizing act may be related to reports of these acts as part of the threat made in regard to not telling. Another type of terrorizing act showed a somewhat different pattern, however. None of the children who disclosed sadistic acts involving urine and feces ($n = 19$) or human torture ($n = 16$) made any reference to these forms of abuse in the first month of therapy. These disclosures began to emerge in the second and third months of treatment and continued to be disclosed for the first time throughout the last quarter of the first year in therapy. It appears that these types of disclosures came later in the therapy process; perhaps they were some of the more frightening and difficult aspects of the experience to divulge.

The children in our sample also tended to disclose ritualistic acts, many of which seemed Satanic in nature, relatively later than they reported other types of abuse. This is consistent with clinical reports (Hunt, 1988; Streiff, 1988). As Table 6.1 indicates, only 12% of the disclosures of the ritualistic acts came in the first month. Forty percent were disclosed in the second and third months of therapy, and initial disclosures of this type continued throughout the first year. Also, new disclosures from children who had previously talked about rituals increased later in treatment and continued to be one of the more talked-about aspects through the first year and beyond. Finally, in subsamples of children who disclosed ritualistic acts and any other type of abuse, the ritualistic act was disclosed later in the greater percentage of cases. Of the 42 children who disclosed ritualistic and terrorizing acts, 88% disclosed the terrorizing first; of the 43 children who disclosed ritualistic and sexual acts, 81% revealed sexual abuse first.

We also examined whether the children tended to disclose less intrusive sexual acts before describing more intrusive acts. A somewhat confusing picture emerged. Table 6.1 illustrates that a high percentage of disclosures of less intrusive sexual abuse came in the first month. Of the 13 children who described sexualized games, 85% did so in the first month, and of the 16 who disclosed fondling, 69% did so in the first month. In contrast, only 37% of the disclosures of the more intrusive abuse, including oral copulation and anal and vaginal intercourse, came in the first month. When we examined subsamples of children who disclosed different types of sexual abuse, there was some evidence that children were able to talk about the least intrusive types (e.g., kissing, sexualized games) before the severely intrusive types (e.g., intercourse, penetration with foreign objects). It may be harder for children to reveal acts involving greater degrees of bodily invasion. However, a particularly salient finding was the high percentage of children who disclosed sexual abuse of different levels of intrusiveness in the same session. Perhaps, once children are able to begin talking about the sexual aspects of abuse, they do not distinguish types. We must be careful not to assume that adults' categorizations of degrees of intrusiveness or seriousness perfectly match children's perceptions.

Other types of abuse disclosed by the children are shown in Table 6.1. One of these was alluding to abuse of others. About a third of the children disclosed observing other children being abused, and two-thirds of those who mentioned this did so in the first month of therapy. However, when we looked at the specific subsample of children who disclosed both seeing another child abused and being abused themselves, no pattern of which disclosure came first emerged. This is contrary to reports in the clinical literature (Goodman, Aman, & Hirschman, 1987; MacFarlane, 1986). Our finding may reflect the therapists' primary interest in discussing their particular clients' abuse. A different result might be found in the investigatory context, where professionals are particularly interested in hearing about other children's abuse experiences, since these provide further evidence against alleged perpetrators. Still, for some children, talking about the abuse of others first may provide enough distance to pave the way for more difficult disclosures.

Another aspect of the RSA children's abuse experience referred to in this questionnaire was their disclosure of having to engage in sexual behaviors with or in some way to abuse other children. This seemed to be one of the more difficult things to talk about. As indicated in Table 6.1, only one child disclosed this during the first month, but 47% of those who disclosed about these acts did so during the next 2 months of treatment. The rest of the initial disclosures regarding molesting others were spread throughout the first year of therapy. Lastly, the pattern of disclosures of being photographed and being transported to other sites followed similar patterns. Approximately one-quarter of the children who made these types of disclosures did so in the first month.

REASONS ASSOCIATED WITH DISCLOSURES

In an attempt to shed light on what facilitates increased disclosures and what tends to decrease a child's ability to talk about abuse, we explored external events that might be associated with disclosure patterns. As previously mentioned, the majority of children in our sample made initial disclosures of some type quite early in treatment. The therapists of the RSA children believed that this occurred primarily because the children had had diagnostic interviews prior to entering therapy. In these interviews, the subject of the alleged abuse had already been broached, and this may have made it easier for the children to proceed with disclosing. It is important to note that these initial evaluations may have also influenced the pattern of disclosures we discovered in therapy, as the children had already witnessed adult reactions to how they disclosed abuse. Parental belief and support were also seen as helpful to the children's disclosing early in the therapy process.

We further explored reasons associated with subsequent disclosures. The most frequently listed reason for the continuing process of disclosures in the RSA group was the occurrence of events that reminded the children of the preschool experiences they had reported (*n* = 13). "Reminders" that seemed to trigger further disclosures included passing the preschool or seeing an object that was associated with the school. Therapists also reported that children tended to increase disclosures in therapy after interviews with other professionals, such as police officers or district attorneys (n = 9). Other reasons identified by the therapists as associated with disclosures in both the RSA and SA sample were parental belief and support, increases in family stability, and a sense of a safer environment (n = 6).

Mixed findings were obtained in regard to whether testifying aided or suppressed disclosure in the RSA sample. For some children (n = 4), being considered as witnesses increased their disclosures; for others, a decision that they would not testify seemed to free them to make more disclosures (n = 4). A few children made subsequent disclosures after hearing the accounts of other children, beginning group therapy, or withdrawing from an allegedly abusive school. Thus, in general, it appears that being exposed to events associated with abusive experiences, family support, stability, and a sense of safety are important issues in a child's continued ability to reveal additional abuse after initial disclosure.

We also looked at what might impede or disrupt an RSA child's disclosure process in treatment. A child's family seemed to be one of the primary determinants in the victim's lack of disclosures (n = 4). Family problems and instability, and parents' discouraging a child from focusing on the past, were seen by the therapists in the RSA sample as obstacles to additional revelations about the alleged abuse. Similarly, therapists in the SA sample listed family disruption or nonsupportive parental reactions as reasons why children stopped talking about their victimization (n = 4). These findings provide further evidence of the critical role played by support and safety in helping children talk about their traumatic experiences.

RETRACTIONS

One of the more confusing aspects of dealing with children who report sexual abuse occurs when they recant allegations. Our data document the existence of recantation in the therapy setting. "Recantation" was defined as any time a child took back or denied a previous disclosure. As indicated in Table 6.2, 16 children, or 25% of the RSA sample, recanted previous abuse allegations during the course of therapy. Three children recanted twice. As also seen in Table 6.2, 38% of the retractions occurred within the first month of treatment. The timing of the remaining recantations was spread out over the next several months, with 31% occurring at some point after the first year of therapy. As shown in Table 6.3, 23% (n = 3) children in the SA sample recanted, a finding striking in its similarity to that for the RSA sample. Retractions in the SA sample are particularly interesting, given that the perpetrator had confessed. The fact that

TABLE 6.2. Children Who Recanted in Therapy: RSA Sample (n = 61)

	Number recanting	Percentage of those who recanted	Percentage of total sample
Months in therapy			
1	6	37.5	9.5
2–3	1	6.3	1.6
4–5	2	12.5	3.2
6–8	1	6.3	1.6
9–11	1	6.3	1.6
12+	5	31.3	7.9
TOTAL	16	100.0	25.4
Children who recanted more than once	3	18.8	14.8
Children who redisclosed	14	87.5	22.2

children recant in the treatment setting makes recantation outside this highly supportive context even more understandable.

A finding of great importance is that 88% of the RSA subjects who recanted made a redisclosure of abuse. Similarly, two of the three recanters in the SA sample redisclosed abuse. Furthermore, not only did children in our RSA sample redisclose after a recantation, but in many instances they talked about new types of abuse not reported prior to the retraction. Our findings provide some evidence in support of the characterization of recantation as an understandable phase within the disclosure process, and not as an end in itself or a synonym for false allegations.

Our questionnaire also asked therapists to consider what events might have been associated with retractions. Three of the recantations in the RSA sample were seen as reactions to the possibility that the children

TABLE 6.3. Children Who Recanted: SA Sample (n = 13)

	Number recanting	Percentage of those who recanted	Percentage of total sample
Months in therapy			
1	0	0	0
2–3	2	67	15
4–11	0	0	0
12+	1	33	8
TOTAL	3	100	23
Children who redisclosed	2	67	15

would testify in court. Another three RSA children recanted after being told that their disclosures needed to be reported to investigators in the system. Two children recanted after interviews with professionals outside of therapy, including a representative of the media and an attorney. One child recanted in response to parental pressure to disclose more, and another retracted statements after a friend who attended the same preschool denied abuse. It appears that a major issue associated with retractions in the RSA group had to do with interactions with the criminal justice system and the children's perceived intrusion of strangers into their world. Just as safety seems to be an important condition for disclosure, perceived lack of safety may be associated with retraction. The only reason for a retraction identified in the SA sample was that a father had encouraged the child to forget what happened. Again, family support emerges as an influence on the children's disclosure processes.

CONCLUSION

To summarize briefly, the children in our sample tended to disclose abuse early in the therapy process. This seemed to be aided by the facts that in most instances the children had been interviewed prior to receiving treatment and that their families were supportive. Vague references to abuse, threats of harm, and less intrusive sexual acts tended to be disclosed earlier than other types of abuse. Abuse revealed somewhat later in the therapeutic process included ritualistic acts; highly intrusive sexual acts; being forced to molest another child; and acts involving urine, feces, and human torture. Family support was a crucial variable in the continuing process of additional disclosures. Approximately one-fourth of the children recanted abuse allegations at some point in therapy, but almost all of them redisclosed later in treatment. Reasons for recantation were seen as including fears associated with court procedures and outside investigations, as well as lack of family support.

We believe that our findings represent an initial step toward empirical understanding of the disclosure processes surrounding children's allegations of sexual abuse. The most obvious limitation of the study is that we examined disclosure in psychotherapy without controlling for different therapist styles. We lacked information surrounding whether and at what point therapists asked about specific types of abuse. Thus, caution is warranted when patterns of disclosure are examined, because they may reflect common therapist agendas. Furthermore, the treatment context we explored does not represent the children's first disclosure experience, since they had undergone investigative interviews (several, in some cases) prior to entering therapy. We also think it essential to state that although exploring patterns has utility, individual differences in child victims should never be ignored. All children bring their unique qualities to disclosure situations. We hope that this report of our descriptive and qualitative data spurs future empirical study of how children talk about traumatic experiences, as the field continues to work toward developing the best methods for serving the needs of child victims.

PART III

Effects
on Children

OVERALL LEVEL
OF DISTRESS

Robert J. Kelly

I N OUR STUDY, we attempted to ascertain whether children reporting child sexual abuse would experience a greater degree of psychological problems than a control group of children who never reported being sexually abused. In the following chapters, we report our findings about specific problem areas, including cognitive and school-related effects, emotional effects, and issues centering around sexuality. We also discuss these findings in relation to major theoretical models, such as the traumagenic dynamics model and the post-traumatic stress disorder model (see Chapters 2, 9, and 12). The present chapter focuses on the overall level of distress experienced by these children. As in all of these chapters, the reported findings are based on data obtained from the following three sources: the parents, the children themselves, and the therapists.

PARENTAL PERCEPTIONS

We first wanted to examine parents' perceptions of how their children were functioning overall, and to do so we used two instruments. The first instrument, the Child Behavior Checklist (CBCL), is a standardized measure that has been used in several studies of sexual abuse, as well as in a variety of other research areas. In the sexual abuse studies, researchers have generally found greater degrees of behavioral disturbance in sexually abused children than in comparison groups of nonabused children (Friedrich, Beilke, & Urquiza, 1987, 1988; Friedrich, Urquiza, & Beilke, 1986; Gomes-Schwartz, Horowitz, & Cardarelli, 1990; Kelley, 1989; Valliere, Bybee, & Mowbray, 1988). Our results were quite similar. For the period of most distress, children who reported experiencing ritualistic sexual abuse (the RSA group) were rated by their mothers as exhibiting significantly more behavior problems than were children who did not report having been abused (the NA group). Moreover, an extraordinarily high percentage (46.4%) of the RSA children scored in the clinical range on this instrument, compared with none of the NA children (see Tables 7.1 and 7.2). Only approximately 2% of the general population falls in this clinical range.

In addition to the Total Behavior Problems score, the CBCL also provides three major subscale scores assessing children's Internalizing behavior, Externalizing behavior, and Social Competence. The internalizing dimension includes fearful, inhibited, withdrawn, depressive, and overcontrolled behaviors. The Externalizing dimension reflects aggressive, antisocial, acting-out, and undercontrolled behaviors. The Social Competence score assesses positive, appropriate behavior related to school and social activities. As shown in Table 7.1, the RSA children had significantly higher scores on the Internalizing and Externalizing scales than the NA children did, and also scored significantly lower on social competence. Moreover, a disproportionately large percentage of the RSA children scored in the clinical range on each of these subscales (see Table 7.2).

A subsample of parents of the RSA children participated in a follow-up approximately 5 years after the children had initially disclosed abuse. These parents did not differ significantly from parents who were not

TABLE 7.1. Maternal Ratings of RSA versus NA Children on the CBCL

Scale	RSA	NA	F^c
Total Behavior Problems			
$\bar{X}$	67.2^a	47.5^b	54.7^{**}
SD	12.5	7.6	
Internalizing			
$\bar{X}$	68.1^a	49.8^b	71.6^{**}
SD	10.2	6.5	
Externalizing			
$\bar{X}$	62.9^a	47.4^b	38.3^{**}
SD	11.4	8.8	
Social Competence			
$\bar{X}$	40.8^d	50.8^e	14.2^*
SD	9.4	11.0	

Note. Lower scores reflect fewer problems, except on Social Competence, on which higher scores reflect fewer problems. Scores are based on period of most distress.
$^a n = 68$; $^b n = 32$; ^{c}Analysis of covariance (ANCOVA) controlling for socioeconomic status (SES); $^d n = 58$; $^e n = 30$; $^* p < .01$; $^{**} p < .001$.

TABLE 7.2. Percentage of RSA and NA Children in the Clinical Range on Maternal CBCL

	Percentage in clinical range		
Scale	RSA (n = 69)	NA (n = 32)	χ^2
Total Behavior Problems	46.4	0.0	19.6*
Internalizing	47.8	0.0	20.6*
Externalizing	37.7	3.1	11.6*
Social Competence	22.0[a]	6.7[b]	2.3

Note. Scores are based on period of most distress.
[a]n = 59; [b]n = 30; *p < .001.

in this follow-up on any demographic variable or on CBCL scores gathered at the initial data collection. It is encouraging to see that most of the children who had been in the clinical range during the period of most distress were no longer in the clinical range by the time of the follow-up. Nonetheless, the percentage of children who were still in the clinical range was still somewhat higher than what would be expected from the instrument norms. Once again, approximately 2% of the general population falls in the clinical range on each of these scales. For the children in the follow-up subsample, 17.1% were still in the clinical range on the Total Behavior Problems scale, 11.4% on the Internalizing scale, and 8.6% on the Externalizing scale. The mean scores on the Social Competence scale, however, were virtually normal, and only one child (3.4%) remained in the clinical range on this scale (see Tables 7.3 and 7.4).

The other parent instrument that we used to obtain an overall picture of the children's functioning was the Behaviors After Diagnostic Interview (BADI) checklist. As noted in Chapter 3, we followed Finkelhor's suggestion of using a combination of standardized, traditional instruments that measure global pathology and nonstandardized instruments that assess abuse-specific sequelae. Thus, we used the abovementioned CBCL together with our own nonstandardized BADI, which taps into both abuse specific and more general behavior problem areas. The BADI includes problems associated with bathing, undressing, sexual play or reenactment, violence, secrets, regressive behavior, and nightmares.

We wanted to answer three questions about overall symptomatology with the BADI, with each question corresponding to the children's behaviors at three different time periods. The first question was whether there was a significant difference in the children's behavior problems after they disclosed ritualistic abuse in their initial diagnostic interviews. We expected that their behavior problems would increase, in part because they reported having been severely threatened with death threats against

TABLE 7.3. Maternal Ratings of RSA Children on the CBCL for Period of Most Distress and at 5-Year Follow-Up

Scale	Most distress	Follow-up	Two-tailed t
Total Behavior Problems[a]			
$\overline{X}$	67.4	56.6	5.6*
SD	11.9	10.8	
Internalizing[a]			
$\overline{X}$	68.1	57.3	6.2*
SD	9.8	10.3	
Externalizing[a]			
$\overline{X}$	63.4	54.7	5.1*
SD	11.0	9.6	
Social Competence[b]			
$\overline{X}$	40.9	48.6	−5.7*
SD	8.5	7.9	

Note. Lower scores reflect fewer problems on all scales except Social Competence, on which higher scores reflect fewer problems.
[a]n = 35; [b]n = 29; *p < .001.

themselves or their parents if they ever disclosed their abuse. We were able to collect predisclosure data on 20 children, after their parents gave us permission to analyze the behavioral questionnaires they completed immediately preceding the children's initial diagnostic interview. This analysis showed that the children were exhibiting a large number of behavior problems before that initial interview ($\overline{X}$ = 7.9 out of 41 BADI behaviors). We then compared these data with the BADI questionnaires these parents filled out approximately 3 years later, in which they were asked to retrospectively rate their children's behavior in the first month following the diagnostic interview. According to these retrospective accounts, the number

TABLE 7.4. Percentage of RSA Children in CBCL Clinical Range at Period of Most Distress and at 5-Year Follow-Up

Scale	Percentage in clinical range	
	Most distress	Follow-up
Total Behavior Problems[a]	45.7	17.1
Internalizing[a]	45.7	11.4
Externalizing[a]	40.0	8.6
Social Competence[b]	17.2	3.4

Note. Scores are maternal ratings for those mothers who participated in both the initial data collection and follow-up.
[a]n = 35; [b]n = 29.

of behavior problems did indeed rise significantly after the diagnostic interview ($\overline{X}$ = 12.3; p < .005).

The second question we attempted to answer with the BADI was whether the RSA children were exhibiting a higher number of behavior problems than the NA children during the first month following the RSA children's initial diagnostic interview. We predicted that the RSA children would exhibit more behavior problems, both as a result of their reportedly severe abuse, and as a result of disclosing the abuse despite reported death threats against doing so. For this analysis, we compared the retrospective data from 69 RSA mothers and 32 NA mothers. NA mothers were asked to base their ratings on their children's "behavior in early 1984." As predicted, we found that the RSA children exhibited many more behavior problems during that period (11.5 vs. 1.9; p < .001). A similar analysis involving 40 RSA fathers and 24 NA fathers also showed a significantly higher number of overall behavior problems observed in the RSA children (9.8 vs. 2.5; p < .001). When the NA group was used as a control for the predisclosure BADI, it could be seen that the RSA group exhibited many more behavioral difficulties ($\overline{X}$ = 7.9) before disclosure than did nonabused controls ($\overline{X}$ = 1.9).

Our third BADI question was whether the RSA children would still be exhibiting more behavior problems than the NA children at the time of our psychological assessments, which took place approximately 3 years after the initial diagnostic interview. Despite the fact that almost all of the RSA children in our sample had received psychotherapy, we predicted that they might still have a higher degree of behavior problems. Analyses showed that both the RSA and NA groups exhibited significantly fewer BADI behaviors at this 3-year follow-up. This finding resulted in part from developmental changes over this time period; however, according to the mothers' ratings, the RSA children were still exhibiting significantly more of these behaviors at the time of this follow-up (4.3 vs. 1.1; p < .001). This difference did not reach significance in the smaller sample of fathers' ratings (2.6 vs. 1.8; p < .08, one-tailed).

CHILD MEASURES

It is clear from the parent data that many RSA parents perceived their children as exhibiting severe levels of overall distress just prior to the diagnostic interview, during the period of most distress following the interview, and in some cases at the 3-year and 5-year follow-up periods. We wondered whether this distress would be directly observable in the children during our psychological assessment procedures, which took place approximately 3 years after the diagnostic interviews. We planned to measure overall distress levels in the children through the use of four instruments. Once again, we decided to use a combination of standardized and nonstandardized but abuse-specific measures.

The first measure we used was a brief screening measure developed by Beery (1982), called the Developmental Test of Visual-Motor Integration (VMI), which assesses the presence of gross abnormalities in visual–motor skills. We predicted that there would be no differences between groups on this measure, but we wanted to document this finding for two reasons. First, there has been some speculation that child sexual abuse may lead to neuropsychological problems in some victims, as has been found for some victims of physical abuse. Although this may be true in some cases, we did not expect that the sexual abuse reported by children in this study would lead to such effects. Second, we wanted to rule out the possibility that differences in our other child data were caused by the confounding effects of visual–motor deficits. As expected, no differences were found between groups on the VMI, with both the RSA ($\overline{X}$ = 52.0) and NA ($\overline{X}$ = 56.5) groups falling well within the normal range ($F < 1.0$, n.s.).

The second measure was the Draw-A-Person (DAP) task, in which children were asked to draw a picture of a person, and then to draw a picture of a person of the opposite sex. These drawings were then scored for "emotional indicators" according to a widely used scoring system developed by Koppitz (1968, 1984). Our primary analysis involved the sum of the 12 indicators reported by Koppitz, which significantly discriminated between clinical and nonclinical groups in her studies. These indicators include items such as missing body parts, missing facial features, distortion of body parts, and the like. Trained raters were blind as to the group status of the children. As shown in Table 7.5, children in the RSA group showed significantly more emotional indicators than children in the NA group did (all p's < .055). This was true for drawings of a male figure as well as for those of a female figure, and

TABLE 7.5. Indicators of Emotional Distress in the Human Figure Drawings of RSA and NA Children

Drawing	RSA (n = 62)	NA (n = 32)	F
Both drawings	1.04	0.61	2.88a*
Male drawing	1.08	0.56	2.75a*
Female drawing	1.00	0.66	2.61*
Same-sex drawing	1.10	0.63	3.66a*
Opposite-sex drawing	0.98	0.59	3.23*

Note. Scores reflect mean number of 12 emotional indicators with discriminant validity reported by Koppitz (1984) for the Draw-A-Person.
aANCOVA controlling for SES.
*p < .055, one-tailed.

was also true for analyses focusing on figures of the same sex and the opposite sex as the child (Waterman, Kelly, Erhardt, McCord, & Oliveri, 1988). As discussed more fully in Chapter 10, one additional finding was the strikingly high percentage of drawings by the RSA children in which the raters were not able to determine the sex of the person depicted.

We conducted an additional analysis on the DAP, based on Naglieri's (1988) method for scoring nonverbal intelligence. As predicted, the two groups were virtually equivalent on these scores ($F < 1.0$, n.s.). Thus, our findings on Koppitz's emotional indicators do not appear to have been influenced by differences in nonverbal ability.

Figures 7.1 through 7.4 provide a sample of some of the distortions and/or abuse-related themes in drawings by children in the RSA group. Figure 7.1 is a self-portrait made by a 6-year-old girl, who depicted herself thinking about her alleged molesters while playing with her toy duck. When asked

FIGURE 7.1. Drawing by a 6-year-old RSA girl for the Draw-A-Person (DAP) task.

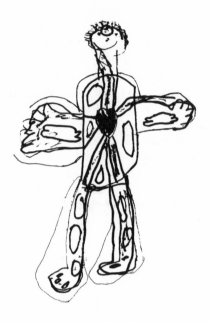

FIGURE 7.2. Drawing by a 6-year-old RSA boy for the DAP.

what the girl in the drawing is thinking and feeling, the child stated that she is thinking about "bad guys trying to hurt the babies," and feeling "nothing." One of the perpetrators is drawn holding a pointed knife-like object. This is one of several drawings in which children made negative references to alleged perpetrators.

Figure 7.2, drawn by a 6-year-old boy, shows a gross sense of boundary violation: the child drew a transparent image in which the internal organs are visible, even though the child stated that this boy is dressed. Figure 7.3 is a primitive, developmentally immature drawing by an 8-year-old girl, who deleted all body parts except for the head. This child named the person in the

FIGURE 7.3. Drawing by an 8-year-old RSA girl for the DAP.

FIGURE 7.4. Drawing by an 8-year-old RSA boy for the DAP.

drawing "Koo Koo Brain," who is thinking "that she has a head" and feeling "that she's stupid." The final drawing, Figure 7.4, was drawn by an 8-year-old boy and is one of several drawings made by RSA children that lack facial features and give a sense of an outer shell or facade around hollow characters without any defining sense of self-identity. (See Chapter 10 for additional drawings.)

The third child measure that allowed for an assessment of overall distress was one of three versions of a widely used, standardized self-concept scale developed by Susan Harter (Harter, 1985; Harter & Pike, 1984). No differences were found on this measure for the younger children in the study, who had not yet completed second grade. However, significant differences were found on the older children's version of this measure. RSA children exhibited significantly poorer self-concept, than NA children as measured by the mean subscale z score ($p < .05$, one-tailed) as well as the individual Global Self-Worth subscale ($p < .053$, one-tailed), even after differences in socioeconomic status were controlled for (see Table 7.6).

The final child measure assessing overall distress was the Incomplete Sentence Test, a nonstandardized test that we devised to examine children's attitudes toward peers, school, adults, family, their sense of self, and their reactions to affection or touch. Children were asked to complete

TABLE 7.6. Self-Concept Scores of RSA and NA Children (Older Cohorts)

Subscale	RSA ($n = 49$)	NA ($n = 21$)	F
Scholastic Competence			
X̄	0.17	0.61	0.88[a]
SD	1.10	0.79	
Social Acceptance			
X̄	0.24	0.53	1.17
SD	1.08	0.93	
Athletic Competence			
X̄	–0.02	0.16	0.43
SD	0.98	1.17	
Physical Appearance			
X̄	0.05	0.84	6.85[a]**
SD	1.04	0.68	
Behavioral Conduct			
X̄	–0.10	0.33	1.98
SD	1.30	0.81	
Global Self-Worth			
X̄	0.15	0.73	2.70[a]*
SD	1.02	0.49	
Mean z Score			
X̄	0.08	0.53	3.18**
SD	0.85	0.53	

Note. Scores reported are standarized z scores calculated from age norms on the Self-Perception Profile for Children (Harter, 1985).
[a]Ancova controlling for SES.
*$p < .053$, one-tailed; **$p < .05$, one-tailed.

sentences such as "The kids in my neighborhood are . . . ," and "My face is . . . ," and so on. Each sentence was then scored by trained raters according to whether the response was negative, neutral, or positive in tone. For example, a completed sentence such as "The kids in my neighborhood are cool" would be scored as positive, whereas a sentence such as "The kids in my neighborhood are mean" would be scored as negative. As with the DAP, raters were unaware of the children's group status. We were actually a bit surprised to find such consistent differences in the responses of the RSA children. The total score for the RSA children was significantly less positive than it was for the NA children ($p < .05$, two-tailed), suggesting that the RSA children may have developed a more pessimistic view of their world than that of their nonabused counterparts. This finding seems particularly discouraging, given our fears that children will lose some youthful optimism when they are abused.

These data suggest that the "loss of innocence" resulting from reported sexual abuse does not just pertain to lost sexual innocence, but may also extend to a loss of viewing the world optimistically as a fair and safe place.

A few of the children actually made reference to their alleged perpetrators in their answers to the incomplete sentences. For example, one child completed a sentence this way: "Sometimes I dream about McMartin, *like how [alleged perpetrator's name] always killed the animals.*" On another item the same child responded: "I think the Devil *is a bad person, and I don't think [alleged perpetrator's name] should copy him.*"

At the end of the sentence completion task, we asked all the children to make three wishes. Once again, a few of the children's wishes related to their reported abuse. These included the following: "I wish that [alleged perpetrator's name] will stay in jail 'til he dies. I hope he never hurts me again"; "I wish I could go back in time and kill [alleged perpetrators' names]"; "I wish I was protected from everything and nobody could kill me and I just had to die of old age." We did not conduct any systematic analysis of the children's three wishes, but it seemed that the wishes of the RSA and NA children were more similar than dissimilar, with the exception of those wishes referring to the alleged abusers.

There was one child measure that did not show differences in distress levels between RSA and NA children, and that was the Roberts Apperception Test for Children (RATC). Although this test does not include a measure of overall distress per se, it is important to mention here that there were no differences between groups on any of the individual clinical scales. The discriminant validity of the RATC has not been consistently demonstrated in other studies, so it may be that our results reflect the test's inability to discriminate reliably between clinical and nonclinical groups. However, we are reporting this "negative finding" in order to be thorough in our assessment of the children, and also for comparison with future studies that may use the RATC, which we believe has important clinical uses with both abused and nonabused children.

THERAPIST QUESTIONNAIRES

Having seen generally consistent evidence of high levels of distress for many children in both the parent and child data, we examined the therapist data for the RSA children in order to compare the familial findings with the perspective of professionals who had worked intimately with the children but who were outside the children's family systems. Perhaps the most direct measure of overall distress level was the Children's Global Assessment Scale (CGAS; Shaffer et al., 1985). Using behavioral descriptions given in this scale, each child's therapists was asked to rate the child's level of general functioning for two time periods: the time of most distress, and the time of termination from therapy (or currently [i.e., 3 years after the diagnostic interview], for the few children who were still in therapy). According to the therapist ratings, most of the children were experiencing a good deal of impairment at the time of most distress. The mean score for these children was 54.8, which corresponds to the following category description (relevant for scores between 51 and 60): "Variable functioning with sporadic difficulties or symptoms in several but not all areas . . ." (Shaffer et al., 1985, p. 748). Moreover, 38.2% of these children had a CGAS score of 50 or below, which corresponds to this description:

> Moderate degree of interference in functioning in most social areas or severe impairment of functioning in one area, such as might result from, for example, suicidal preoccupations and ruminations, school refusal and other forms of anxiety, obsessive rituals, major conversion symptoms, frequent anxiety attacks, poor or inappropriate social skills, frequent episodes of aggressive or other antisocial behavior, with some preservation of meaningful relationships. (Shaffer et al., 1985, p. 748)

It is encouraging to see that most of these children greatly improved over time, in the opinion of their therapists. For the second rating period, the average CGAS score had climbed to 73.9, which corresponds to "No more than slight impairment in functioning at home, at school, or with peers . . ." (Shaffer et al., 1985, p. 747). Although 13.3% continued to score at or below 60, only 3.0% of the children scored at or below 50.

Therapists also completed a modification of the Teacher Report Form of the CBCL, parallel to the parent version discussed above. We did not want to risk stigmatizing the RSA children by asking their teachers to complete the teacher CBCL. Thus we obtained this information from the therapists, and asked them to rate the children's behavior at the time of most distress. Like the parent CBCL, this version provides a Total Behavior Problems score as well as measures of Internalizing and Externalizing behaviors; unlike the parent CBCL, it includes no Social Competence scale.

The degree of behavioral symptomatology described in these therapist ratings was dramatic. As with the parent CBCL, approximately 2% of the general population would be expected to fall into the clinical range on these scales. However, the average score for the RSA children on all three therapist scales fell into or close to the clinical range. The percentage of RSA children in the clinical range for Total Behavior Problems was a remarkable 47.6%. An even higher percentage, 57.1%, fell into the clinical range on the Internalizing scale, whereas 28.6% were seen as falling into the clinical range on the Externalizing scale.

It is not clear why more children would score in the clinical range on the Internalizing scale than on the Externalizing scale. It may be that these children were more fearful and withdrawn, or it may be that internalizing behaviors appear more in the context of individual therapy, as opposed to externalizing, acting-out behaviors that may be expressed more often in a group context. It is conceivable that scores on the Externalizing scale were artificially low, since the children were generally not observed by therapists in any type of group setting, whereas the norms for the instrument are based on ratings made by teachers, who obviously do observe children in a group setting and may be more likely to observe externalizing behaviors. It is also noteworthy that a parallel finding of higher therapist ratings on the Internalizing than on the Externalizing scale was also obtained for the children in the Reno sample, who reported sexual abuse only (the SA group; see Chapter 12).

We also wondered whether some gender-related difference was influencing these scores. Some research has suggested that boys tend to externalize their problems, whereas girls are more likely to internalize theirs (see Eme, 1979; Friedrich et al., 1986). However, the percentage of boys and girls falling into the clinical range on each of these two scales was virtually equivalent ($\chi^2 < 1.0$, n.s.).

Finally, we wondered whether our asking therapists to describe the children at their period of most distress artificially increased their pathology scores. Although this may have been true to a small extent, the data from the NA parents suggested that using the period of most distress rather than the traditional rating period did not account for much of the extremeness in these scores. Despite the fact that NA parents were asked to rate their children for the period of most distress, fewer than 3.2% of these children fell into the clinical range on either Total Behavior Problems (0.0%), the Internalizing scale (0.0%), or the Externalizing scale (3.1%).

CONCLUSION

The parent, child, and therapist data definitely provide much evidence for the belief that many of the RSA children suffered high levels of overall distress following their alleged abuse experiences. The children seem to have experienced the most distress after disclosing their abuse, which they reportedly did despite having been threatened with death threats against themselves or their parents if they were to disclose. The parent and therapist measures that used "period of most distress" as the rating period consistently showed dramatically high percentages of distressed children, compared to the NA group or to normative samples.

It is somewhat encouraging to see that most children improved over time, according to parent and therapist ratings, although a disturbingly high percentage of children continued to show impairment at the follow-up periods. According to parent data from the 5-year follow-up sample, 17.1% of this seemingly representative subgroup of children still scored in the clinical range on a standardized behavior problems scale.

Other studies of sexual abuse have often found differences between abused and nonabused children on parent ratings, whereas differences on actual child measures are less often reported. This is probably influenced by many factors: Parent data are usually easier to collect and are therefore included in more studies; children's measures often do not discriminate between groups because they are susceptible to children's presenting a socially desirable view of themselves when tested by strangers; parents of abused children often become very concerned about their children's behavior, and may conceivably be more likely to notice and report unusual behavior and to characterize such behavior as related to abuse, and so forth. Thus, the fact that many of the child data in this study showed statistically significant differences between the RSA and NA children is both noteworthy and unsettling.

The data presented in this chapter suggest that the RSA children's experience of trauma led to disturbance in several domains, including behavioral functioning, emotional functioning, self-concept, social competence, and attitudes toward the world around them. In the chapters that follow, we examine more closely the specific symptoms exhibited by these children within these domains.

We think it is also important to mention that, as in all previous studies of sexual abuse, some children in our study did not show significant symptomatology, and appeared to be coping quite well during their early years. In later chapters we will take a closer look at these children and examine the mitigating factors that may have led to their better outcomes.

COGNITIVE AND SCHOOL-RELATED EFFECTS

Robert Lusk

IN THE LITERATURE on the initial and long-term effects of child sexual abuse, sexually abused children have been noted to exhibit cognitive and school-related problems that appear related to the abuse. In the sections of this chapter, cognitive and school-related effects of sexual abuse suggested by the literature are reviewed; these were used as a basis for some of our predictions. Other predictions were derived from the traumagenic model of sexual abuse (Finkelhor, 1987), from literature on the effects of post-traumatic stress disorder (PTSD), and from studies on attributions (see Chapters 2 and 9 for a discussion of the traumagenic model and the PTSD literature). After the relevant literature in each section is reviewed, the predictions we made and the results we obtained are described.

INTELLIGENCE

Although school performance of sexually abused children has been discussed by a number of authors, intelligence per se has rarely been addressed. Both Meiselman (1978) and Weinberg (1955) reported that the incest victims they studied appeared to be of average intelligence, but neither specified how this determination was made. Only two studies to date have apparently compared the IQ scores of sexually abused children to those of nonabused children. Basta (1986) compared 32 molested children (half of whom were incest victims) to 16 nonmolested children on the Wechsler Intelligence Scale for Children—Revised (WISC-R;

Wechsler, 1974). His study found significantly higher Full Scale and Verbal WISC-R IQs in the nonabused group. However, the molested children's mean IQ was in the high end of the average range relative to the WISC-R normative sample (109.9), whereas the control group's mean IQ was significantly higher than average (117.6). Furthermore, the nonabused children were significantly higher than the sexually abused children in socioeconomic status (SES), and this variable was not controlled for.

Mannarino and Cohen (1986) administered the Stanford–Binet (third edition) to younger children and the WISC-R to older children in a sample of 45 sexual abuse victims (there was no comparison group). They found the mean IQ to be 92.9 (this is in the low end of the average range); the SES of the sample was "diverse" (p. 19). It is difficult to know whether this result was lower than would be expected, given the lack of a control group. Thus, the limited data available suggest that sexually abused children tend to be of average intelligence, but may demonstrate poorer performance on the WISC-R than their nonabused peers.

We predicted that the children who reported ritualistic sexual abuse (the RSA group) would not differ from the nonabused children (the NA group) in intelligence. As noted above, we had little reason to believe in advance that sexual abuse would affect intelligence per se. Intelligence was measured by four subtests of the WISC-R: Vocabulary, Similarities, Block Design, and Object Assembly.

Verbal, Performance, and Full Scale deviation quotients (DQs) were computed from WISC-R scaled scores, according to the procedure outlined by Sattler (1988). These DQs, like IQs, have a mean of 100 and a standard deviation of 15. As we predicted, there were no significant differences between groups on Full Scale or Performance DQs (with SES taken into account), although the NA children's Full Scale scores tended to be higher (see Table 8.1). However, contrary to our prediction, the NA children scored significantly higher on Verbal DQ, even when SES was controlled for.

ACHIEVEMENT AND
SCHOOL-RELATED PROBLEMS

Many authors have noted school-related problems in clinical observations of child sexual abuse victims (Adams-Tucker, 1981, 1982; Burgess & Holmstrom, 1978; DeFrancis, 1969; Meiselman, 1978). These problems are frequently unspecified, but include underachievement (Johnston, 1979; Perlmutter, Engel, & Sager, 1982; Yates, 1982), learning disabilities

TABLE 8.1. Intelligence and Achievement

Variable	Group[a]		Statistics[b]
	RSA	NA	
Mean WISC-R Full Scale deviation quotient (DQ)	112.29	116.66	$t = -1.87$
Mean WISC-R Verbal DQ	113.81	122.71	$F = 7.98**$
Mean WISC-R Performance DQ	108.00	108.00	$t = 0.00$
Mean PIAT Math standard score (SS)	111.32	116.37	$t = -2.27*$
Mean PIAT Reading Recognition SS	112.11	114.83	$t = -1.33$
Mean PIAT Reading Comprehension SS	113.03	114.32	$t = -0.63$
Mean PIAT Spelling SS	108.60	111.71	$t = -1.32$
Mean PIAT General Information SS	107.77	113.53	$F = 3.41$
Mean PIAT Total Test SS	111.02	113.85	$t = -1.52$
Mean WISC-R–PIAT Discrepancy	1.16	2.42	$t = -0.51$

[a]n's = 62–66 in the RSA group, and 34–35 in the NA group.
[b]Analysis of covariance (with SES partialed out) was performed if the variable significantly correlated with SES for the combined groups in these and all subsequent analyses. Otherwise, t tests were performed.
*$p < .025$; **$p < .01$.

(Dixen & Jenkins, 1981; Heims & Kaufman, 1963; Rosenfeld, Nadelson, Krieger, & Backman, 1977), and truancy (Weiss, Rogers, Darwin, & Dutton, 1955). However, we are aware of only five empirical studies to date that have addressed school problems. Both Peters (1976) and Anderson, Bach, and Griffith (1981) found significant problems with school functioning and truancy in sexually abused children, but neither had comparison groups. Conte and Schuerman (1987) noted that 15% of their sample had academic problems; they did not specify the prevalence in the nonabused control group. Tong, Oates, and McDowell (1987) gave the Teacher Report Form of the Child Behavior Checklist (CBCL; Achenbach & Edelbrock, 1986) to teachers of sexually abused children; they rated the abused children as significantly lower than nonabused controls on all dimensions of adaptive functioning, and as significantly more disturbed on a number of behavior problem subscales. Finally, Laird, Eckenrode, and Doris (1988) are collecting data on a sample of 500 sexually abused, physically abused, and neglected children; they are using the Iowa Test of Basic Skills (a standardized achievement test), among other instruments. Reading and math scores appear to be significantly below average for the abused and neglected children as a whole; separate scores for the sexually abused children alone are not yet available. Therefore, although some evidence exists, it cannot be firmly concluded that child sexual abuse causes academic problems.

Achievement

Consistent with clinical literature and the traumagenic model, we predicted that the RSA children would demonstrate poorer school achievement than their NA peers. Achievement was measured by the Peabody Individual Achievement Test (PIAT; Dunn & Markwardt, 1970). Furthermore, we predicted that the RSA children would demonstrate a greater discrepancy between intelligence and achievement than their NA peers.

Contrary to our prediction, the only significant difference in achievement between groups was found on the PIAT Math subtest (see Table 8.1). However, it should be noted that the groups did not significantly differ on the Math subtest score when intelligence was partialed out. Although the mean score on all subtests was higher for the NA children, the group differences were not significant. Also contrary to our prediction, there was no significant difference between groups on discrepancy between intelligence and achievement.

School Performance/School Behavior Problems

Also on the basis of the traumagenic model, we predicted that subjective ratings of school performance and school-related behavior problems by mothers would be worse for the RSA children than for their NA peers (particularly since the RSA was reported in a school context). School performance was measured by the School subscale of the Social Competence portion of the CBCL; school behavior problems were assessed by a subgroup of items on the CBCL.

As we predicted, school performance (as rated by mothers on the CBCL) was significantly poorer for the RSA group (see Table 8.2). On average, mothers of RSA children rated them at about the 30th percentile (T-score of 44) on school adaptive functioning, compared to ratings at about the 50th percentile by mothers of NA children. On the subset of CBCL items that were judged to represent school behavior problems (e.g., "Disobedient at school," "Truancy, skips school"; note that this subset is not derived from factor analysis, and may not be valid), the RSA children were rated as having significantly more problems than their NA peers.

Attitudes about School

Finally, we predicted that the RSA children would have more negative and fearful attitudes about school than their NA peers. We predicted this because the children studied reported that the abuse occurred in a school setting; we also predicted it for reasons implied by the

TABLE 8.2. School Performance, Behavior, and Attitude

Variable	Group[a]		Statistics
	RSA	NA	
Mean CBCL School *T*-score[b]	43.98	51.21	*t* = −3.23***
Mean sum of CBCL school behavior items[b]	1.47	0.13	*t* = 5.95****
Mean sum of BADI school attitude items (for past month)[b]	0.39	0.03	*t* = 2.29**
Mean net sum of Incomplete Sentence Test School subscale items	0.74	2.27	*t* = 3.13***
Proportion of Negative Incomplete Sentence Test School subscale items	28.9%	9.1%	χ^2 = 4.07*

[a]*n*'s = 55–76 in the RSA group, and 29–34 in the NA group.
[b]Ratings were from mothers only.
*$p < .045$; **$p < .025$; ***$p < .002$; ****$p < .001$.

traumagenic model. Attitudes about school were measured by the School subscale of the Incomplete Sentence Test and the Behaviors After Diagnostic Interview (BADI) checklist.

Child Data

Incomplete Sentence Test items were scored independently by two psychologists or graduate students unaware of the children's group membership. There were significant group differences on the School subscale of this test, with the NA children showing more positive school-related attitudes (see Table 8.2). In addition, there was a significantly higher proportion of negative attitude responses in the RSA group (29%, vs. 9% in the NA group).

Parent Data

Also as we predicted, the RSA group showed significantly more school attitude problems in the past month (reported by mothers on the BADI questionnaire) than the NA group (see Table 8.2). However, it should be noted that a majority of mothers reported no problems with school attitude on this measure.

SELF-ESTEEM

Although clinicians frequently report that sexually abused children have poor self-esteem (e.g., Herman & Hirschman, 1977; Katan, 1973; Steele

& Alexander, 1981; Van Gijseghem, 1978), research findings in this area have been mixed. For example, Conte and Schuerman (1987), Gold (1986), and Tong et al. (1987) found differences in self-esteem between sexual abuse victims and nonabused children; Cohen and Mannarino (1988), Gomes-Schwartz, Horowitz, and Sauzier (1985), and Mannarino, Cohen, and Gregor (1989) did not. Furthermore, no one has yet reported results on scholastic self-concept.

Consistent with clinical findings, the traumagenic model, and the literature on PTSD, we predicted that the RSA children would have poorer scholastic self-esteem than their NA peers. Self-esteem was measured in older children (third grade or over) by the Self-Perception Profile for children (Harter, 1985), which provided Scholastic Competence and Global Self-Worth scores (see Chapter 7 for a discussion of other self-concept findings). These were converted into standardized z scores, to allow for comparisons across all age groups (the norms differ by age).

Contrary to our prediction, there was no significant difference between groups on the Scholastic Competence subscale when SES was controlled for.

ATTENTION AND CONCENTRATION

Problems with attention and concentration have been found both initially and in the long term in victims of child sexual abuse. Shaw and Meier (1983) studied young victims and found significant problems with attention and concentration; Johnston (1979), in clinical observations, also noted that sexually abused children seemed to have problems concentrating on tasks. However, it is difficult to estimate the actual proportion of sexually abused children with problems in this area. Conte and Schuerman (1987) compared 369 sexually abused children of various ages to 318 nonabused children recruited from the same community and found that parents and/or social workers rated only 14% as unable to concentrate. In contrast, Lindberg and Distad (1985b) studied 27 incest victims aged 12–18, and concluded that all had problems with attention and concentration.

At any rate, it appears that this may be a significant problem for victims of sexual abuse, and one that can obviously have negative effects on related variables (e.g., school performance). Furthermore, problems with attention and concentration may continue for many years after the abuse ceases. Lindberg and Distad (1985a) also studied 17 adult women who were incest victims as children, and noted that many experienced problems with concentration in adulthood.

Consistent with the PTSD model, we predicted that the RSA children would have more problems with attention and concentration than the NA children. Attention and concentration were measured by items on the modified CBCL and an item on the Brief Psychiatric Rating Scale for Children (BPRS-C; Overall & Pfefferbaum, 1982) filled out by psychological testers.

Parent Data

We examined a sum of CBCL items (completed by mothers for the period of most distress in the past 2 years) that asked about problems related to attention and concentration (e.g., "Can't concentrate," "Daydreams; gets lost in thoughts"). It is again important to note that this group of items was not derived from factor analysis, and therefore was based solely on our subjective judgment. The RSA children were rated as having significantly more problems with attention and concentration than their NA peers (see Table 8.3).

Tester Data

Attention and concentration problems were also measured by the tester rating on Distractibility from the BPRS-C. The mean rating for the RSA children was significantly higher than that for the NA children (see Table 8.3). It should be noted that these problems were typically rated in the very mild to mild range for the RSA children, so they were not viewed as severe.

ATTRIBUTIONS/LOCUS OF CONTROL

It can be predicted from the traumagenic model (Finkelhor, 1987) that a sense of powerlessness is likely to result from sexual abuse. This powerlessness may be manifested in several ways. Powerlessness may result in "learned helplessness" and changes in attributions made by a child (e.g., a greater tendency to attribute causality in general to external factors). In turn, these may lead to reduced achievement and an increase in school-related problems.

Many clinicians have observed helplessness or powerlessness as an effect in child victims of sexual abuse (Courtois & Watts, 1982; Gross, 1979; Jiles, 1981; Knittle & Tuana, 1980; Lindberg & Distad, 1985b; Summit, 1983). Summit (1983) and Knittle and Tuana (1980) have commented that sexually abused children tend to develop a "helpless victim" mentality, which affects them in other situations. Furthermore,

TABLE 8.3. Attention and Concentration

Variable	Group[a]		Statistics
	RSA	NA	
Mean sum of CBCL attention/ concentration problem items[b]	2.36	0.58	$F = 12.07$**
Mean BPRS-C Distractibility rating (from tester)	1.39	0.61	$t = 2.08$*

[a]n's = 61 RSA and 31 NA for the first variable, and 51 RSA and 23 NA for the second variable.
[b]Ratings were from mothers only.
*$p < .05$; **$p < .001$.

Lindberg and Distad (1985b) conclude that many of the observed symptoms of sexual abuse (or incest, in their case) may be attempts to "assert some control over helplessness created by the incest" (p. 521).

One empirical study to date has examined the attributions of child sexual abuse victims. Gold (1986) compared attributions of 103 adult women molested as children to 88 controls; subjects were recruited through advertisements. Gold found that the sexually abused women were more likely to attribute good events to external factors. Apparently, prior to the present study, no one has yet published research that empirically examines the attributions or locus of control of children reporting ritualistic sexual abuse. As Conte and Schuerman (1987) wrote, "we do not know the attributional beliefs of child victims of sexual abuse and how these beliefs are associated with the effects of such experiences" (p. 211).

Consistent with the traumagenic model, we predicted that the RSA children would have a more external locus of control than the NA children in the cognitive domain. We also predicted that they would make fewer internal attributions in these domains. Locus of control was measured in older children by the Why Things Happen questionnaire (Connell, 1985), which includes subscales for Internal Control and Powerful Others in the cognitive domain.

We calculated z scores for the Internal Control and Powerful Others scores (since they are normed by age). Contrary to our prediction, there was no significant between-group difference on any of these scores.

INTERPRETATIONS

Intelligence and Achievement

It was not surprising that the groups did not significantly differ in global intelligence. As discussed earlier, we had little reason to believe that reported ritualistic sexual abuse would affect intelligence per se. It is interesting to note, however, that the mean difference in prorated full-scale intelligence (Full Scale DQs) favored the NA group by about 4 points, and that Verbal DQs were significantly higher in this group, even when SES was controlled for. This finding is difficult to explain, but may result at least partially from factors other than intelligence per se (e.g., poorer attention and concentration).

It is more surprising that almost no significant group differences were found in achievement (although mean differences consistently favored the NA group). There are several possible interpretations of this finding. It must be considered that the measure of achievement used, the PIAT, is a screening test. Thus, rather than being based on school records over a period of time (which were impossible to obtain), the achievement measure came years after the reported abuse, typically took less than 45 minutes to administer, and was obtained in a one-on-one testing situation. As a result, this measure could not be considered sensitive to past deficits, which may have resolved by themselves over time or may have been remediated through educational interventions implemented after the reported abuse, or to chronic problems (e.g., "tuning out" in a classroom) that might not be apparent under these conditions. Anecdotal information suggests that many of the children in the RSA group attended relatively prestigious, academically oriented private schools at the time of the testing. Thus, their academic program may have helped to ameliorate any delays in achievement.

It should also be noted that although the clinical literature on school problems in sexual abuse victims mentions underachievement as a symptom, empirical studies report an increase in school problems, but do not focus specifically on achievement (Finkelhor & Browne, 1986). Thus, the finding of school problems (but not lower achievement per se) is not inconsistent with the existing clinical literature. In addition, this result is not necessarily inconsistent with the traumagenic model, which predicts school problems, but not specifically poorer achievement.

School Performance and Behavior

Maternal ratings indicated that the RSA children had significantly more severe problems with school performance and behavior than the NA group. This finding is consistent with the literature reviewed on sexual abuse, and helps provide support for the traumagenic model. However, it must also be noted that the RSA children reported abuse in a school (albeit a preschool) setting, and therefore it cannot be concluded that the reported abuse alone resulted in these problems. In sum, these data suggest that the RSA children may at this point have been achieving on par with their NA peers; however, they were still exhibiting school behavior problems, even after a number of years had passed.

Attitudes about School

Consistent with the traumagenic model and clinical literature, the RSA children showed significantly poorer school-related attitudes than the NA children on a projective measure; they also showed more attitude problems as rated by mothers. Despite this finding, in an absolute sense their projective attitudes on the School subscale of the Incomplete Sentence Test (e.g., "Most of the time, school is ...") were rated as positive overall (i.e., the mean was 0.74, with zero being neutral). However, nearly 30% of the RSA children had negative overall ratings, whereas fewer than 10% of the controls did. This finding is consistent with effects predicted by the traumagenic model of sexual abuse: The dynamic of betrayal, particularly when it is reportedly paired with a school setting, may well lead to poorer school-related attitudes. If a child is betrayed by trusted caretakers in a school setting, he or she therefore may develop mistrust of school personnel, and fear or dislike of classmates or other things related to school. In sum, like school-related behavior problems, attitudes about school appear to be negatively affected by reported preschool ritualistic sexual abuse.

Locus of Control

Contrary to prediction, locus of control was not more external (i.e., a higher score on the Powerful Others subscale of the Why Things Happen measure for the cognitive domain) for the RSA children; nor was the Internal Control score lower, as was also predicted. There are several possible explanations for these findings. One is that the reported abuse did not cause the RSA children to develop a more externally oriented locus of control, despite the fact that this would be predicted by the powerlessness dynamic of the traumagenic model and supported by other research. Perhaps a more likely explanation is that psychotherapy fostered self-efficacy in these children, which resulted in a more positive, internal locus of control. A third explanation comes from the traumagenic model itself: It predicts that powerlessness may result in a need to control, which could result in answering Why Things Happen items in ways that reflect less Powerful Others control. Thus, some children may have been attributing more control to Powerful Others, whereas others may have been attributing less; in effect, they may have canceled each other out. Finally, it is possible that other dimensions of locus of control (e.g., stability) that were not measured are affected by ritualistic sexual abuse.

Attention and Concentration

Attention and concentration problems were rated as significantly more serious by mothers of RSA children on the CBCL (for the time of most distress in the past 2 years); this finding provides support for the PTSD model. Ratings of distractibility made by examiners at the time of the final testing session were also significantly higher for the RSA children. It should be noted that the finding of greater attention and concentration problems is consistent with the traumagenic model, but is not specifically predicted by it. It is, however, directly predicted by the literature on PTSD.

Self-Concept

Contrary to predictions suggested by most literature to date (including the traumagenic and PTSD models), as well as to our findings for global self-concept, no group differences were found in scholastic self-concept. It appears that other areas of self-worth (e.g., those having to do with physical appearance) may be more affected by sexual abuse than is scholastic self-worth.

THEORETICAL IMPLICATIONS

Consistent with the traumagenic model, the RSA children exhibited more school-related behavior problems and showed poorer school-related attitudes. However, inconsistent with the model, no differences were found in cognitive locus of control or scholastic self-concept. The PTSD model predicted differences in attention and concentration, which were found, but did not provide specific predictions for other areas.

Thus, it can be argued that the results of this study provide limited overall support for both models, but qualifications must be attached. First, not all predictions were supported, as noted above. Second, there are two observed effects that the PTSD model does not account for (school-related behavior and attitude problems), and one (attention/concentration problems) that the traumagenic model does not account for. Therefore, these models (particularly the PTSD model) do not completely account for cognitive and school-related effects of reported child sexual abuse, and may need to be expanded in this area. It would not be difficult for the traumagenic model to be expanded to account for problems with attention and concentration. Perhaps these problems could be viewed as an effect of either the betrayal or the traumatic sexualization dynamic.

On the other hand, it would be more difficult to expand the PTSD model to include the school-related effects noted. As Finkelhor (1988) argues, the PTSD model is really too narrow to account for all of the effects of sexual abuse; his traumagenic model, if modified, appears much more promising as a comprehensive descriptive model.

CLINICAL IMPLICATIONS

Several important clinical implications arise from these findings. First, these data indicate that there are indeed cognitive and school-related effects of reported ritualistic sexual abuse; literature on clinical treatment to date has largely ignored these variables, focusing instead on emotional and behavioral effects. This study suggests that it is important to focus on cognitive and school-related variables in treatment as well. This is undoubtedly especially true for children who are abused in a preschool (or other school) setting. Specific implications include more routine assessment of school-related behavior problems, attitudes, and functioning; and assessment for PTSD symptoms, including attention and concentration problems. Parent ratings and projective sentence completion items proved useful in eliciting these problems in the present study. Assessment might also include discussions with a child's teacher(s), review of school records, and classroom observation. Moreover, psychoeducational interventions might be considered (e.g., educational therapy or behavioral management in the classroom).

Second, this study suggests that although cognitive and school-related effects appear worse shortly after ritualistic sexual abuse is reported, they persist for years afterward, despite intervening therapy. Thus, these concerns may need to be addressed on a long-term basis. Perhaps parents of victims should be encouraged to monitor their children's school-related attitudes and fears as well as scholastic functioning, and to seek consultation if problems appear. Both therapists and parents should attempt to help children separate the experience of abuse from the setting (e.g., school) in which it occurred, so that more positive attitudes toward new school settings may be encouraged. These findings may even suggest that therapists with adult clients who were molested as children should observe these clients for cognitive symptoms.

Finally, it appears that difficulties with attention and concentration may have to be addressed in treatment. This is typically done by helping the victim work through the trauma that has caused these problems (Horowitz, 1974). However, they could probably be addressed through cognitive techniques used with children who have attention deficit disorders (e.g., teaching strategies to help focus attention and maintain concentration).

We can speculate about what the future might hold for these children, given the finding that they appeared to be achieving on par with their peers, but had poorer school-related attitudes and more school behavior problems (even after treatment). While in school, these children might be labeled as "troublemakers" and therefore further stigmatized. We certainly hope that their more negative attitudes toward school will not interfere with their achievement later on, or with any desire to pursue a college education or an advanced degree. Longitudinal research is vital to examine whether negative behavioral and attitudinal responses to school are ameliorated or exacerbated with time and developmental maturation.

EMOTIONAL
EFFECTS

Robert J. Kelly
Sharon Ben-Meir

$\mathbf{A}$S RECENT STUDIES have consistently shown, child sexual abuse frequently leads to a myriad of harmful emotional effects in its victims (for reviews, see Chapter 2; Browne & Finkelhor, 1986). The most frequently cited conceptual frameworks that have been advanced to explain the mechanisms by which child sexual abuse leads to negative emotional sequelae are the post traumatic stress disorder (PTSD) model and Finkelhor and Browne's (1986) traumagenic dynamics model. In the former model, child sexual abuse is equated with other types of traumatic experiences, and a victim's response is understood as a variant of PTSD syndrome. By contrast, Finkelhor and Browne focus on what is unique to sexual abuse encounters, postulating four "traumagenic dynamics" that co-occur exclusively in childhood molestation. These four dynamics are powerlessness, betrayal, stigmatization, and traumatic sexualization.

The PTSD model emphasizes the role of anxiety in the development of negative emotional effects. Pynoos and Eth (1985b) describe this process as one in which "psychic trauma occurs when an individual is exposed to an overwhelming event, and is rendered helpless in the face of intolerable danger, anxiety, or instinctual arousal" (p. 23). It is the individual's experience of acute and overwhelming anxiety, flooding the available coping capacities, that defines trauma. A diagnosis of PTSD as defined in the revised third edition of the *Diagnostic and Statistical Manual of Mental Disorders* (DSM-III-R), requires the presence of four criteria; which we paraphrase here (see American Psychiatric Association, 1987, p. 250, for the complete description).

1. The occurrence of a recognizable stressor that would be expected to evoke significant distress in most persons (such as an incident of child sexual abuse).
2. Reexperiencing of the traumatic events via intrusive, recurrent memories, dreams, or feelings.
3. A decrease or numbing of responsiveness to the external world, evidenced by constricted affect, diminished involvement in usual activities, and sense of estrangement from other people.
4. At least two of the following secondary symptoms: sleep difficulty, problems with concentration, survival guilt, hyperalertness, avoidance of trauma-related stimuli, or the exacerbation of symptoms with exposure to trauma-related cues and activities.

The traumagenic dynamic model also incorporates anxiety as a core issue for abuse victims, but it proposes a broader paradigm for understanding the diversity of effects often experienced by these victims. According to Finkelhor (1987), "a traumagenic dynamic is an experience that alters a child's cognitive or emotional orientation to the world, and causes trauma by distorting the child's self-concept, world view or affective capacities" (p. 354). Thus, the traumagenic dynamics inherent in child sexual abuse converge to create, in some victims, a variety of negative emotional effects.

In the preceding chapters, we have examined differences between the children reporting ritualistic sexual abuse (the RSA group) and those who never reported being sexually abused (the NA group) in terms of overall distress levels (Chapter 7) and problems related to cognitive ability and school behaviors and attitudes (Chapter 8). The current chapter focuses on more specific emotional effects. Three types of emotional reactions were assessed: (1) fears and anxieties; (2) depression; and (3) anger, hostility, and aggression. For each type of emotional reaction, results are presented according to the three major sources of data: parents, children, and therapists.

FEARS AND ANXIETIES

Parental Perceptions

Four instruments filled out by parents assessed children's fear and anxiety levels: (1) the Louisville Fear Survey; (2) subscales of the Child Behavior Checklist (CBCL); (3) additional items attached to the CBCL, focusing on PTSD symptoms; and (4) the Behaviors After Diagnostic Interview (BADI) questionnaire.

The Louisville Fear Survey (Miller, 1976; Miller, Barrett, Hampe, & Noble, 1972) was used as the primary standardized instrument for assessing children's fear reactions. In using this instrument, we attempted to answer four questions. First, were there any differences in the overall fear levels of the RSA children? The answer to this question was a resounding "yes." As shown in Table 9.1, parents of RSA children rated their children as significantly more fearful than did parents of children in the NA group, F $(1, 95) = 15.5, p < .001$. Although children in the NA group scored very similarly to the standardized norm group used by Miller (1972), children in the RSA group scored even higher than the group of phobic children reported in that study. Thus, RSA children were more fearful than their own control group, Miller's normative sample, and the clinical sample Miller utilized.

The second question to be answered was whether the three factors developed by Miller (1976) in order to classify types of fears would be useful in understanding the types of fears experienced by children in the RSA group. However, children in the RSA group scored significantly higher than children in the NA group on all three fear factors, which are described as fear of Natural Events, fear of Physical Injury, and fears related to Social Stress. These results suggest that the children in the RSA group have became generally fearful, rather than manifesting fears in circumscribed domains.

The third question also related to the specificity of the children's fears. Although their fears were not limited to narrow domains, we were still interested in the specific fears that were most frequently exhibited by children in the RSA group. Table 9.2 lists the rank order of the 10 most common fears, along with the percentage of children who exhibited what parents rated as "an excessive or unreasonable amount of fear." For example, the most frequently exhibited fear was fear of the Devil, which was shown by 36.6% of the children in the RSA group, as opposed to 0.0% of the children in the NA group or 2.5% of children in Miller's (1972) normative sample. As is readily apparent, many of the most frequently

TABLE 9.1. Louisville Fear Survey Scores for RSA and NA Children

Total fears	RSA $(n = 69)$	NA $(n = 29)$	F
$\bar{X}$	131.1	111.4	15.5^{a*}
SD	21.9	12.7	

Note. Scores were calculated from mothers' ratings of children's "current" fears approximately 3 years postdisclosure. Maximum score = 162.
^{a}Analysis of covariance controlling for socioeconomic status.
$^*p < .001$.

TABLE 9.2. Ten Most Frequently Endorsed "Excessive or Unreasonable Fears" of RSA and NA Children

| | | Percentage endorsing item | | |
| | | RSA | NA | |
Rank	Item	(n = 71)	(n = 30)	χ^2
1	Devil	36.6	0.0	12.9***
2	Nightmares	33.8	0.0	11.5***
3	Being criticized	29.6	6.7	5.1*
4	Hell	26.8	0.0	8.2**
4	Dark	26.8	3.3	5.9*
6	Being separated from parents	25.4	6.7	3.5
7	Receiving injections	23.9	3.3	4.8*
8	Being confined or locked up	21.4	0.0	6.0*
9	Sight of blood	21.1	3.0	3.8*
9	Going to sleep at night	21.1	0.0	5.9*

Note. Scores were calculated from mothers' ratings of children's "current" fears approximately 3 years postdisclosure on the Louisville Fear Survey.
* $p < .05$; ** $p < .01$; *** $p < .001$.

exhibited fears seem related to fears that children might be expected to have after being ritualistically sexually abused. It is also noteworthy, given the allegations of Satanic abuse made by many of these children, that two of the most frequently exhibited excessive or unreasonable fears were fear of the Devil and fear of Hell.

The final question involving this fear measure was whether the number of children's fears was related to the types of sexual, terrorizing, or ritualistic abuse acts reported by the children. To answer this question, we obtained Pearson product–moment correlations between the number of abuse acts reported by children within each of the five Sexual Abuse Grid categories (see Chapter 5) and their total fear score. For analyses involving the full RSA sample, the total fear score did not correlate significantly with the number of highly intrusive, intrusive, or less intrusive sexual acts reported by the children. However, the total fear score did correlate significantly with both the number of terrorizing and ritualistic acts reported by these children. As one might expect, children who reported experiencing a greater number of terrorizing and ritualistic acts exhibited a greater number of excessive or unreasonable fears (Kelly, Waterman, Oliveri, & McCord, 1988).

A somewhat different picture emerged when we created separate z scores for boys' and girls' maternal ratings, based on Miller's norms. Boys who reported experiencing a greater number of abusive acts in any of the five Sexual Abuse Grid categories exhibited a greater number of fears (r's ranging from .40 to .51; all p's < .03). However, girls' fear levels did not significantly correlate with the number of acts they reported experiencing within any of the five grid categories (r's ranging from −.09 to .27; all p's nonsignificant). Moreover, although the absolute fear levels of boys and girls were almost identical (both means equaled 131), the boys' z scores tended to be higher than the girls' z scores, because boys in the normative sample (and our control sample) generally exhibited fewer fears than did girls. In other words, both the boys and girls in the RSA sample were extremely fearful, and they exhibited the same degree of fearfulness; however, since boys generally exhibit fewer fears than girls, the difference in fear levels between RSA boys and NA boys was greater than the difference between RSA girls and NA girls, although both were highly significant (p's < .01).

The second instrument completed by parents in order to document fears and anxiety was the CBCL. In Chapter 7 we reported that children in the RSA group showed significantly more pathology than children in the NA group on the four major scales (Internalizing, Externalizing, Total Behavior Problems, and Social Competence). The CBCL also includes a variety of factor subscales, which enabled us to assess more specific behavioral and emotional effects. One of these subscales, Withdrawal, contains items relating to social and emotional withdrawal—an anxiety reaction that is common in people experiencing PTSD. Mothers of children in both groups were asked to rate their children's behavior retrospectively for the period of most distress during the past 2 years. Mothers of children in the RSA group rated their children as significantly more withdrawn than did mothers of children in the NA group, t (1, 99) = 6.77, p < .001. Moreover, 37.7% of children in the RSA group scored in the clinical range on this subscale, as opposed to 0% in the NA group. No differences were found on father ratings on the Withdrawal subscale.

In addition to this standardized CBCL subscale, we also grouped together a series of individual items from either the standard version of the CBCL or the extra items we added to this instrument. These items all related to aspects of PTSD, such as becoming emotionally numb, becoming suspicious, being easily startled, having flashbacks, and having dreams specific to sexual abuse. Children in the RSA group showed significantly more pathology than children in the NA group on all 12 of these PTSD-related items (all p's < .014, two-tailed).

The final parent measure that included an assessment of fears and anxiety was the BADI questionnaire. This nonstandardized instrument assessed a series of nine problem areas, three of which related to fears and anxiety. The first subscale, Withdrawal, included four items assessing clinginess, withdrawal, fear of separation, and fear of strangers. The second subscale, Sleep Problems, assessed sleep problems, nightmares, fear of monsters, fear of naps, and bedwetting. The third subscale, School Problems, assessed specific anxiety related to school, and was included because all children in the RSA group reported having been abused at their preschools. This subscale consisted of five items: "School problems," "Sudden dislike of school," "Refusal to attend school," "Fear of school or teacher(s)," and "Emotionally upset upon returning home." Parents were asked to rate retrospectively whether their children had exhibited specific problem behaviors in these categories during the first month after their diagnostic evaluation (or in early 1984 for control parents), and whether they had exhibited these behaviors during the last month (approximately 3 years after that initial evaluation).

For the first month after their diagnostic evaluation, a significantly higher percentage of children in the RSA group than the NA group exhibited symptoms of Withdrawal, Sleep Problems, and School Problems on both mothers' and fathers' ratings (all p's < .03). For example, 91.4% of the RSA children were rated by mothers as exhibiting at least one Withdrawal symptom, as opposed to 28.1% of the NA children ($p <$ .001). By the time of the 3-year follow-up, a significantly greater percentage of RSA children still exhibited symptoms in all three categories, according to mothers' ratings. Some alleviation of symptoms had occurred, at least in part simply because the children had grown older. For example, 45.7% of the RSA children were still exhibiting at least one Withdrawal symptom, as compared with 11.8% of the NA children ($p <$ .01). By the time of the follow-up, there were no differences on fathers' ratings on the Withdrawal or School Problems subscales, although a significant difference still existed on the Sleep Problems scale ($p < .01$).

Child Measures

Three child instruments assessed children's fear and anxiety levels: (1) the Kinetic Family Drawing; (2) the Rorschach; and (3) the Roberts Apperception Test for Children (RATC).

Chapter 7 has noted that RSA children showed a significantly higher number of emotional indicators than NA children on the Draw-A-Person task. More specific evidence of fears and anxiety came on the other task involving drawings of human figures, the Kinetic Family Drawing. For this task, children were asked "to draw a picture of your family doing something." Once again, trained raters were blind as to group status. Nevertheless, the drawings of children in the RSA group showed a significantly greater amount of "strange and frightening content," such as the presence of scary monsters or grotesque figures, persons in danger, major body parts omitted, heads drawn without a body, or absence of facial features on all figures (Rorty, Waterman, Kelly, Oliveri, & McCord, 1990).

Rorschach responses for a large subsample of children in the RSA and NA groups were analyzed in a doctoral dissertation (Ben-Meir, 1989). No differences were found between the two groups on two indices used to measure anxiety—namely, the Elizur (1949) coding scheme based on verbal content of the protocol, and Exner's (1986) scoring system for the sum of diffuse shading responses (Sum of Y). Initially, we did find a significant difference in the percentage of children who met criteria on the Hypervigilance Index. When we rescored the Rorschachs with raters who were unaware of group status, however, this finding became marginal, $\chi^2 (1) = 2.83$, $p = .09$. Nonetheless, future studies may want to explore this index, since it did appear to yield a higher percentage of hypervigilant children in the RSA group (18.2%) than in the NA group (4.0%).

We would like to add a word of caution to clinicians and researchers who are using the Rorschach with children. Most clinicians and researchers administer the test to children in a clinical context and compare those children's responses with the published norms (Exner, 1986), without the use of a control group. If we had followed this procedure, our RSA and sexual abuse only (SA) groups would have appeared severely disturbed, since their responses were much "worse" than the published norms. However, we then noticed that our control group's responses were also much "worse" than those norms. For example, none of our groups came anywhere near the $X+\%$ or $F+\%$ listed in the national norms or in the norms for Western states (see Ben-Meir, 1989). If these were the only data we had collected, we might have suspected that our control group had a high degree of disturbance, but this speculation was not supported by the other instruments, on which the control group consistently scored very comparably to the published norms. It also may have been that our administration or scoring of the Rorschach was inaccurate, despite the large number of hours we invested under the supervision of a Rorschach expert and the helpful consultation of Dr. Exner himself. We are not Rorschach experts, and we would actually be relieved to learn that the Rorschach results we gathered were indeed very different from those that most professionals would obtain. But we fear otherwise.

An alternative explanation is that the published norms do not provide us with the most accurate prediction of what most "normal" children will score when tested by most trained professionals. If that is true, the potential for overpathologizing children on the basis of their Rorschach responses gives cause for concern. Moreover, since most clinicians and researchers do not use control groups, they do not have a self-correction mechanism in place; that is, they will never know that they are overpathologizing. Thus, we encourage other clinicians and researchers to test some nonclinical children and to compare those results with the published norms, instead of taking those norms at face value.

On the final child measure assessing fears and anxiety, the RATC, no differences were found on the Anxiety subscale. The raters on this instrument were the original test administrators, who were aware of group status. However, since no differences were found between groups, this prior knowledge of group status did not seem to interfere with raters' scoring this measure objectively. As mentioned in Chapter 7, the RATC has not consistently discriminated between clinical and nonclinical groups in other studies, so we do not know whether our "nonfinding" is valid, or whether the test should not be expected to differentiate between children who do and do not report abuse. The measure does appear useful in working with individual children in a clinical setting, since it helps children to discuss potential conflict situations in their lives.

Therapist Questionnaires

Three therapist measures were used to assess children's fear and anxiety levels: (1) a PTSD checklist; (2) subscales of the Teacher Report Form of the CBCL (therapist CBCL); and (3) factor scores on the Brief Psychiatric Rating Scale for Children (BPRS-C). These data were not available for the children in the NA group, since most of these children were not in therapy.

The PTSD checklist was incorporated into the extra items attached to the therapist CBCL. This checklist consisted of the PTSD criteria outlined in the initial draft version of DSM-III-R. Therapists were asked to rate retrospectively the children in the RSA group in terms of their PTSD symptomatology during the period of most distress within the 2 years after the initial diagnostic evaluation. Table 9.3 shows the percentage of children who exhibited each of the PTSD symptoms. In order to attain the diagnosis of PTSD, a child would need to exhibit a certain number of symptoms within each group of criteria (see American Psychiatric Association, 1987, p. 250). Of the 66 children for whom we have complete therapist data, 55 (83.3%) met criteria for this diagnosis, showing overwhelming evidence for PTSD as a common anxiety-related effect in children reporting ritualistic sexual abuse.

Chapter 7 reported that an unusually large percentage of children in the RSA group scored in the clinical range on the four primary scales of the therapist CBCL (Internalizing, Externalizing, Total Behavior Problems, and Social Competence). Like the parent version of the CBCL, the version completed retrospectively by therapists also includes standardized subscales, which enabled us to assess more specific behavioral and emotional problem areas. Three of these subscales focus on anxiety related problems: Anxiety, Social Withdrawal, and Nervous–Overactive. Approximately 2% of children in a nonclinical sample would be expected to

TABLE 9.3. Percentage of RSA Children (n = 66) Exhibiting PTSD Symptoms during Period of Most Distress

Item	Percentage
Persistent reexperiencing	
Recurrent and intrusive recollections	79.3
Recurrent distressing dreams	74.2
Sudden acting or feeling as if event is recurring	53.0
Physiologic reactivity or intense distress	75.8
Persistent avoidance of stimuli associated with trauma, or numbing of responsiveness	
Avoids thoughts or feelings associated with trauma	95.5
Avoids activities or situations that arouse recollections of trauma	87.9
Psychogenic amnesia	74.2
Markedly diminished interest in activities	45.5
Feeling of detachment or estrangement from others	59.1
Restricted range of affect	66.7
Sense of foreshortened future	N/A
Persistent symptoms of increased arousal	
Difficulty falling or staying asleep	78.8
Irritability or outbursts of anger	90.9
Difficulty concentrating	69.7
Hypervigilance	71.2
Exaggerated startle response	56.1
Percentage meeting criteria for diagnosis of PTSD	83.3

Note. Ratings were made by therapists. Criteria were adapted from a working draft of DSM-III-R. NA, not asked.

fall into the clinical range on these subscales. However, in the RSA group, almost two-thirds (65.1%) of the children scored in this clinical range on the Anxiety subscale. An unusually high percentage also scored in the clinical range on the Social Withdrawal (34.9%) and Nervous–Overactive (14.5%) subscales.

The final therapist measure that included an assessment of children's fear and anxiety levels was the BPRS-C, which each child's therapist filled out retrospectively for two time periods: (1) the period of most distress for the child; and (2) the time of termination from therapy (or currently, for the few children who were still in therapy). During the period of most distress, over two-thirds of the children in the RSA group were experiencing at least moderate symptoms of tension (74%), anxiety (79.5%), and sleep difficulties (69.0%), with many children exhibiting symptoms in the severe or extremely severe range. Fortunately, according to the therapists' BPRS-C ratings at the end of therapy, most of these children became less anxious over time. Nevertheless, by the end of therapy, an average of 1 to 2 children out of every 10 were still experiencing at least moderate symptoms of tension (11.0%), anxiety

(21.9%), and sleep difficulties (12.5%). Although this improvement in anxiety level was both statistically and clinically significant, it should be noted that anxiety was one of the symptoms that was most resistant to change.

DEPRESSION

Parental Perceptions

Parental observations of children's depression levels were collected via the Depression subscale of the parent CBCL. This subscale included items such as "Looks unhappy" and "Moody." Once again, parents were asked to rate retrospectively their children's behavior during the period of most distress within the past 2 years. As hypothesized, children in the RSA group were described by their mothers ($\bar{X}$ = 70.3) as being significantly more depressed than were children in the NA group ($\bar{X}$ = 56.2), t (1, 73) = 9.44, p < .001. Moreover, 52.5% of the children in the RSA group were in the clinical range on this subscale, as opposed to 0% of the children in the NA group. A similar pattern was found for the smaller sample of fathers who participated in this study. Fathers of children in the RSA group rated their children as more depressed ($\bar{X}$ = 64.9) than did fathers of children in the NA group ($\bar{X}$ = 57.5), t (1, 51) = 3.82, p < .001. According to fathers' ratings, 33.3% of the children in the RSA group were in the clinical range on the Depression subscale, as opposed to 0% of the children in the NA group.

Child Measures

No evidence for a greater degree of depression in RSA than in NA children was found on the two projective measures used to assess depression levels. On the Rorschach, no significant differences were found on the Rorschach Depression Index (Exner, 1986). Similarly, scores on the Depression subscale of the RATC-C were not significantly different for RSA children ($\bar{X}$ = 62.5) versus NA children ($\bar{X}$ = 59.9).

One related finding concerns the locus of control results presented in Chapter 8. A major theoretical model in the conceptualization of depression is "learned helplessness"—that is, the idea that depressed people "learn" or come to believe that they are helpless against outside forces. As mentioned previously, the older children in the RSA group scored significantly higher than the older children in the NA group in terms of their perceptions of how much control "powerful others" possessed. Given that the children would be expected to feel powerless during horrendous acts of ritualistic abuse such as the ones that they reported, along with the fact that none of the alleged perpetrators had been convicted of any crimes by the time these children were tested, it does not seem surprising that these children may have begun to adopt a form of learned helplessness in which they perceived themselves to be defenseless against the domination of powerful others. Thus, although the projective child measures provided no direct evidence of depression, the RSA children did show some cognitive ideation that might make them more vulnerable to depression later in life.

Therapist Questionnaires

Two therapist instruments assessed depression levels of children in the RSA group. The therapist CBCL contains a standardized Depression subscale, although it is only appropriate for assessing depression in female children who are in the age range of the current study. For the 34 girls with complete data on this instrument, the mean Depression score ($\overline{X} = 77.6$) was the highest mean score of all the subscales. Moreover, almost three-fourths (73.5%) of these girls scored in the clinical range on this subscale.

The BPRS-C assessed depression levels in both girls and boys. During the period of most distress, a very large percentage of children in the RSA group exhibited symptoms of depression. Many of these children scored in the moderate to extremely severe range on the three depression items: depressive mood (65.8%), inferiority feelings (75.3%), and, despite their young age, suicidal ideation (15.1%). Fortunately, by the end of therapy most of these children had become less depressed, although a disturbing number still exhibited moderate to extremely severe depressive mood (15.3%), and inferiority feelings (37.0%). Only one child continued to exhibit at least moderate suicidal ideation.

ANGER, HOSTILITY, AND AGGRESSION

Parent Data

Two parent measures included some assessment of anger, hostility, and/or aggression: (1) the Aggression subscale of the CBCL; and (2) the Aggressive Behaviors subscale of the BADI measure. On the CBCL (which, again, parents rated for the period of most distress), children in the RSA group were described as being significantly more aggressive than children in the NA group by both mothers, t (96) = 6.82, $p < .001$, and fathers, t (52) = 3.24, $p < .002$. Moreover, according to mothers' ratings, 33.3% of the RSA children scored in the clinical range on the Aggression subscale, as opposed to only 3.1% of the NA children. A similar pattern was found in fathers' ratings, with a greater percentage of RSA children (20.0%) falling into the clinical range than NA children (0.0%). By the time of follow-up, 5 years after initial disclosure of abuse, the children in the RSA group had become significantly less aggressive. Only 2 of the 40 mothers (5.0%) and none of the 32 fathers (0.0%) in this subsample of parents who completed follow-up data still rated their children as being in the clinical range on the Aggression subscale.

The Aggressive Behaviors subscale of the BADI includes items such as "Talk or play involving violence" and "Threats of violence towards dolls, pets, siblings, or friends." For the rating period that corresponded to the first month following the children's diagnostic interview, both mothers and fathers of children in the RSA group rated their children as exhibiting more of these symptoms than did mothers and fathers of children in the NA group (p's < .001). Moreover, a significantly greater percentage of children in the RSA group than in the NA group were rated as exhibiting at least one of these behaviors by both mothers (61.4% vs. 12.5%; p < .01) and fathers (54.8% vs. 8.3%; p < .01). Secondary ratings on this measure were also collected to assess how these children were behaving approximately 3 years later. Mothers of children in the RSA group continued to report observing more of these aggressive behaviors than did mothers of children in the NA group, t (93) = 3.73, p < .001, with a significantly higher percentage of children (36.2% vs. 14.7%; p < .04) exhibiting at least one of these behaviors. However, no differences on the Aggressive Behaviors subscale were found in fathers' ratings for this follow-up period.

Child Measures

The two child measures that assessed anger, aggression, and/or hostility were the Rorschach and the RATC. However, neither of these measures supported the hypothesis that children in the RSA group would exhibit more of these symptoms than children in the NA group.

The two measures of aggression on the Rorschach were the Elizur (1949) Hostility score based on Rorschach verbal content, and Exner's (1986) Aggressive Movement (AG) score. These indices tap aggression in fantasy rather than actual aggressive behavior. As reported for the subsample of children in the Ben-Meir (1989) dissertation, children in the RSA and NA groups were virtually indistinguishable on the Elizur scale (t < 1.0). Furthermore, when a cutoff AG score of more than 3 in a record (drawn from Exner's norms for this variable) was used, a significantly greater percentage of children in the NA group produced a "higher than normative" number of AG responses. In fact, none of the RSA children was elevated on AG, as compared with 23% of the NA children, χ^2 (1) = 6.49, p < .01.

The Aggression subscale of the RATC also showed no significant difference for children in the RSA ($\overline{X}$ = 54.1) versus NA ($\overline{X}$ = 52.4) groups (t < 1.0). Both groups scored well within the normal range on this measure. As mentioned previously, the discriminant validity of this measure has yet to be consistently established.

Therapist Questionnaires

As with the construct of depression, therapist ratings of anger, aggression, and/or hostility in the RSA children were derived from the therapist CBCL and the BPRS-C. The mean scores on subscales of the CBCL measuring Aggression ($\overline{X}$ = 66.7) and Self-Destructiveness ($\overline{X}$ = 65.3) were significantly higher than the normative mean ($\overline{X}$ = 50.0). Moreover, a large percentage of children scored in the clinical range on both Aggression (33.3%) and Self-Destructiveness (23.8%).

On the BPRS-C, a significant percentage of RSA children exhibited moderate to extremely severe degrees of uncooperativeness (75.3%), hostility (61.6%), and manipulativeness (32.9%) during the period of most distress. Fortunately, by the end of therapy these symptoms had significantly subsided. Nonetheless, a disturbingly high percentage of children were still exhibiting moderate to extremely severe uncooperativeness (26.0%), hostility (12.3%), and manipulativeness (9.6%) even at this point.

CONCLUSION

The data presented here, especially the data from therapists and parents, overwhelmingly document high levels of negative emotional symptoms in many of the RSA children. More than four-fifths of the children were rated by therapists as meeting criteria for PTSD during the period of most distress. Other emotional effects predicted by the traumagenic dynamic model, such as specific fears, depression, and aggression, were also evident.

Anxiety and fearfulness were consistently found for many RSA children on parent and therapist measures, as well as on some child drawings. Moreover, many of the most frequently exhibited specific fears (fears of the Devil, Hell, being kidnapped, etc.) are consistent with what might be expected for children reporting ritualistic sexual abuse with Satanic elements.

Depression and anger, hostility, and aggression were also consistently found for many RSA children on parent and therapist ratings, although these were not found on the projective tests taken by the children. Children in the RSA group did attribute a greater degree of control to "powerful others" than did children in the NA group—a finding that may have implications for the development of "learned helplessness" and vulnerability to future depression in some children.

Research studies on child abuse have typically found more evidence of child symptomatology in the ratings of parents or therapists than in data collected directly from children. In other chapters we discuss some of our major findings from child data, such as lower scores on a self-concept scale, more negative attitudes on a sentence completion measure, and a very high degree of emotional indicators in children's drawings. This chapter has focused on more specific emotional effects, and the child data discussed here have been restricted mainly to projective measures such as the Rorschach and the RATC, on which very few differences were found. It is our hope that future researchers will develop less global child measures tailored more specifically to emotional sequelae that may be exhibited by children reporting sexual abuse.

CHAPTER 10

EFFECTS ON SEXUALITY

Robert J. Kelly

O NE OF THE CONCERNS most frequently stated by parents of children who reported sexual abuse (the RSA children) was their fear that their children's sexuality might be altered by their reported abuse. Within the framework of the traumagenic dynamic model (Finkelhor & Browne, 1986), it makes intuitive sense to be concerned about the effects of child sexual abuse on sexuality. This model proposes that the dynamics of powerlessness, betrayal, and stigma interact with the fourth dynamic of traumatic sexualization in such a way as to increase the likelihood of certain psychological and behavioral effects on a victim's sexuality. These effects may include aversion to sex, aggressiveness in sex, sexual preoccupations or compulsions, and sexual dysfunction.

Although one might expect that most of the effects proposed in the traumagenic model would be manifested in later adolescence and adulthood, we were interested in determining whether any effect on sexuality would be evident while the children were still young and, in most cases, prepubertal. In previous research, sexual problems such as public masturbation, frequent exposure of genitals, and excessive sexual curiosity have been documented in sexually abused children aged 3 to 12 (Friedrich, Urquiza, & Beilke, 1986; Friedrich, Beilke, & Urquiza, 1987, 1988; Gomes-Schwartz, Horowitz, & Cardarelli, 1990). To examine this issue in our study, we once again looked at pertinent indicators within the data collected from the parents, the children themselves, and the therapists.

PARENTAL PERCEPTIONS

Two parent instruments contain subscales assessing sexual behavior. The first instrument is the Child Behavior Checklist (CBCL), which was analyzed in three different ways. First, there is an empirically based, standardized Sex Problems subscale built into the checklist, but it only has normative information for certain age groups. The only one of these groups that was significantly represented in our samples consisted of girls aged 6 to 11. Thus, we could only use this subscale to compare this specific subsample of children. In doing so, we found that the 6- to 11-year-old girls in the RSA group were rated by their mothers as having significantly more sexual problems (mean *T*-score = 67.7) during the period of most distress than did the 6- to 11-year-old girls who had not been sexually abused (the NA girls; mean *T*-score = 56.5); even after differences in socioeconomic status between groups were controlled for, $F(2, 50) = 14.7$, $p < .001$.

The Sex Problems subscale includes items such as "Behaves like opposite sex," "Plays with own sex parts in public," and "Plays with own sex parts too much" (see Achenbach & Edelbrock, 1983). (The item "Sexual problems" was altered to read "Sexual problems other than abuse," to avoid the confounding problem in other studies of sexual abuse.) Moreover, 46% of the 6- to 11-year-old girls in the RSA subsample scored in the clinical range (*T*-score > 70; i.e., above the 98th percentile) on this subscale, as opposed to only 6% of the NA girls. A similar pattern was found for the smaller group of fathers' ratings, although this finding no longer approached significance once socioeconomic status differences were partialed out.

Since we were interested in determining whether there were effects on sexuality in the RSA group as a whole, rather than just in the 6- to 11-year-old female subsample for which we could use the standardized Sex Problems subscale, we conducted two additional analyses. First, we combined six items from the standard version of the CBCL that clearly asked about sexual problems (i.e., had a high degree of face validity) into what we called Sex Items Scale A. In our second analysis, we combined these six items with five other face-valid sex items that we had attached to the standard CBCL, forming Sex Items Scale B. (We included Scale A as a separate scale to enable other researchers who use the standard CBCL, without our additional items, to make comparisons with these data; it is assumed that they will also alter item 73 to read "Sex problems other than abuse.") No formal scale development was conducted on these scales other than the assurance of face validity. One item from the original Scale B, "Prostitution," was deleted from the analyses because, as expected, no children in either group were rated as engaging in this behavior.

Table 10.1 lists the items that were included in each scale, as well as the percentage of children in each group who exhibited each sexual problem. It is clear from these tables that the RSA children were rated by their parents as exhibiting a significantly higher degree of inappropriate

TABLE 10.1. CBCL Sex Items Scales A and B for Time of Most Distress

Item	Percentage rated as showing behavior		
	RSA[a]	NA[b]	p
Behaves like opposite sex	12.1	0.0	.104
Plays with own sex parts in public	13.8	3.2	.217
Plays with own sex parts too much	29.2	0.0	.002
Sexual problems (other than abuse)	13.8	0.0	.072
Thinks about sex too much	28.8	0.0	.002
Wishes to be opposite sex	9.2	0.0	.195
Does not like how body looks	55.1	22.9	.004
Gave or received affection from people child did not know well	8.7	5.7	.881
Does not like to be touched	44.1	2.9	.001
Shy or uneasy with opposite sex	39.1	5.7	.001
Hated or feared sex or the idea of sex	15.9	0.0	.031

Note. The first six items, which comprise Sex Items Scale A, are from the standard form of the CBCL. Sex Items Scale B consists of Sex Items Scale A plus the remaining five items, which were attached to the CBCL. p levels are based on two-tailed χ^2 analyses using Yates's correction. [a]n's ranged from 65 to 69; [b]n's ranged from 30 to 35.

sexual behavior during the period of most distress than were the NA children. On analyses of both Scale A and Scale B, the mean number of sexual behaviors was consistently high in the RSA sample. Additional analyses showed that these significant differences were true for both boys and girls.

Table 10.1 also illustrates the very disturbing effects on children's sense of body image and body boundaries during the period of most distress. A high percentage of children in the RSA group did not like how their bodies looked (55.1%), and did not want to be touched (44.1%). These findings are consistent with the frequent reports from sexual abuse victims of feeling like "damaged goods" or "dirty" once their bodies had been violated sexually. Also consistent with findings from other studies is the generally heightened degree of sexualization, evidenced by the large percentage of children who were described by their mothers as "Thinking about sex too much" (28.8%) and "Playing with own sex parts too much" (29.2%). The high percentage of RSA children who were described as "Shy around the opposite sex" (39.1%) is also interesting, since it was so much higher than what was reported for the NA children, and thus was not attributable to a developmental phase.

The parents who agreed to a follow-up interview, approximately 5 years after their children's initial disclosure of sexual abuse, were asked to complete these scales once again to assess their children's current sexual functioning. It is heartening to see that these children had indeed decreased their levels of inappropriate sexual behavior. On the standardized Sex Problems subscale, only 13 girls who were still in the 6- to 11-year-old age range had complete CBCL data from both time periods. Nonetheless, the decrease in inappropriate sexual behavior for this small subsample was highly significant, t (1, 12) = 3.87, p < .003. Similar improvements were shown on Sex Items Scales A and B, with sexual behavior becoming more similar to that exhibited by the NA children.

This subsample of parents was also asked to compare their children's sexual behavior during the first year after disclosure with their sexual behavior at the time of follow-up, approximately 5 years later, through ratings on the Parent Reaction Questionnaire. There were no significant differences on the fathers' ratings. However, mothers of RSA children rated their children as being less likely now to touch their genitals in front of their parents, to have sex play with other children, or to walk around nude (all p's < .055).

Since we do not have 5-year follow-up data from the NA sample, we must be very careful in labeling these decreases in sexual behavior over time on the Parent Reaction Questionnaire as indicative of something other than normal developmental changes. To help us interpret these data, it is useful to examine the extremely important study on normal sexual development that has recently been released by Friedrich, Grambsch, Broughton, Kuiper, and Beilke (1991). These authors have empirically documented what clinicians and theorists have previously assumed— namely, that the frequency of certain sexual behaviors differs at various ages. Of particular interest for this study are their data comparing 2- to 6-year-olds with 7- to 12-year-olds, since this is a rough approximation of how old the children in the RSA and NA groups were at the time of disclosure and time of most distress (2 to 6 years) and the time of both follow-ups (7 to 12 years). Among the behaviors that were found to decrease with age in the normative sample were "Touches sex parts in public," "Shows sex parts to children," and "Walks around nude"—items very similar to those used in the Parent Reaction Questionnaire. Thus, we are led to believe that the *decrease* in these behaviors in the RSA children was a reflection of normal sexual development, although our other data suggest that the *absolute level* of certain sexual behaviors was still unusually high.

The third parent instrument that assessed sexual problem areas was the Behaviors After Diagnostic Interview (BADI) questionnaire, which was also collected from both the RSA and NA groups. The six-item Sexual Behaviors subscale within this instrument had some overlap with Sex Items Scales A and B, in that it contained items assessing "Excessive masturbation" and "Preoccupation with genitals." The other four items were not included in those scales, and asked about "Sex play with peers or siblings," "Sexual talk or new words for genitals," "Sexual reenactment with dolls or drawings," and "Pseudomature behavior." Moreover, parents were asked to assess these behaviors for two time periods that were different from those used for the Sex Items Scales (see Tables 10.2 and 10.3).

The first time period was labeled "first month after diagnostic interview" for the RSA group, and "early in 1984" for the NA group. Parents in both groups were asked to rate their children's behavior retrospectively for that time period. The second time period was labeled "during this last month" for both groups, which corresponded to a time period approximately 3 years from the time the RSA children had first disclosed about abuse. Results show that during the first time period, the RSA children were rated as exhibiting a significantly higher number of sexual behaviors than the NA children by both mothers and fathers (both p's < .001). Moreover, a greater percentage of children in the RSA group than in the NA group were described as exhibiting at least one of these six sexual behaviors on both mothers' (46% vs. 9%; p < .01) and fathers' (45% vs. 4%, p < .01) ratings.

For the second time period, this difference was only significant for the larger sample of mothers' ratings. Mothers of children in the RSA group still described their children as exhibiting a higher number of sexual behaviors (p < .04), although there was no longer a significant difference in the percentage of children in the RSA group who were still exhibiting at least one of these six sexual behaviors (26% vs. 18%, n.s.). As shown in Table 10.3, sexualized behavior decreased for most children in the RSA sample. The increased percentage (from 9% to 18%) over time for the

TABLE 10.2. Maternal Ratings of BADI Sex Items for First Month after Disclosure

| | Percentage rated as showing behavior | | |
| | RSA | NA | |
Item	(n = 70)	(n = 32)	p
Excessive masturbation	21.4	3.1	.039
Sex play with peers or siblings	27.1	3.1	.010
Sex talk or new terms for genitals	20.0	3.1	.053
Sexual reenactment with dolls, drawings	21.4	0.0	.011
Preoccupation with genitals	20.0	0.0	.016
Pseudomature behavior	11.4	0.0	.111
At least one item present	45.7	9.4	.001

Note. p levels are based on two-tailed χ^2 analyses using Yates's correction.

TABLE 10.3. Maternal Ratings of BADI Sex Items at 3 Years after Disclosure

Item	Percentage rated as showing behavior	
	RSA (n = 69)	NA (n = 32)
Excessive masturbation	4.3	2.9
Sex play with peers or siblings	7.2	2.9
Sex talk or new terms for genitals	11.6	8.8
Sexual reenactment with dolls, drawings	4.3	0.0
Preoccupation with genitals	8.7	2.9
Pseudomature behavior	8.7	0.0
At least one item present	26.1	17.6

Note. Two-tailed χ^2 analyses using Yates's correction were performed. No percentage differences were significant at 3 years postdisclosure, although RSA children had a high mean number of sexual behaviors

control group was the result of three children being described by their mothers as using "Sex talk or new terms for genitals," which the Friedrich et al. (1990) study suggests is more reflective of developmental change than of any form of sexual problem. Nevertheless, the fact that the mean number of sexual behaviors was significantly greater for the RSA children suggests that at least some of these children had been sexualized to a degree above and beyond what one would expect solely from developmental changes.

We conducted one other analysis on the parent data that yielded interesting results. We collected predisclosure data from the files of 22 children whose parents had given us permission to do so. Our BADI instrument was actually based on the behavior questionnaire used by the original diagnosticians, so that we could compare mothers' ratings of these children made before the initial evaluation with retrospective ratings of these children's behavior for the month following that evaluation. Results show that mothers viewed their children as exhibiting significantly more sexual behaviors after disclosing the abuse to the diagnostician (t = 2.57, p < .02). For example, "Preoccupation with genitals" (from 9.1% to 28.6%), "Excessive masturbation" (from 13.6% to 23.8%) and "Sexual reenactment with dolls or drawings" (from 4.5% to 33.3%) were rated as increasing during this period. There are several possible explanations for this finding. It may be that mothers' retrospective ratings of their children's behavior during that time were not as accurate as the predisclosure ratings. It might also be that mothers became more sensitized to and aware of their children's sexual behavior after their children made disclosures of abuse to the diagnostician. Alternatively, the actual sexual behavior of the children may have increased as a result of being asked about, and disclosing, sexual abuse.

The parent interviews provided more qualitative data regarding parents' fears about how their children's sexuality would be affected. Several parents of boys expressed concern that their sons would become gay or that they would become child molesters themselves. One boy's mother stated:

My number one fear is that [child's name] will grow up and molest other children, and that's really hard to even admit. It's very difficult for me to say that, but that is the greatest fear I have. . . . My other fear is that he'll grow up and think he's gay because he's been sodomized, and when he recounts all that and thinks about it, I'm afraid he's going to say, "Oh, my God, I'm gay and I never knew it."

That mother also described a commonly reported fear about acquired immune deficiency syndrome (AIDS):

I'm also concerned about AIDS. I'm afraid that since it's a disease that maybe doesn't show up for, what, 7 years . . . I'm afraid that could happen. . . . That's something I would like to have done, is have him tested . . . just for my peace of mind.

One girl's mother expressed concerns regarding relationships, pregnancy, and motherhood:

I really do worry about her relationships as she gets older. I worry [about] how she views sex. . . . I think there will be times in her life where she will have to reenter therapy and work through those things, because I don't think that's an issue now with her, but I think when she's older it might be an issue. One of the disclosures she made was that one of the male perpetrators had threatened her that when she was pregnant with her first baby when she grew older, that he would kill that baby and it would be his. And I'm concerned that that belief will come back when she has children. I think when she does have children . . . that there will be certain fears that come up in her, you know, of seeing her own children go through that same age period where she was hurt, and that kind of thing.

CHILD MEASURES

Three child instruments assessed aspects of sexuality. The first instrument, the Draw-A-Person (DAP), involves having each child draw a picture of a person, and then having that child draw a person of the opposite sex. As discussed in Chapter 7, the drawings of RSA children contained significantly more emotional indicators than did the drawings of NA children. We also examined the sexual content of these children's drawings. Fifteen items were combined into the Sexual Content scale, with raters who were unaware of group status scoring whether each item was present. No difference was found in the number of Sexual Content items present. However, a few interesting results were found in the individual item analyses. The most striking finding was that the scorers were unable to determine the sex of the male figure in 30% of the RSA children's drawings, as compared with only 6% of the NA children's drawings ($p < .02$). Although a somewhat similar pattern was found in children's drawings of female figures (24% undeterminable for RSA vs. 16% undeterminable for NA), this difference was not significant.

A less subtle question regarding sexual content in the children's drawings was whether there would actually be group differences in the number of children who included genitals in their drawings. We did not find statistically significant differences on this item. No children in the NA group drew genitals, whereas three children (5%) in the RSA group drew genitals on the female figure (e.g., see Figure 10.1), and two children (3%) in the RSA group drew genitals on the male figure. Although the group difference was not statistically significant, we do find it interesting

FIGURE 10.1. Drawing by a 7-year-old RSA boy for the Draw-A-Person (DAP) task.

that genitals, while rarely drawn by children in either group, were only drawn by RSA children.

What may have happened is that a percentage of children reacted to their experiences in two divergent ways. A small percentage saw sexual cues or sexual content more frequently than is usual. A higher percentage may have reacted in the opposite direction, not wanting to see or show any awareness of sexual content. Perhaps for these children issues regarding sexuality were so emotionally loaded and difficult to tolerate that they preferred to draw genderless, sexless figures. Drawing clear gender distinctions would have necessitated thinking about sexuality, which may have been overwhelming or anxiety producing to them.

One other finding was counterintuitive. The male figure drawings of children in the NA group were more likely to be drawn with their legs pressed together than were those of children in the RSA group (28% vs. 8%; $p < .02$). We had assumed that if any difference existed on this item, the RSA children would be more likely to draw legs pressed together, since this feature had been postulated as a possible indicator of sexual content by other clinicians. However, the statistical significance of this item may have been due to chance, given the number of individual item analyses that were conducted. No differences were found on this item for the female figure.

Figures 10.2 and 10.3, both drawn by a 5-year-old (65-months-old) girl, are examples of drawings that contain both sexual content and

FIGURE 10.2. Drawing by a 5-year-old RSA girl for the DAP.

FIGURE 10.3. Another drawing by the same 5-year-old RSA girl.

abuse-related themes. This child named the boy in Figure 10.2 "Ben," and when asked what the boy is doing, stated that he is "standing, waiting for a teacher. I forgot his clothes on [*sic*]." When asked what the person is thinking, she replied, "He's thinking the teachers have a plan of doing something to the kids." When asked how he is feeling, she stated, "He's feeling bad." When the tester asked the child's relationship to the person in the drawing, the child answered, "He's my friend. He could be my boyfriend." The child later drew a picture of her black girlfriend, whose name she could not remember (Figure 10.3). The child described this girl as "feeling a little sad like Ben did," and thinking "that the teachers are going to chain her up in a few minutes. That's what the teachers are feeling too." Figure 10.4, drawn by a 6-year-old (73-months-old) girl, also combines sexual content and abuse-related themes. This child drew her alleged perpetrator, who is thinking and feeling "nothing" and "showing the parts of his body."

Figure 10.5, drawn by an 8-year-old (102-months-old) girl, does not include explicit sexual content but raises the question of how this girl viewed males. When asked to draw a picture of a male after she had drawn a female, this child drew a picture of a crab with long claws, which she named "Crabby Grabby Crabby." She described him as "pinching" and

FIGURE 10.4. Drawing by a 6-year-old RSA girl for the DAP.

thinking "about a nice tasty something to eat—crunch, crunch, crunch." The child was very hesitant in telling the tester her relationship with this character, finally answering, "I made him up."

The second child instrument assessing some aspect of sexuality was the Self-Perception Profile for Children, which was completed by children in the third grade or above (Harter, 1985). This instrument contains a Physical Appearance subscale, which is not included in the self-concept scale completed by younger children in our samples. The items on this subscale assess whether children are happy with the way they look; whether they are happy with their height and weight; and whether they wish their body, hair, face, or general physical appearance were different. In line with the "damaged goods syndrome" alluded to previously, as well as the parent ratings of children's dissatisfaction with how they look, we

FIGURE 10.5. Drawing by an 8-year-old RSA girl for the DAP.

hypothesized that there would be differences between groups on these child ratings of attractiveness and body image. As predicted, we found that the RSA children had significantly lower scores on the Physical Appearance subscale than did the NA children ($p < .05$, one-tailed).

One other nonstandardized child instrument, the Incomplete Sentence Test, contained four items that explored children's attitudes toward their bodies and toward being hugged or kissed. Several children in the RSA group seemed to have negative attitudes in this area. Six RSA children answered, "My face is *ugly*." Another child stated; "I think my body is *dead*." Many of the RSA children also responded negatively to the item "When someone touches me I. . . ."; this may have resulted in part from the abuse prevention training many of the children were given, which included discussions of "good" and "bad" touch. Some of the children may have assumed that their therapists or testers were implying "abusive touch" whenever the word "touch" was used. Or some of these children may have been developing an aversion to physical contact, similar to that reported by many adult survivors of child sexual abuse. Despite the fact that the incomplete sentence "When someone touches me I. . . ." is neutral, approximately one-third of the RSA children gave negative endings, such as *"feel icky"*; *"feel weird"*; *"feel angry"*; *"feel funny"*; *"feel unhappy"*; *"feel nervous"*; *"freak"*; *"say get away from me, pull their hand away, and punch them in the face"*; and *"kick them or punch them because I don't like them touching my body."* A similar phenomenon occurred with another item; "When someone I know hugs me, it feels. . . ." Again, several children responded negatively (*"oogie—terrible"*; *"weird"*; *"bad"*; *"gross"*; *"I don't like it"*). The negative endings on this last item are especially worrisome, since the item usually pulls for positive responses. It appears that these open-ended responses were providing us with qualitative data on the distressing "aversion to touch behavior" reported by parents. As previously shown in Table 10.1, 44.1% of the children were described by their parents as "not wanting to be touched" during their period of most distress.

In a parent interview, one mother described this behavior:

A lot of times he thinks things are going to be worse than they are, like a lot of times if I turn to touch him, he'll flinch. . . . And we're an affectionate family, so it's not like he's never been held or loved, but he'll still jerk. . . . like he's going to get beaten or something.

THERAPIST QUESTIONNAIRES

Since the NA group did not have therapist data, we could not make direct comparisons of therapist ratings of inappropriate sexual behavior between the two groups. In addition, the therapist version of the CBCL does not include a standardized Sex Problems scale. However, we were able to get some sense of the therapists' observations of children's sexual behavior by attaching one item, "Inappropriate sexual behavior," to the Brief Psychiatric Rating Scale for Children that therapists completed. Therapists were asked to rate children on this item on a scale ranging from 0 ("No symptom present") to 7 ("Extremely severe"). Ratings were made for two time periods: the time of most distress, and the time of termination from therapy (or currently, for the few children who were still in therapy). At the time of most distress, 47.2% of the children were rated as exhibiting at least some degree of inappropriate sexual behavior. By the end of therapy, this percentage had decreased, although a disturbingly high percentage (36.1%) still exhibited this behavior. One optimistic note, however, is that for most of these children this behavior was described as being mild or very mild.

CONCLUSION

As predicted by the traumagenic dynamic model, the RSA children did appear to have become inappropriately sexualized, especially in the first month following their disclosures of abuse, as well as during their period of most distress in the 3 years following the abuse. The most consistent data documenting this behavior came from parent ratings, although additional support for this conclusion came from the children's drawings and (Physical Appearance subscale) self-concept scores, as well as from therapist observations. The parent and therapist data seem to suggest that this behavior decreased over time, although data from all three sources suggest that some degree of inappropriate sexual behavior continued, above and beyond that which was attributable to developmental changes. Among the most disturbing findings were the high degrees of body image dissatisfaction and fear of boundary violation exhibited by the RSA children. These issues are frequently reported by adults molested as children. Although it is beyond the scope of this study, the question of whether effects on sexuality will continue to be manifested at different developmental phases in these children's lives is an important question that remains unanswered. Parents were especially fearful that their children's experience might have a severe negative impact on their sexuality in adulthood. Several parents seemed particularly concerned that their children might become perpetrators, or that their sexual orientation might be altered.

I would like to add some words of comfort for these parents, based on my work treating adults who have been sexually abused. I do think it is very important for abuse victims to explore feelings of rage and aggression. However, most people who are abused do not go on to molest children (see Bolton, Morris, & MacEachron, 1989; Finkelhor, 1984; Lew, 1988). On the other hand, many of the men who have come to me have discussed the harmful effects of having people assume that they are "at risk" for offending simply because they were abused. Some are even reluctant to seek therapy, because they fear that therapists will hold this assumption. Others have shared painful stories of relatives' and neighbors' telling them that they will never allow their children to be alone with the clients, simply because they assume that survivors of abuse will inevitably perpetuate some perpetration cycle. These instances are chilling examples of how the stigmatization associated with being an abuse victim can be long-lasting, and even more of an issue for abuse survivors than any presumed urge to molest children. It is my hope that parents and therapists will take an active role in examining their own misconceptions about the perpetration cycle, so that the more subtle cycle of stigmatization can be minimized. Second, researchers who have sought to determine the causes of sexual orientation have generally been unable to find a consistent environmental event in the backgrounds of gay, bisexual, or heterosexual adults (see Bell, Weinberg, & Hammersmith, 1981; Money, 1988). I believe the most helpful stance that a child's parents can take is to support the child in being whoever he or she truly is, and not hinder this development with stated or unstated fears about how he or she may have been damaged. Once again, I encourage parents not to underestimate the effects their own prejudices and fears can have in the interaction of the stigmatization and traumatic sexualization dynamics on their child's development.

EFFECTS ON INTERPERSONAL RELATIONSHIPS

Mary Kay Oliveri

$\mathbf{Y}$OUNG CHILDREN are particularly dependent upon and vulnerable to the influences and experiences afforded by the relationships in their world, specifically to those created by the adults who care for them. All children are affected by the quality and the valence of their relationships with parents and caretakers. Something is known about the effects upon children when they experience harm within the context of these relationships. Little is known about the effects of the types of abusive relationships with preschool teachers alleged by the traumatized children in this study.

Children who experience trauma often rely first upon their parents and caretakers for support. When these caretakers are themselves the source of trauma, it is generally anticipated that the children's present and future relationship world will be colored by such events. The closer such an adult is to a child, the more intense this effect is thought to be. The more threatening and violent the caretaker's misuse of the child, the more likely the child is to experience present symptomatology and longer-term difficulties in relating to others in a trusting manner (Finkelhor, 1986; Russell, 1986; Brenner, 1984).

Placed in an overwhelming situation with a trusted adult, a child may withdraw, become anxious about social contacts, or act in a younger or more regressed manner. On the other hand, the child may cope in the opposite way, suddenly behaving in an overly mature or more exaggerated style. In some cases, the child may act toward others, adults and children, in the way he or she was treated. And finally, any given child may shift between and among many of these responses, casting relationships differently from moment to moment and person to person. As children grow and develop, they often become vulnerable to—and may even unwittingly select—relationships and experiences similar to the abusive ones they encountered when younger. This pattern, too much like painting by numbers, may persist even into adulthood (Russell, 1986).

In the case of ritualistic sexual abuse, all of these possibilities apply. A unique set of circumstances arose for the children in this project who reported ritualistic sexual abuse (the RSA group). They were exposed to the alleged abuses by trusted caretakers in a preschool setting. They were particularly young and vulnerable, experiencing one of their first daily or weekly separations from family and extended family members. They also reported being threatened and shown in a terrifying manner how their parents or other family members would be harmed if the children revealed anything about the physical, sexual, and verbal abuses they experienced. Furthermore, all of this occurred in the context of one of their first developmentally significant experiences with other children. At times, they were encouraged or forced, by their own reports, to engage in violent or sexual acts with other children. Because of the young age of the children and the threats experienced by them at the hands of trusted caretakers, there was a concern that the children in the RSA group might be more likely to experience relationship difficulties.

In fact, it was predicted that relationship issues for the RSA children would be more tinged with emotion—specifically, with more negative emotion—than for those children who had not experienced any such abuse (the NA group). This might be most evident in relationships outside of the family, particularly with other adults in a school setting, since the alleged abuse occurred in a (pre)school setting. Family relationships might also be seriously affected by the stress of the secrecy the children were encouraged to maintain in order to protect family members. Protection for these children and their families was reversed from that occurring in more usual development. RSA children felt a need to protect their parents, for fear that only by so doing would they stave off the reported threats of harm to themselves or family members. Therefore, parents were unable to protect their children from the abuses that the parents did not know were occurring in the lives of their children. In addition to the hypothesis that stress or difficulty would be present in family and school relationships, it was anticipated that all relationships, including those with peers, might be problematic for the RSA children as a result of the reported preschool abuses.

THE CHILDREN'S PERCEPTIONS

It is critical to turn to the children themselves in order to understand the impact that their experiences may have had upon their sense of the world around them. One of the instruments that each child completed with the help of an adult was the Incomplete Sentence Test. As noted in earlier chapters, children responded to a series of open-ended statements, such as "My mother . . ." and "School is . . ." by filling in their thoughts and feelings. These responses were then coded by raters unaware of the children's group membership as positive, negative, or neutral, and were summed to give scores in several relationship domains. The higher a score, the more positive a child's perception in a given domain; the lower a score, the more negative the child's perception.

The results, displayed in Table 11.1, give support for several of the hypotheses listed above. The RSA group rated the domains of School, Family, and Adults significantly more negatively than did the NA group. Therefore, there is support for specific effects in the areas of school (the arena in which the abuses reportedly occurred) and family (the area in which trust and protection may have been seriously damaged and developmentally reversed). There is also evidence that adult relationships in general were perceived more negatively by the RSA children than by the NA children. However, there were no differences between the two groups in the domain of peers.

Some of the children's responses to the Incomplete Sentence Test are of interest and clearly show their ambivalence in the areas of school, family, and adult relationships. Although the stem "School is . . ." was completed by some RSA children as "*fun*," it was most often seen as "*hard work*" and frequently as "*boring*." The stem "My teacher . . .," on the other hand, was sometimes completed as "*is nice*" but was often finished in more negative ways: "*yells*," "*is like a witch*," "*gets mad*," "*makes us work hard*,"

TABLE 11.1. RSA versus NA Children's Mean Incomplete Sentence Test Scores

Category	RSA (n = 76)	NA (n = 33)
Peers	2.64	3.03
General Self	2.30	2.79
School	0.74	2.27**
Adults	3.11	4.18*
Family	2.88	3.67**
Physical Self	0.66	0.76
Affection/Touch	1.04	1.00
Miscellaneous	1.09	1.36
Total score	10.61	13.94**

*p < .05 (two-tailed).
**p < .01 (two-tailed).

"*makes us run,*" and "*has bad days.* And in response to the stem "I hope my teacher . . . ," the RSA children responded "*has better days,*" "*gets fired,*" "*will not be around next year*" more often than did the NA children.

One of the most difficult things seemed to be "Getting up for school . . ." which was described by some children as "*is not exciting,*" "*is tiring,*" "*is very, very hard,*" "*is a lot of work,*" and "*is a bummer.*" And although other adults and activities fared better than teachers and schools did, many mixed feelings were evident. "My parents . . ." was often completed as "*are nice,*" "*are loving,*" and "*are beautiful,*" but frequently also as "*argue,*" "*act strange,*" or "*get mad.*" Other grown men and women might be seen with the same ambivalence as parents, but "Other adults . . ." was often completed as "*are weird,*" or "*are strange.*"

On another measure, the Parent Perception Inventory (PPI) the children rated their parents in such areas as times when the parents thanked the children, took away a privilege, comforted the children, criticized the children, took time to listen or to talk with the children, punished, yelled, spent time with the children, and so on. Positive, negative, and total scores were then calculated for each child's ratings of each parent. These ratings revealed that the RSA children did not see their parents very differently from the way the NA children saw their parents in terms of positive and negative interactions, as shown in Table 11.2. The only significant difference was in the children's perceptions of their mothers: The RSA children gave their mothers less favorable total scores than did the NA children. Thus, the predicted effect on parental relationships was present, but it was only statistically meaningful in terms

TABLE 11.2. **RSA versus NA Children's Mean Ratings of Their Parents on the Parent Perception Inventory**

Perception	RSA[a]	NA[b]
Ratings of mothers		
Positive sum	26.13	27.83
Negative sum	11.20	10.31
Total score	18.54	21.14*
Ratings of fathers		
Positive sum	26.04	27.08
Negative sum	9.08	8.50
Total score	19.72	21.25

[a]For ratings of mothers, n = 76; for ratings of fathers, n = 72.
[b]For ratings of mothers, n = 35; for ratings of fathers, n = 36.
*$p < .05$ (one-tailed).

of the RSA children's perceptions of their mothers as less positive and more negative in overall interaction and discipline.

The differences and similarities between RSA and NA children's perceptions of their parents may have resulted from many factors. The similarities probably stemmed in part from the fact that the RSA parents tended to believe and support their children's reports of the abuse. They also did not blame their children and took action (e.g., therapy) to assure their children the best chances of recovering and moving forward. However, although the RSA mothers were generally experienced as affirming, it must be emphasized that these mothers were also experienced as less approving by their children. Therefore, the differences between the two groups of children may have been due to the RSA children's expectations of more support from their mothers; to their mothers' reactivity to the reported events; or to the likelihood that the children had more contact with mothers than with fathers, which placed the mothers in a position to provide more discipline or limit setting. Also, mothers were more likely than fathers to be responsible for the children's transportation to the preschool and later to therapy. This may have led children to associate their mothers more strongly with the discomfort of the reported abusive events or to perceive that their mothers felt there was something wrong with them that needed to be changed or corrected.

PARENTS' PERCEPTION

Parents were asked to rate their children on a series of items that were used to compute a Social Competence score on the Child Behavior Checklist (CBCL) at the time of most distress. This score was utilized to gain a sense of how capable the parents felt that their children were in the social world. The total Social Competence score is comprised of ratings in three areas. The first subscale, Activities, is made up of items related to the number of sports, other activities, and jobs that children engage in, as well as ratings that reflect their skill and performance quality. Next is a Social subscale, consisting of items related to the number of organizations and friends that the children have in their lives, as well as measures of participation (e.g., frequency and behavior with others and alone). And, finally, the School subscale consists of items related to school problems, special class placement, and the children's repeating of grades (if any). Together, these scales give a view of children's general social competence.

The children in the RSA group received significantly lower parental ratings than the children in the NA group on overall Social Competence. This difference was highly significant for both mothers' and fathers' ratings, as shown in Table 11.3. The four principal CBCL factor scores

TABLE 11.3. RSA and NA Children's Social Competence Scores on the CBCL (Mothers' and Fathers' Mean Ratings)

Scale	RSA[a]	NA[b]
Mothers' mean ratings (T = scores)		
Activities	45.32	47.94
Social	38.82	47.84**
School	43.98	51.21[c]*
Total Social Competence	40.61	50.77**
Fathers' mean ratings (T = scores)		
Activities	45.00	45.82
Social	42.15	44.94
School	45.64	52.35*
Total Social Competence	41.84	50.19[d]*

[a]For mothers, n's ranged from 59 to 69; for fathers, n's ranged from 37 to 41.
[b]For mothers, n's ranged from 29 to 32; for fathers, n's ranged from 16 to 18.
[c]Analysis of covariance (ANCOVA) controlling for socioeconomic status.
[d]ANCOVA controlling for child age.
*$p < .01$ (two-tailed). **$p < .001$ (two-tailed).

have been discussed at length elsewhere (see Chapter 7). Essentially, for the period of most distress, the RSA group was rated as functioning more poorly and as falling more often into the clinical range not only on the Social Competence Factor, but on the Total Behavior Problems, Internalizing, and Externalizing factors as well. These findings seem to suggest that the RSA children became more reactive and less competent in general.

It is particularly interesting to look at the individual subscale scores that go into the Social Competence factor. Upon inspection, it becomes apparent that the two groups did not differ meaningfully in the type and level of their social activities in general. However, the Social and School subscale results provide a different picture: The RSA mothers gave their children significantly lower scores on these subscales than the NA mothers gave their children. RSA fathers displayed similar trends, but only rated their children as significantly less competent on the School subscale. Thus, mothers and fathers in the RSA group concurred that their children displayed less competence in the area of school performance. Only RSA mothers, however, perceived a significant difference in the area of peer interaction when compared with NA mothers' perceptions.

It is important to note that the mothers' ratings of the children offer the first support for differences between the two groups in the area of social or peer interactions at the time of most distress. Because of the strong possibility that mothers spent more time with their children and other children, and participated with and observed their children more often in organized activities, the mothers' lower Social Competence rating for the RSA group is very meaningful. And, finally, it should be noted that the RSA group showed considerable improvement in Social Competence ratings at the time of follow-up. Despite the magnitude of the reported abuse in early life, over time the children's experiences in nonabusive relationships with others, with their families, and with therapeutic activities seemed to contribute to improvement in the social domain.

SUMMARY

An examination of the data presented in this chapter suggests that the RSA children's reported experiences during their preschool years resulted in a real vulnerability for these children in the area of relationships. The RSA children tended to perceive their mothers in a less positive manner. Also, these children behaved in ways that caused their parents to judge them as less competent in the social world than NA youngsters were judged to be by their parents. The RSA children were particularly likely to experience school-related factors in a negative manner, and to be judged by both their mothers and their fathers as less competent in school-related areas than children in the NA group. Moreover, the RSA children gave more negative responses to items related to family and adult relationships in general. There were no differences in the children's perceptions of their peers. However, mothers in the RSA group rated their offspring as less accomplished in peer group relations and activities than mothers in the NA group rated their children. Therefore, the predictions of disruption in school, family, adult, and peer relationships have been partially upheld.

At follow-up 5 years after their reported abuse, the RSA children showed marked improvement in all areas of the Social Competence factor on the CBCL. Over time, these children appear to have experienced a healing process in terms of their skill and capacity to move more effectively in their relationship worlds. There were clearly significant differences between the RSA children and the NA children at the time of most distress for the former. The RSA children exhibited difficulty in relating to or experiencing comfort with adults in general, school, and family, as shown on the Incomplete Sentence Test items. Of particular interest is the finding that the RSA children perceived less comfort from or constructive interaction with their mothers. What remains to be seen is how far the effects of these experiences at the time of most distress and those acquired during the healing process can reach over the children's life course. At this writing, these children are only now approaching the developmental phase of their lives that will launch them into sexual relationships, the search for mates, and the creation of their own families. These types of relationships could not be assessed during the present study, given the children's ages. We hope that as these children grow, develop, and expand their relationship worlds, their corrective experiences will assist them toward success in their future relationships.

CHAPTER 12

COMPARISON OF EFFECTS OF REPORTED RITUALISTIC AND NONRITUALISTIC SEXUAL ABUSE

Jill Waterman

ALTHOUGH CHILD SEXUAL ABUSE in day care and preschool settings is not common, there have been reports of such cases in every large community in the United States. Some of these cases involve allegations of ritualistic abuse. In the only national study of sexual abuse in day care settings, Finkelhor, Williams, and Burns (1988) found that 83% involved single perpetrators. The 17% of cases involving more than one perpetrator are clearly the most serious ones. Multiple-perpetrator cases (1) involve the most children and the youngest ones; (2) have the most intrusive sexual activities; and (3) have the highest likelihood of pornography and ritualistic abuse. In this chapter, effects of reported ritualistic sexual abuse in preschool are compared with effects of sexual abuse in preschool without ritualistic elements; the chapter specifically examines the factors of *severity* and *specificity* of effects.

As discussed earlier, the sample reporting sexual abuse only (the SA group) consisted of 15 children molested in a preschool/day care setting by a single male perpetrator who admitted to more abuse than the children disclosed. No allegations of ritualistic or terrorizing acts were made in this group, and the perpetrator is currently serving four life terms in prison. A subsample of the group reporting ritualistic sexual abuse (the RSA group) was picked through propensity-matching techniques to provide the closest demographic match to the SA group, since the children in the SA group were older at time of testing (although disclosure in both the RSA and SA groups occurred at about the same time), and had lower socioeconomic status (SES) and IQ than the RSA group. These 15 children comprised the "RSA match" group. Demographic data for both groups are given in Table 12.1.

Since a perfect match was not made, age and/or SES were covaried in any analyses where these variables were significantly correlated with effects variables. As detailed in Chapter 5, there were no significant differences in categories of sexual abuse reported by the two samples, but there were highly significant differences in terrorizing and ritualistic acts. The RSA group reported high levels of these acts, and the SA group reported no terrorizing acts and only one ritualistic act (singing or chanting reported by one child).

SEVERITY OF EFFECTS

Information on children's level of functioning is available from three sources: parents, therapists, and children. Each source of data is examined separately here, and then general conclusions are drawn.

Parental Report

Each child's parents filled out the Child Behavior Checklist (CBCL), rating the child at time of most distress. Because of the small number of fathers from whom data were available in the SA sample (only 5 fathers participated), maternal ratings were used in the analyses described here. As shown in Table 12.2, mothers of the RSA match group saw their children as exhibiting significantly more Internalizing problems and Total

TABLE 12.1. Demographic Data on the SA and RSA Match Samples

Item	SA (n = 15)	RSA (n = 15)
Mean age (years)	13.1	11.7**
Gender (% girls)	60	53
Hollingshead SES (mean score)	36.5	43.1*
Full Scale IQ	103.1	108.3
Mother's ethnicity (% caucasian)	100	100
Father's ethnicity (% caucasian)	90	93

*p = .04; **p = .02.

TABLE 12.2. Maternal CBCL Ratings of SA and RSA Match Children at Time of Most Distress

Subscale	SA (n = 11)	RSA (n = 14)	F
Total Behavior Problems			
$\bar{X}$	57.1	68.9	7.72[a]*
SD	11.8	13.3	
Internalizing			
$\bar{X}$	58.3	68.2	8.35[a]*
SD	10.2	10.1	
Externalizing			
$\bar{X}$	55.8	63.7	n.s.[b]
SD	10.1	10.5	
Social Competence			
$\bar{X}$	37.8[c]	38.6	n.s.
SD	9.2	9.6	

[a]Analysis of covariance (ANCOVA) controlling for SES.
[b]ANCOVA controlling for child age.
[c]n = 10.
*$p < .05$.

Behavior Problems than the mothers of the SA group saw their children as showing. There were no significant differences between groups on the Externalizing and Social Competence scales. It should be noted that a score is in the clinical range if equal to or greater than 70; the RSA match group's *mean* score was close to the clinical cutoff for both the Internalizing and Total Behavior Problems scales.

Therapist Ratings

The Teacher Report Form of the CBCL was modified slightly and was filled out by therapists of children in both groups; Table 12.3 details the results. The therapists of the RSA match children saw their clients as exhibiting significantly more Externalizing problems and Total Behavior Problems than the therapists of the SA children saw their clients as showing. Although no group differences were found on Internalizing problems, therapists' mean scores for Internalizing problems were in the clinical range for *both* groups. In comparing parents' and therapists' ratings for the two groups, it appears that the main discrepancy was on the Internalizing scale in the SA group; therapists rated the children as having many more of these problems than did the parents. It is possible that internalizing problems such as withdrawal or depression may have been displayed more intensely in the therapeutic situation, where the focus was

TABLE 12.3. Therapist CBCL Ratings of SA and RSA Match Children at Time of Most Distress

Subscale	SA (n = 14)	RSA (n = 15)	F
Total Behavior Problems			
$\overline{X}$	62.9	69.0	4.45*
SD	6.2	9.1	
Internalizing			
$\overline{X}$	71.1	73.9	n.s.
SD	8.1	8.6	
Externalizing			
$\overline{X}$	58.4	64.1	4.47*
SD	6.6	7.9	

*$p < .05$, one-tailed.

on a child's internal state, than in the home situation, where parents might be expected to notice externalizing behaviors more often since they tend to be more disruptive.

Therapists also rated children on the Children's Global Assessment Scale (CGAS), both for time of most distress and for the current time or termination of therapy (whichever applied). On the CGAS, a respondent gives a global score on a scale from 1 to 100 to describe a child's functioning. As detailed in Table 12.4, there were no differences between groups at time of most distress, with both the sample SA and the RSA match sample showing considerable diminution of functioning. However,

TABLE 12.4. Therapists' CGAS Ratings of SA and RSA Match Children

Time period	SA (n = 14)	RSA (n = 15)	F
Time of most distress			
$\overline{X}$	57.0	55.7	n.s.
SD	12.2	8.0	
End of therapy[a]			
$\overline{X}$	81.8	73.9	3.68*
SD	10.1	11.8	
Change score			
$\overline{X}$	24.8	18.2	3.81*
SD	6.3	11.1	

Note. Children's Global Assessment Scale (CGAS) is a 100-point scale, with higher scores indicating better adjustment (Shaffer et al., 1985).
[a]For the few children still in therapy, ratings were based on current functioning.
*$p < .05$, one-tailed.

by the end of therapy (or at the current time, if children were still in treatment), the SA group showed significantly higher functioning and significantly more change than did the RSA match group.

Very similar findings were reported by therapists on the Brief Psychiatric Rating Scale for Children (BPRS-C), as displayed in Table 12.5. Again, there were no differences between groups on total mean score at the time of most distress, but when rated for the end of therapy (or the current time, if children were continuing in treatment), the RSA match group was perceived as continuing to exhibit significantly more problems than the SA group. It should be noted that over time, therapists perceived large decreases in psychiatric problems for both groups.

Children's Measures

Children were compared on a variety of measures. For purposes of looking at differences in severity of effects between the SA and RSA match groups, this section examines results for self-concept, emotional indicators, and general positivity of attitude. Children filled out the Self-Perception Profile for Children, a measure of self-concept developed by Harter (1985). As Table 12.6 displays, RSA match children had significantly lower Global Self-Worth and Physical Appearance scores than did SA children. No significant differences were obtained on the other subscales.

A different type of index of functioning was obtained by scoring the children's Draw-A-Person (DAP) human figure drawings for emotional indicators, according to the system developed by Koppitz (1968). Raters were unaware of group membership status. For the female drawing and for both drawings combined, the RSA match group displayed more emotional indicators than did the SA group, as shown in Table 12.7. Interestingly, although the same trend existed for the male drawing, the difference was not significant; one speculation is that since children reported male

TABLE 12.5. Therapists' Mean Ratings of SA and RSA Match Children on Brief Psychiatric Rating Scale for Children (BPRS-C)

Time period	SA (n = 13)	RSA (n = 15)	t
Time of most distress	2.62	2.49	−0.22
Treatment termination	0.67	1.25	2.81*

Note. If a child was still in therapy, then rating was for the current time, 2 to 4 years after initial abuse disclosures. On the BPRS-C, each of 21 symptoms is rated for severity on a 5 point scale, with higher ratings indicating more severe symptomatology.
*p = .009.

TABLE 12.6. Self-Concept Scores of SA and RSA Match Children

Subscale	SA (n = 13)	RSA (n = 14)	F
Scholastic Competence	0.00	–0.21	n.s.
Social Acceptance	0.14	0.16	n.s.
Athletic Competence	0.15	–0.04	n.s.
Physical Appearance	0.53	–0.23	3.14**
Behavioral Conduct	–0.67	–0.43	n.s.
Global Self-Worth	0.34	–0.42	2.45*

Note. Scores reported are standardized z scores calculated from age norms on the Self-Perception Profile for Children (Harter, 1985).
$*p < .065$, one-tailed; $**p < .05$, one-tailed.

perpetrators in both SA and RSA match cases, there may have been less difference in their human figure drawings of males than in their drawings of females, who were alleged to have been perpetrators only in the RSA match group. Koppitz (1968) has stated that having two or more emotional indicators in a DAP drawing is clinically significant; it is disturbing that the RSA match children's mean scores were in the clinical range.

Parallel findings were obtained from ratings of a version of the Incomplete Sentences Test, scored for negative, positive, and neutral responses; again, raters were unaware of group membership status. Significant differences were obtained for the total score, and for the General Self and School subscales. In all cases, the RSA match group gave more negative answers than the SA group, as shown in Table 12.8.

TABLE 12.7. Indicators of Emotional Distress in the Drawings of SA and RSA Match Children

Drawing	SA (n = 14)	RSA (n = 11)	F
Male drawing			
$\overline{X}$	1.43	2.27	2.32
SD	1.09	1.68	
Female drawing			
$\overline{X}$	0.86	2.18	6.66*
SD	1.03	1.54	
Both drawings			
$\overline{X}$	1.14	2.23	6.83*
SD	0.86	1.21	

Note. Scores reflect mean numbers of emotional indicators based on the Koppitz (1968) scoring system for the Draw-A-Person.
$*p < .05$.

TABLE 12.8. Responses of Sexually Abused SA and RSA Match Children on the Incomplete Sentence Test

Subscale	SA (n = 15)	RSA (n = 15)	F
Peers			
$\bar{X}$	3.07	2.20	1.62
SD	1.79	1.94	
General self			
$\bar{X}$	3.87	2.60	2.57*
SD	1.55	2.64	
School			
$\bar{X}$	0.73	−0.27	4.03[a]**
SD	1.62	2.22	
Adults			
$\bar{X}$	2.60	2.00	0.34
SD	2.72	2.90	
Family			
$\bar{X}$	2.60	1.80	0.99
SD	1.88	2.48	
Physical self			
$\bar{X}$	0.53	0.00	1.50
SD	1.06	1.31	
Affection/Touch			
$\bar{X}$	1.20	1.07	0.11
SD	0.78	1.39	
Total			
$\bar{X}$	12.20	7.73	2.86*
SD	5.49	8.64	

Note. Responses were scored as positive, negative, or neutral. For each subscale, number of negative responses were subtracted from number of positive responses.
[a]ANCOVA controlling for child age.
*$p < .06$, one-tailed; **$p < .05$, one-tailed.

In summary, it appears that in our samples, reported ritualistic sexual abuse had more severe effects than sexual abuse without terrorizing and ritualistic elements. Data from parents, therapists, and the children themselves were consistent in showing more severe problems and less optimal functioning for the RSA match group than for the SA group.

SPECIFICITY OF EFFECTS

Utilizing David Finkelhor's (Finkelhor & Browne, 1986) model of traumagenic dynamics in examining effects of child sexual abuse, we made differential predictions for the two groups. We hypothesized that because of the nature of the reported abuse and the events that followed in the aftermath of disclosure, some of the traumagenic dynamics might be different for the SA and RSA groups. In general, the predictions were based on the disclosures of children to therapists that were detailed on the Sexual Abuse Grid (see Chapter 5). Because of the variation in experience of the children within each group, any one dynamic may not have been true for a particular child.

In the following sections, the ways in which the four traumagenic dynamics may have been involved for the RSA versus the SA children are detailed. In addition, evidence for the behavioral and psychological manifestations of each dynamic is presented. As outlined below, it appears that the RSA and SA groups were generally similar on the dynamics of traumatic sexualization and betrayal, but were quite divergent on the dynamics of stigmatization and powerlessness.

Traumatic Sexualization

1. *Child is rewarded for sexual behavior inappropriate to developmental level.* SA—definitely true; RSA—definitely true. In both preschool groups, sexual behavior obviously inappropriate for the children's very young ages was reportedly rewarded.

2. *Offender exchanges attention and affection for sex.* SA—definitely true; RSA—definitely true. In both groups, children engaging in sexual activities reported receiving attention and affection in exchange for sex. In the SA group, attention and affection were the main methods used to obtain compliance. Although similar methods were used in the RSA group, these children also reported being subjected to terrorizing and ritualistic acts.

3. *Offender transmits misconceptions about sexual behavior and sexual morality.* SA—definitely true; RSA—definitely true. This was probably a particularly powerful element because of the young age of the children, many of whom would have difficulty understanding sexual morality at any level.

4. *Sexual activity is conditioned with negative emotions and memories.* SA—possibly true; RSA—definitely true. Because of the terror and threat involved with sexual activity reported in the RSA group, we would expect much more negative conditioning of emotions and memories in this group than in the SA group. However, some negative conditioning may also have occurred for the SA group, particularly in light of the storm of disturbance and controversy that disclosure of any multiple-victim case of sexual abuse stirs up.

In summary, we felt that the both the SA children and the RSA children were likely to be quite sexualized. We also thought it possible that some members of the RSA group would experience sexual inhibition or aversion, because of the terrorizing and ritualistic elements reported to be involved in their sexual abuse.

To examine these predictions, we reviewed three measures of sexualization. First, the Sex Problems subscale of the CBCL was examined (for the appropriate group, girls aged 6 to 11), using maternal ratings. The SA group received a mean score of 64.50, and the RSA group had a mean score of 73.75. These scores were not significantly different. Since a score of 70 is considered to be in the clinical range, received by only 2% of the population, it is clear that both groups were highly sexualized in the aftermath of disclosure of sexual abuse. The RSA group's mean score was in the clinical range, whereas the SA group's score was close to the clinical range.

Since the standardized Sex Problems scale applied only to girls 6 to 11 years old, many of our subjects were not included. Therefore, we additionally created a scale of the six face-valid items on the CBCL Sex Problems scale, and examined differences between all subjects in the RSA and SA groups on this scale (see Chapter 10 for details about the scale). Both groups exhibited some sexual behaviors, but there were no significant differences between the RSA match and SA groups on any individual item or on an overall score, as displayed in Table 12.9.

The scores of the two groups on the Sexual Behaviors subscale of a symptom checklist developed for the study (Behaviors After Diagnostic Interview, or BADI) and filled out by mothers were also compared. Two time frames were looked at: (1) 1 month after disclosure, and (2) within the last month (generally about 3 years after disclosure). Results are given

TABLE 12.9. Percentage of CBCL Face-Valid Sex Items Endorsed for RSA Match and SA Groups

Item	SA (n = 10)	RSA (n = 13)
Behaves like opposite sex	20.0	7.7
Plays with own sex parts in public	0.0	7.7
Plays with own sex parts too much	10.0	30.8
Sexual problems (other than abuse)	0.0	15.4
Thinks about sex too much	10.0	30.8
Wishes to be of opposite sex	0.0	15.4
Endorses at least one of sex items above	40.0	30.8

Note. All between-group comparisons were nonsignificant (χ^2 analyses). Scores are based on maternal ratings.

in Table 12.10. Again, there were no significant differences between the RSA match and SA groups on sexual behaviors. Approximately 25% of the children exhibited sexual behaviors in the first month after disclosure, most commonly excessive masturbation or sex play with other children. Very little sexual behavior was reported for either group for ratings of the last month. This decrease in sexual behavior may have been the result of psychotherapy or may have indicated a natural suppression (or more skill at keeping such behaviors hidden from parents) that occurs developmentally with increasing age.

With regard to traumatic sexualization, it appears that our predictions were confirmed. Both the RSA match group and the SA group seemed to be quite sexualized for some period after disclosure of sexual abuse; much of the overt sexual behavior then diminished over time. There were no significant differences between the RSA match and SA groups on any measure of sexualization.

Betrayal

1. *Trust and vulnerability are manipulated.* SA—definitely true; RSA— definitely true. Although different mechanisms were said to be utilized in the two groups, in both cases the relationship with trusted and liked child

TABLE 12.10. Percentage of Sexual Behaviors Items Endorsed on BADI Symptom Checklist for SA and RSA Match Children

Item	SA (n = 9)	RSA (n = 14)
Excessive masturbation		
Postdisclosure	25.0	28.6
Last month	11.1	0.0
Sex play with peers or siblings		
Postdisclosure	25.0	28.6
Last month	0.0	7.1
Sex talk, or new names for genitals		
Postdisclosure	0.0	21.4
Last month	0.0	14.3
Sexual reenactment with dolls or drawings		
Postdisclosure	12.5	14.3
Last month	0.0	0.0
Preoccupation with genitals		
Postdisclosure	12.5	28.6
Last month	0.0	0.0

Note. All between-group comparisons were nonsignificant (χ^2 analyses). Scores are based on maternal ratings.

care providers was reportedly exploited to allow sexual abuse. The SA perpetrator reported that he looked for lonely children who were very needy of attention and affection, and utilized the relationship that developed for sexual gratification. For the RSA group, terror and threat made the children feel very vulnerable, though at times many apparently liked the attention from the alleged perpetrators.

2. *Expectations that others will care for and protect a child are violated.* SA—definitely true; RSA—definitely true. In both groups, caretakers (teachers and day care workers) entrusted with nurturing very young children violated their charge by molesting the children. The effects may have been somewhat more pronounced for the RSA group, both because of the nature of the alleged abuses and because children reported being told that their parents could be killed, so that their primary source of nurturance was threatened as well as their substitute source (preschool).

3. *Child's well-being is disregarded.* SA—somewhat true; RSA—definitely true. Obviously, a child's well-being is disregarded to some extent in any situation involving sexual abuse. However, it would appear that the SA perpetrator's attempts to secure cooperation mainly through special attention may have represented relatively less disregard for the children's well-being than the reports that the RSA perpetrators coerced cooperation by threats of death to parents, animal sacrifices, physical abuse, and the like.

4. *There is a lack of support from parents.* SA—generally untrue; RSA—generally untrue. Once disclosure of sexual abuse in preschools occurred, both groups of parents were generally very supportive (see Chapters 5, 14, and 16). Of course, since the abuses were reported in out-of-home situations without involvement of relatives, it would be easier for families to believe and support their children than would be the case in an incest situation.

We did not expect to find differences in manifestations of betrayal between the two groups; we thought that both groups had experienced some betrayal, with RSA children perhaps being somewhat less trusting than SA children because of the events occurring in the aftermath of the disclosures. However, since parents in both groups were generally highly supportive, we felt that the degree of betrayal experienced by both SA and RSA groups would be somewhat less than that experienced by incest victims.

Because there is some overlap between manifestations of betrayal and those of stigmatization and powerlessness, we did not specifically examine betrayal, since we were not predicting group differences. For example, isolation was expected for both betrayal and stigmatization, whereas depression and aggression were expected for both betrayal and powerlessness. The reader is directed to the other sections for information about group differences on these behavioral and psychological manifestations.

Stigmatization

1. *Offender blames, denigrates victim.* SA—not true; RSA—definitely true. There was a major group difference, since the SA offender confessed, while the alleged offenders in the RSA group maintained their innocence and denigrated the children.

2. *Offender and others pressure child for secrecy.* SA—probably true; RSA—definitely true. There was reportedly pressure for secrecy in both groups, but of different types: In the SA group, the pressure involved potential loss of attention and acceptance by the perpetrator, whereas in the RSA group, children reported that death threats and animal sacrifices were used to assure secrecy.

3. *Child infers attitudes of shame about activities.* SA—possibly true; RSA—probably true. Although there is no hard evidence about this, it is likely that the young age of the victims may have led to less shame than if they were older and more aware of social norms about sexual behavior. However, some of the acts that RSA children reported, such as drinking urine, eating feces, and participating in Satanic rituals, would probably bring feelings of shame to anyone.

4. *Others react with shock to disclosure.* SA—somewhat true; RSA—definitely true. Families and communities were certainly shocked by the allegations of preschool sexual abuse in both groups. Because of the bizarre nature of some of the reports, as well as the ongoing community controversy, this was probably more of a factor for the RSA group.

5. *Others blame child for events.* SA—not true; RSA—slightly true. Although parents in neither group blamed the children to any significant extent, the RSA group may have felt somewhat blamed, both by the alleged perpetrators and by the community backlash in which some felt the children had been led to tell false stories or had fabricated them.

6. *Victim is stereotyped as "damaged goods."* SA—somewhat true; RSA—definitely true. Any young victim of child sexual abuse experiences some of the feeling of being "damaged goods." This is probably more true for the RSA group, because (1) RSA children reported being subjected to more intrusive types of sexual activities (such as anal and vaginal intercourse and foreign object penetration), while the most intrusive sexual abuse for the SA group involved oral–genital contact (which of course leaves less permanent and obvious physical sequelae); (2) RSA children reported Satanic rituals, which confused

them about their moral values and self-worth; and (3) some RSA children were publicly identified as sexual abuse victims through their parents' (and in some cases, their own) participation in media appearances both locally and nationwide.

It appeared that both the RSA and SA groups suffered some stigmatization, but the RSA group appeared to have had to deal with considerably more stigmatization than the SA group, both because of the bizarre nature of many of the reports of sexual, terrorizing, and ritualistic acts, and because of the ongoing and highly public controversy surrounding the abuse disclosures. Therefore, we predicted that the RSA match group would show more manifestations of stigmatization than would the SA group.

According to the traumagenic model, psychological and behavioral manifestations of stigmatization that might be expected for preadolescent children would include (1) isolation; (2) guilt and shame; and (3) lowered self-esteem. Several other manifestations of stigmatization, such as drug or alcohol abuse, criminal involvement, self-mutilation, and suicide, would generally not be seen until adolescence or adulthood.

Isolation

Isolation would be expected to follow from stigmatization because children would feel different from others and have a poor self-concept, making it difficult for them to feel part of a group. To examine this manifestation, data from therapist ratings on the BPRS-C for time of most distress and for the time at termination of treatment (or at the current time, 2 to 4 years after disclosure, if the children were still in treatment) were examined, along with data from the Social Withdrawal subscale of the CBCL, completed by both mothers and therapists.

On the BPRS-C, there were no differences between groups at time of most distress on the Withdrawal subscale. However, for the time of treatment termination (or currently, if the children were still in treatment), there was a trend for RSA match children to exhibit more withdrawal than SA children ($p = .06$).

As shown in Table 12.11, there were no significant group differences in therapist ratings on Social Withdrawal on the CBCL. However, it is clear that both RSA match and SA groups were quite socially withdrawn, since the mean scores in each group were close to the clinically significant range of 70. On maternal ratings, the RSA match group mean score was also close to the clinical range, and there was a trend for the RSA match group to show more Social Withdrawal. This trend might have reached significance if there were more subjects in the two groups.

TABLE 12.11. CBCL Mean Social Withdrawal Subscale Scores for SA and RSA Match Children

	SA[a]	RSA[b]	t
Maternal ratings	62.45	67.79	1.33*
Therapists' ratings	65.64	67.53	0.76

*p = .09, one-tailed
[a]For maternal ratings, n = 11; for therapists' ratings, n = 14.
[b]For maternal ratings, n = 14; for therapists' ratings, n = 15.

Guilt and Shame

To enable us to examine guilt and shame as manifestations of stigmatization, therapists were asked to rate whether the children ever, sometimes, or often experienced the feelings of guilt and shame. As predicted, RSA match children were rated by therapists as having significantly more feelings of guilt than were SA children ($t = 2.50$, $p < .02$), and a similar nonsignificant trend was found for shame as well.

Ratings on two relevant items were also obtained from parents. On maternal ratings of whether the child "blamed self for things," the predicted difference was obtained; RSA match children were seen as blaming themselves significantly more often than SA children ($t = 2.14$, $p = .02$). Similarly, RSA match children were rated as "feeling too guilty" significantly more than SA children ($t = 1.90$, $p = .04$).

Self-Esteem

Children who experience much stigmatization would be expected to have lower self-esteem than children who do not feel stigmatized, and findings from both the children themselves and the therapists confirmed this prediction. As previously presented in Table 12.6, RSA match children had significantly lower Global Self-Concept scores than SA children, and also saw themselves as significantly less physically attractive than their SA counterparts.

Confirmatory evidence for the lower self-esteem of the RSA match children comes from therapists' ratings on the BPRS-C. Specifically, RSA match children were rated higher on the Inferiority Feelings subscale than were SA children ($t = 2.30$, $p = .03$) at treatment termination (or currently, if still in treatment).

In summary, there appears to be evidence that RSA match children suffered more severe effects of stigmatization than did SA children. The RSA match children had lower self-concepts and more feelings of guilt (and also possibly more feelings of shame). Children in both groups appeared to be somewhat socially withdrawn and isolated; there was a trend for RSA match children to be seen as more withdrawn than SA children.

Powerlessness

1. *Body territory is invaded against the child's wishes.* SA—probably true; RSA—definitely true. Because of the terror and force involved in the RSA group, the reported bodily invasion would obviously have occurred against the children's wishes. Although the context was more positive for the SA children, we can assume that at least some of them participated against their own wishes, regardless of rewards. Since young children cannot give informed consent about sexual activities in any case, on some level all sexual abuse involves the children's body territory being invaded against their wishes, even if aspects of the abuse are enjoyable to the children.

2. *Vulnerability to invasion continues over time.* SA—definitely true; RSA—definitely true. In both groups, the abuse was generally reported to have occurred over a period of months or years.

3. *Offender uses force or trickery to involve child.* SA—less true; RSA—definitely true. Both force and trickery were allegedly used in the RSA group. No force was reported to have been used in the SA group, but there may have been subtle manipulation that could be viewed as trickery.

4. *Child feels unable to protect self and halt abuse.* SA—probably true; RSA—definitely true. The effects here were probably more substantial for the RSA group, where children were faced with death threats to themselves and their parents if they disclosed what was happening to them.

5. *There is repeated experience of fear.* SA—generally untrue; RSA—definitely true. Again, the threats and terrorizing activities in the RSA group involved repeated experiences of fear. No similar fear-evoking activities were reported in the SA group, although it is certainly possible that some of the children experienced fear even in the relatively "supportive" milieu in which the sexual abuse occurred.

6. *Child is unable to make others believe.* SA—less true; RSA—definitely true. Although children generally had little or no trouble making their parents believe their abuse allegations, the RSA group faced years of deep community division, including a great deal of skepticism and disbelief. The SA children were spared these reactions by the perpetrator's confession.

As the list above shows, the RSA group experienced every one of the dynamics that are purported to be involved in the development of powerlessness, whereas the SA group had some of the dynamics and not others. As a result, we thought that the RSA group would show more of the manifestations of powerlessness than the SA group. In Finkelhor's traumagenic model (Finkelhor & Browne, 1986), the psychological and behavioral manifestations of powerlessness are thought to be (1) anxiety and fear; (2) aggressive behavior and delinquency; (3) depression; and (4) lowered sense of efficacy and control. Children's symptomatology in each of these areas was examined, and comparisons were made between the RSA match and SA groups.

Anxiety and Fear

Several measures of anxiety and fear were gathered from the parents, therapists, and children to examine the hypothesis that the RSA children would be suffering more anxiety and fear than the SA children. Fears were measured by the Louisville Fear Survey, a questionnaire filled out by mothers. As shown in Table 12.12, both the RSA matches and the SA group were highly fearful. Both sexual abuse samples appeared to be much more fearful than the normative sample, and were somewhat more fearful even than a sample of phobics collected by Miller (1974). Contrary to expectations, there were no significant differences in fearfulness between the RSA match and SA groups.

Anxiety was examined by means of several measures. Symptoms of post-traumatic stress disorder (PTSD) were compared, and subscales of the CBCL were examined. PTSD items were added to the CBCLs filled out by both parents and therapists. Table 12.13 gives the results for therapist ratings of PTSD symptoms. In the RSA match group, 80.0% of the children met criteria for PTSD, whereas 35.7% of the SA children met the criteria. The RSA children scored significantly higher on 7 of the 15 PTSD items listed, including "Recurrent and intrusive recollections," "Recurrent distressing dreams," and "Hypervigilance."

TABLE 12.12. Louisville Fear Survey Total Scores for Original Normative Samples and Current Samples

	Miller (1974)		Current samples (1990)	
	Norms (n = 249)	Phobics (n = 67)	SA (n = 8)	RSA (n = 14)
$\overline{X}$	114.5	124.9	131.9	126.6
SD	19.8	21.6	18.2	19.1

Note. Current samples' scores were calculated from mothers' ratings of children 3 to 4 years after disclosure of abuse.

TABLE 12.13. Percentage of SA and RSA Match Children Rated by Therapists as Experiencing Symptoms of PTSD

	SA (n = 14)	RSA (n = 15)	χ^2
Meets PTSD diagnostic criteria?	35.7	80.0	4.17*
Individual items that discriminate groups			
Recurrent and intrusive recollections	14.3	80.0	10.02***
Recurrent distressing dreams	21.4	80.0	7.74**
Sudden acting or feeling as if event is recurring	0.0	53.3	7.81**
Physiologic reactivity or intense distress	35.7	73.3	2.76*
Restricted range of affect	28.6	66.7	2.82*
Irritability or outbursts of anger	42.9	86.7	4.36**
Hypervigilance	14.3	73.3	7.99**

*$p < .05$; **$p < .01$; ***$p < .001$.

Similarly, several items related to PTSD from maternal ratings also discriminated between the RSA match and SA groups: "Sudden panic or anxiety attacks" ($t = 1.89$, $p = .04$); "Emotionally numb" ($t = 2.08$, $p = .025$); and "Spaced out" ($t = 1.77$, $p = .05$). Although there were no differences between groups on the CBCL Anxiety and Nervousness subscales, the RSA group displayed significantly higher scores than the SA group on the Obsessive scale ($t = 2.19$, $p = .02$).

In conclusion, it appears that the RSA and SA children showed similar reactions on some aspects of fear and anxiety, while the RSA group was higher on other aspects. Both groups were generally highly fearful. Although they did not tend to differ on such things as nervousness, the RSA group appeared to have more symptoms of PTSD (recurrent memories and dreams, hypervigilance, etc.) and, possibly related to these, more obsessive symptoms. It is somewhat difficult to tease out the effects of the type of reported sexual abuse from the outcome in examining the high percentage of PTSD in the RSA group. It is possible that the fact that the perpetrator in the SA group admitted his acts and is in prison has helped the children to process the trauma and move on with their lives. In contrast, no alleged perpetrators in the RSA group were ever convicted, and in fact some remain in the communities where the abuse allegations occurred; therefore, ongoing PTSD symptoms such as hypervigilance may be an expected result.

Aggressive Behavior

The dynamic of powerlessness is also hypothesized to be related to increased aggressive behavior and delinquency. Mechanisms for this may include identification with the aggressor, modeling, and displaced expression of anger. Ratings on subscales of the CBCL, the BPRS-C, and the BADI relating to aggression were compared for the SA and RSA match samples to examine the hypothesis that the RSA group, having experienced more powerlessness in the abuse experience, would show more aggressive behavior. As Table 12.14 details, the RSA match group scored higher on aggressive behavior than the SA group on both maternal and therapist ratings on the CBCL. It is perhaps of special concern that the RSA mean score on the Cruel subscale was very close to the clinical range, indicating that the children who reported extremely cruel and sadistic acts being performed on them were seen by others as exhibiting cruelty themselves.

Similar findings were obtained from the therapists' ratings on the BPRS-C, as displayed in Table 12.15. Although there were no significant group differences for ratings at time of most distress, all items relating to aggression were rated significantly higher for RSA match children than for SA children at treatment termination (or currently, if still in psychotherapy). Both groups appear to have experienced a great lessening of aggressive behavior since the time of most distress, but it appears that the RSA match children showed less diminishment over time than did the SA children.

On the BADI symptom checklist filled out by mothers, the two items concerning aggression were compared between groups, both for the time period of 1 month after disclosure and for the last month before initial data collection (2 to 3 years after disclosure). There was a trend for the RSA group to score higher on all items (see Table 12.16), but the difference was only significant for "Violent talk or play violence" 1 month

TABLE 12.14. CBCL Mean Subscale Scores Relating to Aggressive Behavior for SA and RSA Match Children

	SA	RSA	F
Maternal ratings			
Aggressive	60.45	65.79	0.57a
Delinquent	59.45	64.43	2.98a*
Cruel	58.14	69.29	4.73a*
Hyperactive	60.73	68.43	4.04a*
Therapists' ratings			
Aggressive	59.50	65.40	5.15a*
Delinquent	57.00	64.75	13.69**

Note. Ratings based on time of most distress. n's vary slightly for different subscales, based on age of child.
aANCOVA controlling for child age.
*$p < .05$, one-tailed; **$p = .003$, one-tailed.

TABLE 12.15. Therapists' Mean BPRS-C Ratings Relating to Aggression for RSA Match and SA Children

	SA[a]	RSA (n = 15)	t
At time of most distress			
Uncooperativeness	3.29	3.20	−0.12
Hostility	2.14	2.73	0.92
Hyperactivity	0.86	1.73	1.66
At treatment termination[b]			
Uncooperativeness	0.85	1.73	2.63*
Hostility	0.38	1.40	3.71*
Hyperactivity	0.08	0.67	2.63*

[a]At time of most distress, n = 14; at treatment termination, n = 13.
[b]Or currently (2 to 4 years after disclosure), if still in therapy.
*p = .02, two-tailed; **p = .001, two-tailed.

after disclosure. Similar to what is said above in regard to the Cruel subscale, it is distressing that in the last month (2 to 4 years after disclosure of abuse), 28.6% of the RSA match group were reported to have made violent threats, whereas that behavior had ceased in the SA group.

Depression

A third hypothesized concomitant of powerlessness is depression. Depression is thought to result from the experience of powerlessness, because the child can do little to change the situation and is made to feel badly about himself or herself. Our main sources of data for this manifestation were the Depression scales of the CBCL from maternal and therapist ratings. The mean scores for Depression on the BPRS-C were also compared. For therapist ratings on the CBCL, there was a significant difference in the predicted direction, as shown in Table 12.17; in fact, the

TABLE 12.16. Percentage of BADI Symptom Checklist Items Relating to Aggressive Behavior Endorsed for SA and RSA Match Children

Item	SA	RSA	χ^2
Violent talk or play violence			
Postdisclosure	0.0	57.0	4.93*
Last month	11.1	21.4	n.s.
Threats of violence			
Postdisclosure	25.0	42.9	n.s.
Last month	0.0	28.6	n.s.

Note. From maternal ratings.
*p = .01 (one-tailed).

TABLE 12.17. CBCL Mean Depression Subscale Scores for SA and RSA Match Children

	SA[a]	RSA[b]	F
Therapist ratings	63.25	84.13	19.84c*
Maternal ratings	62.00	70.71	n.s.

[a]For therapist ratings, n = 8; for maternal ratings, n = 2.
[b]For therapist ratings, n = 8; for maternal ratings, n = 7.
[c]ANCOVA controlling for child age.
*p = .001.

mean score for the RSA group was extremely high (84 when a score of 70 is clinically meaningful). On maternal ratings of Depression on the CBCL, the mean score of the RSA match children was in the clinical range as well (70.71); only 2 SA children were rated on this subscale, so statistical comparisons were not meaningful. In general, for these ratings at time of most distress, the SA group appears to have been somewhat depressed and the RSA group seems to have been moderately to severely depressed.

On therapists' ratings on the BPRS-C, both groups appeared depressed on ratings at time of most distress, and there were no significant differences between the groups. However, for ratings at time of treatment termination (or 2 to 4 years after disclosure, if the children were still in treatment), the RSA match children were significantly more depressed than the SA children ($t = 2.13$, $p = .04$).

Lowered Sense of Efficacy and Control

The last manifestation of powerlessness examined was lowered sense of efficacy and control. Children's responses on Why Things Happen, a locus of control measure developed by Connell (1985), were compared between groups. It was expected that both groups of children might have a lowered sense of control, but we thought that the terrorizing elements involved in the reported ritualistic sexual abuse would cause the RSA group to feel less in control than the SA group. As Table 12.18 displays, there were no differences between groups on Internal Control or Unknown Control. Interestingly, the RSA group showed a significantly higher score for control by Powerful Others than the SA group, although both groups scored lower than Connell's normative group. This finding would seem to parallel the children's experience: In the SA group sexuality led to affection and special favors, whereas in the RSA group children reported that powerful adults threatened to kill the children's parents, sacrificed animals, and performed Satanic rituals. Moreover,

TABLE 12.18. Locus of Control Scores for SA and RSA Match Children

Scale	SA ($n = 13$)	RSA ($n = 14$)	F
Unknown Control			
$\bar{X}$	−0.49	−0.30	n.s.
SD	0.80	1.10	
Powerful Others Control			
$\bar{X}$	−0.53	−0.16	3.88[a]*
SD	0.72	1.06	
Internal Control			
$\bar{X}$	0.18	0.01	n.s.[a]
SD	0.94	0.88	

Note. Scores reported are standardized z scores calculated from age norms on Why Things Happen, a locus of control measure (Connell, 1985).
[a]ANCOVA controlling for child age.
*$p < .05$, one-tailed.

these "powerful others" were never convicted of any offenses, possibly adding to the RSA children's perceptions of the reported perpetrators' powerfulness, in comparison to the convicted and jailed perpetrator in the SA case.

In summary, it appears that the RSA match children had many behavioral manifestations of powerlessness. They suffered from PTSD, and showed more aggressive behavior and more depression than SA children. In addition, their symptoms showed less improvement over time than did those of the SA children. This may have been the case because the RSA children continued to experience powerlessness for many years after the reported abuse because of the ongoing controversy and legal procedures; by contrast, the SA children and families experienced "swift justice," in that the perpetrator was quickly sentenced to four life terms in prison. As a consequence, perhaps the SA children were able to move on with their lives and heal from the trauma, while the RSA match children remained embroiled in the abuse issues for years.

CONCLUSIONS

Severity

When we examine the findings from parental ratings, therapist measures, and child data, it appears that in our samples the functioning of the RSA children was considerably more severely affected than that of the

SA children. On a variety of indices of functioning, the SA group appeared to be doing better than the RSA match group.

Specificity

To summarize the information obtained on the specificity of effects on reported ritualistic and nonritualistic sexual abuse, predictions were generally supported. We expected few differences between the two groups on traumatic sexualization, and none were found. It is possible to speculate that differences between groups may emerge with increasing age, although we have no empirical basis on which to evaluate this possibility. Specifically, it may be that sexual abuse without terrorizing and ritualistic elements may lead to sexual behavior that is relatively free of aggression, whereas ritualistic sexual abuse that includes physical abuse and terror may lead to more aggressive sexual behavior later on. Certainly, the high aggression scores of the RSA match sample relative to the SA children do little to discredit this speculation.

We had predicted that there would be no group differences in betrayal, and did not examine the specific behavioral manifestations separately because of overlap with other dynamics. However, to the extent that the high depression and aggression scores for the RSA match group in comparison to the SA group discussed as manifestations of powerless-ness are also predicted as manifestations of betrayal, the RSA match group may have experienced a greater sense of betrayal as well.

For the dynamic of stigmatization, we expected the RSA match group to show more behavioral and psychological manifestations than the SA group. These predictions were generally confirmed. The RSA group had lower self-concepts, and experienced more guilt and self-blame, than the SA group. There was a trend for the RSA match children to be more socially withdrawn and isolated as well.

The contention that the RSA children would experience more powerlessness and all its associated symptoms than would the SA children was largely supported. The biggest conceptual differences in the abuse dynamics between the RSA group and the SA group, as elucidated earlier, were for the dynamic of powerlessness. As interesting theoretical support for the traumagenic model, the strongest empirical differences between the two groups were similarly found on manifestations of powerlessness.

The most significant effects linked to powerlessness that the RSA children displayed were anxiety (specifically of the type involved in PTSD) and aggression. The RSA match children were highly hypervig-ilant, had a high frequency of recurrent dreams and memories, and were described as "spaced out" and "emotionally numb." Similarly, they were seen by parents and therapists as more aggressive in general than the children in the SA group were perceived. Of particular concern was the high score on the Cruel subscale of the CBCL obtained by the RSA match group. It appears that although depression was a problem for both groups in the aftermath of the abuse, the effects were more pronounced for the RSA group. Similarly, both groups appeared highly fearful.

In summary, the children reporting ritualistic sexual abuse seemed to be as sexualized as the children experiencing sexual abuse without ritualistic elements. The RSA children generally seemed to experience more stigmatization (especially expressed as low self-esteem and guilt) and more powerlessness (exhibited mostly as anxiety and aggression) than the SA children. Although the findings appear to provide support for the traumagenic dynamics model, they may actually reflect greater overall disturbance in the RSA group rather than the specific hypothesized effects.

Possible Alternative Explanations

Although the group differences in findings presented above can probably be attributed to the terrorizing and ritualistic elements of the reported abuse experience, there are two other possible alternative explanations. First, differential outcomes for children may have resulted from variations in family response to the abuse that allegedly occurred in the preschool setting. Family response has been found to be one of the most potent factors in determining how a child is affected by child sexual abuse (Summit, 1983; Gomes-Schwartz, Horowitz, & Cardarelli, 1990).

In our study, it is unlikely that family response accounted for the differences between the SA and RSA match groups. In ratings by therapists of parents' response to the abuse, there were few differences between groups; however, on support of children, RSA mothers were seen as significantly more supportive than were SA mothers (see Chapter 16). Therefore, it appears that if family response accounted for group differences, the RSA group might be expected to be suffering *fewer* ill effects of the abuse than the SA group, rather than *more*, as was the case.

A second alternative explanation for our findings is that differences in community or legal response may have influenced the effects on children in the RSA and SA groups. There certainly were differences in both legal and community response in the two situations. In the SA group, the perpetrator admitted to all his acts, actually disclosing *more* acts per child than the children themselves reported. As mentioned previously, he is serving four life terms in prison. As a result of his confession, the community completely believed the children's accounts of their molestation; no children had to testify at any legal proceeding; and the outcome of the case was decided promptly. In addition, some families received substantial monetary settlements in civil lawsuits. Therefore, children and families were able to go on with their lives, processing the abuse experience and (let us hope) putting it behind them to move on to developmentally appropriate activities in growing up.

In contrast, in the RSA group, the accused perpetrators denied all allegations, and in one case the legal proceedings dragged on for 7 years. The community was (and, indeed, still is) strongly polarized over the issue of whether the abuse occurred at all, and the horror of the allegations of terrorizing and ritualistic acts made it difficult for some even to consider whether such activities might have occurred. With no resolution at all in some of the cases, and with the most famous case being almost continually in the news for so many years without any clear resolution, it was difficult for RSA families and children to do as the SA group did—put what happened behind them and get on with the business of growing up.

It is not really possible at this time to tease apart the effects of the reported ritualistic sexual abuse itself from the effects of the controversial legal and community response to the allegations in contributing to outcome for children. Our best guess is that both sets of factors were important. Perhaps later follow-up will allow us to analyze separately the effects of the abuse itself and the effects of the societal aftermath.

Effects
on Others

IMPACT ON
PARENTS

Jane McCord

RAUMATIC EVENTS, such as the experience of discovering that one's child has been abused, have a long-term impact on the way one views the world. We conducted family interviews approximately 5 years after the reported abuse had been disclosed. At that time, the parents of both the children who reported ritualistic sexual abuse (the RSA group) and the children who reported sexual abuse only (the SA group) completed a Parent Reaction Questionnaire after they had been interviewed on the impact of the abuse experience on themselves and their families. Many of these families had had to face the criminal justice system, medical and mental health professionals, child care workers, the mass media, and their personal belief systems in unprecedented ways. The experience left them with an altered view of social institutions and the world in which they lived.

Mothers and fathers of the RSA and the SA children were asked to rate, on a 7-point scale from "not at all trusted" to "highly trusted," their trust in various institutions and professionals. Information was requested for two different times: "before suspicion of child abuse" and "currently."

Table 13.1 presents the data on the 44 RSA mothers and the 28 RSA fathers who completed the Parent Reaction Questionnaire. Also included in this table are the 11 SA mothers who completed the questionnaire; only 3 SA fathers completed the items, so they are not included in this presentation. (To recapitulate the differences between the two groups, the reported experiences of the RSA children, unlike those of the SA children, involved multiple perpetrators and ritualistic or Satanic practices. In addition, the alleged perpetrators in the RSA cases either were not brought to trial or were not convicted.)

TABLE 13.1. Parent Reaction Questionnaire: Comparisons of Parents' Trust in Professionals and Institutions "Before Suspicion of Child Abuse" and "Currently"

	Significant increase or decrease in trust		
Item	RSA mothers (n = 44)	RSA fathers (n = 28)	SA mothers (n = 11)
1. Legal system	Decrease	Decrease	Same
2. Religion	Decrease	Decrease	Same
3. Police	Decrease	Same	Same
4. Medical doctors	Decrease	Same	Same
5. Teachers	Decrease	Decrease	Decrease
6. Babysitters	Decrease	Decrease	Decrease
7. Psychotherapists	Same	Same	Same
8. Media	Decrease	Decrease	Same
9. Belief in Satanic cults	Increase	Increase	Increase
10. Belief in a just and fair world	Decrease	Decrease	Decrease

MOTHERS OF CHILDREN REPORTING RITUALISTIC SEXUAL ABUSE

The RSA mothers rated their levels of trust in the various groups prior to the reported abuse moderate to moderately high. This seems to represent a generally optimistic view of the professions and institutions surveyed. They indicated moderately high trust in the legal system, religion, the police, medical doctors, teachers, therapists, and the media prior to the discovery of the abuse. There was even a moderate belief in the existence of Satanic groups. Finally, these women stated that they had had a moderately high belief in the world as a just and fair place.

These mothers, however, held radically different views at the follow-up survey, 5 years after abuse was disclosed. They had significantly less trust in all the professional groups except for psychotherapists. There had been significant drops in their level of trust in the legal system, the police, medical doctors, and even religion.

In summarizing her feelings about the legal system, one mother stated, "I think the justice system is a joke. . . . You think someone commits a crime and they pay for it. . . . It doesn't work that way at all. And maybe it can't work any way." According to another mother, "the justice system totally failed." Much of the disillusionment of these women came from the court's failure to accommodate child witnesses. As yet another mother stated, "I don't think the legal system is set up for child witnesses. And it's not there to protect them. . . . When the system was set up hundreds of years ago they didn't think that there was abuse of children." In considering her trust in our system of justice, one mother said, "I don't think I would never not trust a lawyer again . . . but I think that in a situation like if I was raped . . . I think that I would be very leery of going through court and testifying and all that." Few of these mothers had had personal experience with the legal system before, and the experience of seeing what can and does happen in the justice system left them shaken.

Many of the mothers in this RSA group also had contact with members of the local police force or the Los Angeles County Sheriff's Department who were investigating the cases. These experiences seemed to vary, with an overall decrease in their trust of the investigative process. One mother stated, "Initially, when I made the report, I felt like they were supportive and helpful. And sometimes, some particular people I felt were . . . totally unsympathetic, and even beyond unhelpful, into trying to screw it up." Another mother expressed her feelings this way: "I think in certain ways their hands were tied. It was all so new for everyone. They really didn't know how to investigate properly."

In addition, these mothers experienced a decrease in their level of trust in religious institutions. Some of the alleged abuse of some of the children in the RSA group was reported to have happened in churches or in church-sponsored preschools. People who were suspected of being involved in the abuse were also members of local churches and this created feelings of distrust in the parents of the children. These experiences seemed to leave many of the mothers feeling ambivalent at best about religious institutions, even though many expressed positive feelings about how their own churches responded to the crisis and were supportive of them.

These mothers also had a general decrease in their faith in medical doctors. These mothers came into contact with doctors in different settings related the reported abuse. They dealt with the children's regular pediatrician, and some of them also had their children diagnostically evaluated by other pediatricians who specialized in sexual abuse examinations. For some mothers, the disillusionment seemed to stem from pediatricians' not picking up on the possibility of sexual abuse earlier and having dismissed symptoms as due to other causes (i.e., poor hygiene). Others felt that doctors did not believe them or were unsympathetic. Still another source of frustration was the lack of clear results from diagnostic evaluations. Although many of the mothers expressed positive feelings about how they had been treated by physicians, they seemed to lose faith in doctors after realizing how little was known at the time about identifying sexual trauma and interpreting the results.

Moreover, these mothers indicated a dramatic decrease in their level of trust in teachers. This was only to be expected, since teachers were the ones who were reported to have abused the children. This was also true for babysitters; in the RSA group, some babysitters had also been implicated in molesting the children. Therefore, these two groups were seen as particularly untrustworthy. Mothers spoke of how they would "check out" schools or child care workers more carefully in the future, and would never feel completely confident of the trustworthiness of these professionals again.

These mothers' faith in therapists, however, remained in the moderately high range. They seemed to feel supported and believed by the therapists, and again and again expressed the opinion that the therapists had been the most helpful to them. Although most of the children were no longer in therapy, many of the mothers stated that they would return to the former therapists should their children experience problems in the future.

Another item on the Parent Reaction Questionnaire dealt with parental faith in the media. The RSA mothers, showed a significant drop on this item, from moderate levels of trust in the media before any knowledge of the child abuse to a moderately low level of trust at the time of the interview. One mother stated, "I think it's been real hard for me recently. It's just society's attitude, you know. Seeing all these injustices with the kids, or all those in the media and on television discounting what they've said." The media was generally supportive of the families' position in the beginning, but more time and space was given to the defendants' side of the story as time passed, and some of the families experienced feelings of betrayal. Others felt that the media did not accurately represent the facts. One mother stated, "I think they sensationalized it. I think they were irresponsible." An interesting sidelight is that a *Los Angeles Times* reporter, David Shaw, won a Pulitzer Prize for a series of articles criticizing the media's failure in its coverage of the McMartin case.

Another issue that emerged in the RSA group was that of alleged Satanic practices. According to one mother, "This experience has opened my eyes that . . . there's a lot more than I could have thought of. And actually before this, I never really thought of it. . . . I just never thought it was right in my backyard."

A final item on the Parent Reaction Questionnaire asked the parents about their belief that the world was a just and fair place. It was this overall sense of basic trust that the mothers rated as the most affected. When asked about this sense of trust, one mother said, "I don't know if there's a better word than paranoid. You just don't know who to trust." Another mother stated, "I scrutinize people a lot closer [now]." Similar thoughts were echoed by a third mother: "I'm just more aware. And not real trusting."

FATHERS OF CHILDREN REPORTING
RITUALISTIC SEXUAL ABUSE

Table 13.1 also compares the trust levels "before suspicion of child abuse" and "currently" for 28 fathers in the RSA sample. A profile similar to that of the mothers was found for the fathers, although the differences were less dramatic than for the mothers.

For the RSA fathers, the greatest difference between their prior and current opinions was the increase in their belief in Satanic cults after their experience with the allegations that surfaced from the preschools in this study. One father said, "[I]t seems to me that it's a lot more than the general public knows about. It seems to be more than I would expect." Other sources for this increased awareness of Satanic cults seemed to be (1) media coverage of the issue and (2) other sexual abuse cases from across the country that included allegations of Satanic or ritualistic practices.

Of all the institutions that they encountered, the RSA fathers lost the most trust in the legal system. According to one RSA father,

As far as our justice system is concerned, . . . that's probably frustrated me more than anything because I could see this happening from day one, and it has happened. . . . I said we're not going to go through this stuff, it's not fair. I'm not going to have somebody cross-examine my kid and say, "You wore a blue dress to school that day and we know you wore red that day so we're going to throw the case out of court." . . . I have no faith in the justice system at all. I think it's a joke.

As was true of the RSA mothers, the fathers indicated a significant drop in their trust levels of teachers and babysitters. As one father said, ". . . It has made me cynical . . . certainly more cautious. Cynical and more cautious about institutions that care for children." The fathers, however, lost less faith in the police and seemed more forgiving of the errors and understanding of the problems involved. One RSA father stated,

All of a sudden (the police) were asked to be instant experts in the subject of child abuse, and I don't think there were any instant experts, and so I think they screwed up a lot of things but I don't think they screwed them up because they were just totally inept.

Like the RSA mothers, the fathers had not lost trust in psychotherapists, and it was this professional group (along with medical doctors) for which these men retained the most respect. They did, however, lose a significant degree of trust in the media, and also indicated a significant drop in their belief that the world is a just and fair place after their experience with the abuse of their children.

MOTHERS OF CHILDREN REPORTING SEXUAL ABUSE ONLY

Parents from the SA sample were also administered the Parent Reaction Questionnaire. This case differed from the RSA preschool cases in that there was a single perpetrator who pled guilty and is currently serving time in prison. There were no allegations of ritualistic abuse and no lengthy legal proceedings. There were also differences in how these parents said they were affected by the abuse of their children, as compared to the RSA parents.

Table 13.1 indicates how the beliefs and trust in the various professions and institutions of the 11 mothers of the SA children changed after they discovered that their children had been sexually abused in preschool. As might be expected, their trust was most affected in the areas applying directly to their situation. They lost significant trust in teachers and babysitters after learning of the abuse; their view of the world as a just and fair place also decreased significantly after the molestations were disclosed. Finally, these mothers were also more likely to believe in the existence of Satanic cults subsequent to their children's experience. This seems somewhat surprising, since such allegations were not raised in this case. Perhaps widespread publicity and a greater awareness of child sexual abuse cases could account for some of this difference.

There was clearly less loss of faith in other professions and institutions among these women than among the RSA parents. There were no significant differences between their levels of trust before they knew their children had been molested and at the time of the survey on feelings about the legal system, the police, medical doctors, therapists, the media, and religion. It would appear that the impact of this type of case was more limited than that of the cases in the RSA sample.

COMPARISON OF MOTHERS AND FATHERS WHOSE CHILDREN REPORTED RITUALISTIC SEXUAL ABUSE

We also looked at how different groups compared to each other in loss of faith in various institutions. As indicated in Table 13.2, the RSA mothers' change scores (difference in levels of trust "before disclosure" and

TABLE 13.2. Parent Reaction Questionnaire: Differences between Change
Scores of RSA Mothers and RSA Fathers from "Before Disclosure" to "Currently"

Item	Significant difference in change scores
1. Legal system	Mothers > fathers
2. Religion	None
3. Police	Mothers > fathers
4. Medical doctors	Mothers > fathers
5. Teachers	Mothers > fathers
6. Babysitters	Mothers > fathers
7. Psychotherapists	Mothers > fathers
8. Media	Mothers > fathers
9. Belief in Satanic cults	None
10. Belief in a just and fair world	Mothers > fathers

Note. n = 26 in each group. A higher change score indicates a greater loss of trust.

"currently") are compared to the RSA fathers' change scores. As can be
seen, the mothers experienced significantly more loss of faith in the legal
system, the police, medical doctors, teachers, babysitters, and the media
than did the fathers. They also lost significantly more faith in a just and
fair world than did the fathers. These findings suggest that although both
mothers and fathers show significant loss of trust in various professional
groups and institutions when this type of traumatic event is experienced,
mothers may experience even more loss of trust and be even more affected
by children's reported victimization. This finding of a differential impact
may have implications both for treatment of individuals in families and
for interventions with couples.

COMPARISON OF MOTHERS IN THE TWO
GROUPS REPORTING SEXUAL ABUSE

In addition to looking at how gender differences affect mothers' versus
fathers' world views after children have reported abuse, we also compared
the change scores of the RSA mothers and the SA mothers. Since the
perpetrator in the SA case pled guilty and went to jail, whereas there were
no convictions in the RSA cases, parents perceived that justice was
rendered in the SA case but not in the RSA cases. This was reflected in
the differences in the change scores between the RSA mothers and the
SA mothers, as indicated in Table 13.3. The RSA mothers lost
significantly more faith in the legal system, religion, medical doctors, and
the media than did the SA mothers. This probably reflects their increased
involvement with these professions and subsequent disillusionment. As

TABLE 13.3. Parent Reaction Questionnaire: Differences between Change Scores of RSA Mothers and SA Mothers from "Before Disclosure" to "Currently"

Item	Significant difference in change scores
1. Legal system	RSA > SA
2. Religion	RSA > SA
3. Police	None
4. Medical doctors	RSA > SA
5. Teachers	None
6. Babysitters	None
7. Psychotherapists	None
8. Media	RSA > SA
9. Belief in Satanic cults	RSA > SA
10. Belief in a just and fair world	RSA > SA

Note. A higher change score indicates a greater loss of trust.
RSA n = 44; SA n = 11.

might be expected, the RSA mothers had a significantly greater belief in Satanic cults than did the SA mothers. The RSA mothers also experienced a significantly greater loss of belief in a just and fair world, as compared to the SA mothers.

CONCLUSIONS

In conclusion, these results indicate that important differences in level of trust, feelings of betrayal, and world views existed, depending on the type of case and the gender of the parents. Women tended to suffer more loss of faith than did the men. This may have been due to mothers' relatively closer involvement than the fathers with the children, or to differences in coping strategies utilized by men and women. It also seems that the RSA parents were much more profoundly affected by the entire experience, because of the sense of betrayal they experienced in many different areas (i.e., a lack of a conviction through the criminal justice system and the resulting frustration that comes with a lack of public validation). Perhaps most striking, however, was the disillusionment involved with the loss of the belief in a just and fair world, experienced by the vast majority of parents in both groups.

CHAPTER 14

IMPACT ON FAMILY RELATIONSHIPS

Jill Waterman

MAJOR TRAUMATIC EVENTS in the life of a child have repercussions in many areas of a family's functioning. Not only may they affect the child in a variety of areas, but they may have a significant impact on other family members; major family relationships may be affected as well. For example, when a child has reported sexual abuse, parent–child relationships may be changed in a myriad of ways. A parent may become very protective and unable to allow the child out of sight, or a may become concerned about physical touch with the child. Similarly, the marital relationship may be affected, and the adults' sexuality may become uncomfortable because it reminds parents of their child's sexual trauma.

To examine some of the effects of reported child sexual abuse in preschools on family relationships in our study, we looked at two different types of information. First, the Family Inventory of Life Events (FILE) was filled out by parents of the children reporting ritualistic sexual abuse (the RSA group) and sexual abuse only (the SA group) at the time of the initial data collection, 2 to 3 years after disclosure of the abuse; the FILE was completed again by a subset of parents from the two abuse groups who participated in a follow-up approximately 5 years after initial disclosure of alleged abuse. Parents of non-abused controls (the NA group) also filled out the FILE during the initial data collection phase. This questionnaire asks about various categories of life stress related to family issues.

Second, we administered a semistructured interview and an accompanying measure called the Parent Reaction Questionnaire to a subset of parents in the RSA and SA groups as part of the follow-up 5 years after disclosure. Information was obtained from 44 mothers and 28 fathers in the

RSA group, and from 11 mothers and 3 fathers in the SA group. The information to be covered in this chapter falls into the following categories: (1) changes in family stressors; (2) changes in parenting practices; (3) changes in the marital relationship; (4) abuse-related issues in the marital relationship; (5) and changes in closeness to extended family members.

FAMILY LIFE STRESSORS

Scores on the FILE were compared between the RSA group and the NA group for ratings at time of initial data collection. The RSA match group (see Chapter 12) was also compared with the SA group, and the scores obtained initially were compared with those gathered at follow-up 5 years later for the subset of parents who participated at both points. As shown in Table 14.1, the RSA mothers obtained significantly higher scores on both Marital Strains and Intrafamily Strains, as well as for Total Life Events than did the NA mothers. In contrast, when the two abuse groups (RSA match and SA) were compared, there were no significant differences between groups on any stress category.

When stressors among parents who participated both in the initial data collection and in the follow-up were examined, overall stressors decreased significantly by the follow-up for RSA mothers and fathers, as shown in Table 14.2. Interestingly, neither the Marital Strains nor

TABLE 14.1. Life Stress Scores for Families of RSA and NA Children

Stress subscale	RSA ($n = 72$)	NA ($n = 33$)	F
Marital Strains			
$\bar{X}$	0.61[a]	0.15	2.92[b]*
SD	0.89	0.57	
Intrafamily Strains			
$\bar{X}$	4.40	2.67	9.24[b]**
SD	2.91	2.23	
Total Life Events			
$\bar{X}$	11.46	6.82	11.39[b]***
SD	6.19	3.25	

Note. All scores are maternal ratings on the FILE (McCubbin, Patterson, & Wilson, 1981). The total score includes other strains, such as work transitions, illness, etc. We were especially interested in intrafamily strains, and this is also the best validated subscale.
[a]$n = 71$.
[b]Analysis of covariance controlling for socioeconomic status.
*$p < .05$, one-tailed; ** $p < .01$, two-tailed; *** $p < .001$, two-tailed.

TABLE 14.2. Comparisons of Mean FILE Scores for RSA and SA Families at Initial Data Collection and at Follow-Up

	Time 1	Time 2	t
RSA mothers (n = 34)			
Total Life Events	11.15	8.74	3.21*
Intrafamily Strains	3.91	3.26	1.34
Marital Strains	0.48	0.33	1.09
RSA fathers (n = 15)			
Total Life Events	10.0	6.93	3.38*
Intrafamily Strains	3.53	3.00	0.98
Marital Strains	0.53	0.27	1.29
SA mothers (n = 7)			
Total Life Events	9.28	11.43	−1.34
Intrafamily Strains	4.14	4.86	−0.85
Marital Strains	0.57	0.28	1.00

*$p < .01$.

Intrafamilial Strains subscales showed a similar significant decline. There were no significant differences for the SA mothers in stressors between initial and follow-up measurements. From the findings, it appears that disclosures of sexual abuse may cause a great deal of stress and conflict both in the marital relationship and in the parent–child relationship, even if the reported abuse has occurred in a setting outside the family.

EFFECTS ON FAMILY RELATIONSHIP PATTERNS

Three types of comparisons were made in examining the information on family relationships obtained from the parent questionnaires at the time of follow-up, 5 years after initial disclosure. First, we examined how behaviors and feelings changed over time. For most of the areas to be assessed, each child's parents were asked how things had changed in the first year after the child's disclosure and how they were now. For a few topics, parents were also asked to compare the period prior to the child's disclosure with the two time periods noted above. Second, we looked for differences between the RSA and SA groups in effects on family relationships of the abuse experience. Third, we looked for differences between mothers and fathers in the RSA group, utilizing the scores of the 27 couples for whom we had information from both mothers and fathers. Since only 3 fathers in the SA sample filled out the questionnaire, their responses were generally dropped from analyses, although some interesting trends are described.

Parenting Practices

Independence Allowed for Children

Parents were asked about a series of possible child care and independence situations, and rated how willing they were to allow their children to participate in each situation on a 7-point scale (1 = "much less willing"; 4 = "about as willing as before abuse"; 7 = "much more willing"). Mothers and fathers in both the RSA and the SA groups were all much less willing to allow their children independence (e.g., to stay overnight at a friend's house; to start a class or join a team without a parent's being present) or to entrust their care to someone outside the family in the first year after disclosure than they were prior to the abuse. There did not seem to be any reluctance to allow the children to be cared for by extended family members. In rating the current period at follow-up, approximately 5 years after the abuse disclosures, parents in general were significantly more likely to allow their children independence than they were in the first year after abuse. However, some parents still had difficulty with this issue, as one mother detailed:

> I either walk or drive my child to school. She's getting older, she'll be in sixth grade. I still don't want her by herself. If there's a friend she can walk with, then we can make arrangements. But as far as sending her out on her own, I can't do it.

A general trend was for parents to be extremely reluctant to utilize preschool or day care facilities for their younger children. As one mother stated, "My youngest son is almost $4^1/2$ and bored with being at home. But there's no way I'll put him in preschool—no way."

The fact that on most items, parents were more willing to allow their children to participate outside the home at follow-up than they were prior to the reported abuse probably reflects developmental trends. Although parents were asked to try to report only abuse-related changes and not developmental changes, it was often difficult to ignore the major effects of developmental growth. In light of this, it is particularly interesting to note that all respondents were still less likely to leave their children with anyone outside the family than they were prior to the abuse. Mothers in the SA group were significantly less likely to allow their children to stay overnight at a friend's house or to allow them to go out of sight in a public place (such as a park) during the first year following disclosure than were RSA mothers. There were no significant differences on these items between mothers and fathers in the RSA group.

Affection and Sexual Behavior in the Home

In examining changes in frequency of physical expressions of affection from parent to child, such as hugging and kissing, we found that both mothers and fathers in the RSA group responded to their children's disclosure with more affectionate expressions than prior to the abuse, and that this increase continued to the follow-up. In contrast, in the SA group, the disclosure caused a more moderate increase in the amount of affectionate behavior toward the children. When mothers in the two groups were compared, SA mothers reported that there was no difference between prior to the abuse disclosure and follow-up in the frequency with which they kissed their children, while RSA mothers asserted that they kissed their children more frequently at follow-up; this group difference was significant ($p = .002$).

Regarding parental affection in front of the children, mothers in the RSA group reported that they kissed and hugged their spouses significantly less often in front of the children in the first year after disclosure than they did at the time of follow-up ($p < .01$); none of the other parental groups saw significant differences. The RSA mothers perceived more of a decrease at follow-up from the first year after disclosure in hugging and kissing their spouses in the children's presence than their mates perceived ($p = .01$), and there was a similar trend regarding parental perceptions of parents' walking around nude in front of the children. Both parents rated these behaviors as occurring less often at follow-up than they did several years ago, again probably reflecting developmental trends. In general, as children approach adolescence, we would expect less parental nudity and perhaps less overt sexually tinged affection between parents, in response to the children's increased interest in and sensitivity to these issues.

Parents were also asked about their comfort level in showing physical affection to the children prior to the abuse reports, in the first year after disclosure, and at the time of follow-up, as detailed in Table 14.3. Interestingly, mothers in the RSA group rated themselves as very comfortable showing physical affection at all time periods, with no significant differences between time periods. In contrast, RSA fathers rated themselves as significantly less comfortable showing physical affection to their child in the first year after abuse disclosure than they were prior to the disclosure or at follow-up. A pattern similar to that of the RSA fathers was found for the SA mothers. In the first year after abuse disclosure, but not prior to disclosure or at follow-up, SA mothers reported significantly less comfort with physical affection than did RSA mothers ($F = 16.49$, $p = .000$; covariate of child age: $F = 23.22$, $p = .000$).

TABLE 14.3. RSA and SA Parents' Comfort in Showing Physical Affection to their Children

Group	Before disclosure (a)	First year after disclosure (b)	Follow-up (c)	Significant difference?
RSA mothers	1.32	1.11	1.14	No
RSA fathers	1.64	2.11	1.57	b > a; b > c
SA mothers	1.36	2.91	1.36	b > a; b > c

Note. 1 = "very comfortable"; 7 = "not at all comfortable."

Among the RSA couples, mothers were significantly more comfortable in expressing physical affection at all three time periods than were fathers. Fathers showed significantly more change in comfort with physical affection between the preabuse period and the first year after disclosure, and again between the first year after disclosure and at the time of follow-up, than did mothers. In addition, fathers attributed significantly more of the change in comfort with physical affection to the abuse situation than did mothers ($t = -3.78$, $p < .001$). It appears that for fathers, the sexualization of their children through reported abuse made them uncomfortable with physical affection toward the children for a period of time, possibly because such affection might be perceived as sexual. As one father stated, "All of a sudden I saw my young daughter as a sexual person, and this scared the hell out of me. I got nervous about getting too close to her." Another father said,

> I'm very careful how I'm physically affectionate with her now. And I think in the back part of my mind I'm sensitive to the sexual abuse issue, especially with the father and daughter. It's on my mind whenever I'm physically affectionate with her; I'm saying, you know, "be careful where you touch and how you touch and how you kiss and all that." And I think on some level, it's probably that the sexual abuse issue has probably affected me more than it has her.

The same process did not appear to occur for the RSA mothers.

Discipline Style

In discipline style, both mothers and fathers in the RSA group reported that they became more lenient in discipline in the first year after disclosure, as shown in Table 14.4. However, whereas RSA mothers felt

TABLE 14.4. RSA and SA Parents' Discipline Style

Group	Before disclosure (a)	First year after disclosure (b)	Follow-up (c)	Significant difference?
RSA mothers	4.48	3.39	4.59	b < a; b < c
RSA fathers	5.18	3.75	4.43	b < a; c < a
SA mothers	4.45	4.18	4.72	No

Note. 1 = "very lenient"; 7 = "very strict."

at follow-up that they had returned to their earlier, somewhat stricter style, fathers continued to be significantly more lenient than they were prior to the abuse. It appears that there were significant differences prior to abuse disclosure (mothers were more lenient), but that these differences no longer existed after disclosure, since both parents reported very similar styles of discipline in the first year after disclosure and at the time of follow-up. There were no significant differences in discipline style over the three time periods in the SA group.

Marital Relationship

Marital Satisfaction

Both mothers and fathers in the RSA group reported a significant increase in marital dissatisfaction during the first year after abuse disclosure; there was a similar though nonsignificant trend for the SA mothers as well. Table 14.5 details the groups' ratings on marital issues. Mothers in both groups felt that their marriages were more satisfying at the time of follow-up than they were prior to the abuse, although the

TABLE 14.5. Marital Satisfaction among RSA and SA Parents

Group	Before disclosure (a)	First year after disclosure (b)	Follow-up (c)	Significant difference?
RSA mothers	2.55	3.87	2.18	b > a; b > c
RSA fathers	2.22	2.63	2.41	b > a
SA mothers	3.00	3.89	2.14	No

Note. 1 = "very satisfied"; 7 = "very dissatisfied."

difference was only significant in the RSA group. In examining the RSA couples' ratings, fathers were much more satisfied with their marriages in the first year after abuse disclosure than were the mothers ($t = 2.98$, $p <$ .006); there were no differences for other time periods. From the comments of the parents, it appeared that the fathers frequently withdrew or continued with "business as usual" as a way to cope in the first year after abuse disclosure, while mothers wanted to discuss the abuse events and developments extensively during that time period. Many mothers reported that they were extremely frustrated by the unresponsiveness of their husbands at the time, since they felt as if they needed a great deal of support.

When changes in closeness to one's spouse were examined, both RSA and SA mothers reported a decrease in such closeness in the first year after disclosure, while RSA and SA fathers indicated an increase during this time period (Table 14.6). The RSA mothers perceived significantly less closeness with their spouses than did the RSA fathers in the first year after disclosure ($t = -2.86$, $p = .008$). All parental groups reported increases in closeness between the first year after disclosure and the time of follow-up, and these increases were significant for all groups except the SA fathers (of whom, it must be remembered, there were only 3).

As for changes in marital status over the period from abuse disclosure to the initial data collection about 3 years later, marriages in the RSA group were clearly more affected than those in the SA and NA groups, as detailed in Table 14.7. Out of 71 RSA mothers reporting marital status, 4 were separated or divorced over the 3-year period, as compared with none of the NA mothers. One SA mother remarried, while none divorced over the period. It is also clear from the table that in general, the RSA and NA groups were mostly composed of intact families, while over half of the mothers in the SA group were divorced at both time periods.

TABLE 14.6. Effect of Abuse on Closeness with Spouse among RSA and SA Parents

Group	First year after disclosure	Follow-up
RSA mothers	3.73	5.03***
RSA fathers	4.15	5.07**
SA mothers	3.56	5.56*

Note. 1 = "much more distant"; 7 = "much closer."
*$p = .05$; **$p = .01$; ***$p = .0001$.

TABLE 14.7. Parents' Marital Status at Time of Abuse disclosure and at Time of Initial Data Collection

Group and status	Percentage at time of disclosure	Percentage at time of data collection
RSA (n = 71)		
Married	84.5	78.9
Separated	2.8	2.8
Divorced	11.3	16.9
Never married	1.4	1.4
SA (n = 12)		
Married	33.3	41.7
Divorced	66.7	58.3
NA (n = 33)		
Married	87.9	87.9
Separated	6.1	0.0
Divorced	6.1	12.1

Note. For the NA group, the first period rated was "in early 1984." The initial data collection took place approximately 3 years after disclosure of abuse.

Sexual Relationship

All groups of parents reported that their sexual relationship was worse in the first year after disclosure; however, a significant improvement was noted by the time of follow-up for all groups, as shown in Table 14.8. Among the RSA couples, the mothers reported that the sexual relationship was significantly worse in the first year after disclosure than their husbands reported it to be ($t = -3.70$, $p < .001$). Many mothers (and a few fathers as well) commented that in the first months after disclosure, when their husbands initiated sexual activity, the mothers "flashed" on their children in the sexually abusive situation and could not continue.

TABLE 14.8. Effect of Abuse on Sexual Relationship among RSA and SA Parents

Group	First year after disclosure	Follow-up
RSA mothers	2.28	4.73***
RSA fathers	2.93	4.21**
SA mothers	3.00	4.44*

Note. 1 = "much worse"; 4 = same"; 7 = "much improved."
* p = .05; ** p = .01; *** p = .001.

Communication with Spouse

Similar to the pattern reported above for closeness with spouse, both SA and RSA mothers reported slightly worse communication with their spouses in the first year after disclosure, while RSA fathers reported either no change in communication or a slight improvement during this time period. This finding was true both for general communication and for communication related to parenting. All groups felt that communication improved from the first year after disclosure to the time of follow-up; there were significant improvements on both general communication and communication about parenting for RSA mothers and fathers. SA mothers' improvement scores reached significance only for general communication.

Parental Reactions to Abuse

Parents were also asked to examine several issues relating to their own and their spouses' reactions to the reported abuse. There was a steady decrease in both SA and RSA groups in how much time couples spent discussing the matter. About 70% of RSA mothers and fathers reported discussing the alleged abuse for at least some time every day in the first month after disclosure, and approximately 40% of both parents in the RSA group continued to discuss it daily during the first year after disclosure. At follow-up, about 20% of the mothers and 32% of the fathers in the RSA group reported that they still discussed the alleged abuse with their spouses at least once a week. Although figures for the first month after disclosure were not much different in the SA group, at follow-up none of either the mothers or the fathers in the SA group reported discussing the abuse with their spouse at least once per week. These results undoubtedly reflect the fact that the perpetrator in the SA group confessed and was quickly placed in prison for life, whereas 5 years after disclosure, when the follow-up parental ratings were obtained, legal proceedings against some of the alleged perpetrators in the RSA group were dragging on seemingly interminably.

In addition, parents were asked to examine differences between their own and their spouses' reactions to the abuse disclosure in certainty of belief and in preoccupation or distress about the abuse disclosure. As Tables 14.9 and 14.10 show, the mothers in both the SA and RSA groups were perceived by themselves and their spouses as being more certain that the reported abuse happened, and as generally feeling more preoccupied with and distressed about it, than the fathers. The SA and RSA groups did not differ on these reactions. However, there were significant differences between RSA mothers and fathers in both certainty of belief ($t = -5.38$,

TABLE 14.9. Differences between RSA Spouses on Belief and Distress about Reported Abuse

	RSA mothers	RSA fathers
Differences in extent to which respondent versus spouse believed child had been abused		
1 = I was much more certain	19.5%	0.0%
2 = I was somewhat more certain	9.8%	0.0%
3 = I was slightly more certain	19.5%	0.0%
4 = No differences	51.2%	46.4%
5 = Spouse was slightly more certain	0.0%	32.1%
6 = Spouse was somewhat more certain	0.0%	17.9%
7 = Spouse was much more certain	0.0%	3.6%
Mean score (couples only)	3.03	4.81*
Differences in extent to which respondent versus spouse was preoccupied or distressed by child's abuse disclosure		
1 = I was much more preoccupied/distressed	48.8%	0.0%
2 = I was somewhat more	19.5%	3.7%
3 = I was slightly more	22.0%	3.7%
4 = No differences	7.3%	14.8%
5 = Spouse was slightly more	2.4%	7.4%
6 = Spouse was somewhat more	0.0%	37.0%
7 = Spouse was much more	0.0%	33.3%
Mean score (couples only)	1.85	5.81*

Note. n = 27 in each group.
* $p < 001$.

$p = .000$) and preoccupation and distress about the abuse disclosure ($t = -11.22, p = .000$). It seems clear that the mothers were more affected by the reported abuse than the fathers, perhaps because they spent more time with the children, or perhaps because mothers in general are more likely to focus on feelings about problems, whereas fathers may be more likely to avoid distressing feelings.

Relationships with Extended Family Members

Mothers in general tended to perceive little effect of the reported abuse on closeness with extended family members, whereas RSA fathers tended to perceive it as somewhat increasing closeness with their extended families. There were no significant differences between mothers in the SA and RSA groups. However, among the RSA couples, fathers were significantly more likely to perceive increased closeness to extended family members than were mothers ($t = 2.37, p = .03$).

TABLE 14.10. Differences between SA Spouses on Belief and Distress about Abuse in First Year after Disclosure

	SA mothers	SA fathers
Differences in extent to which respondent versus spouse believed child had been abused		
1 = I was much more certain	30.0%	0.0%
2 = I was somewhat more certain	10.0%	0.0%
3 = I was slightly more certain	0.0%	0.0%
4 = No differences	60.0%	100.0%
5 = Spouse was slightly more certain	0.0%	0.0%
6 = Spouse was somewhat more certain	0.0%	0.0%
7 = Spouse was much more certain	0.0%	0.0%
Differences in extent to which respondent versus spouse was preoccupied or distressed by child's abuse disclosure		
1 = I was much more preoccupied, distressed	70.0%	33.3%
2 = I was somewhat more	10.0%	0.0%
3 = I was slightly more	0.0%	0.0%
4 = No differences	10.0%	33.3%
5 = Spouse was slightly more	0.0%	0.0%
6 = Spouse was somewhat more	0.0%	33.3%
7 = Spouse was much more	10.0%	0.0%

Note. Although 11 SA mothers were involved, only 3 SA fathers participated.

SUMMARY

In summary, it appears that the reported abuse had a major impact on some aspects of family relationships. In general, both marital and parent–child stress increased. Parents tended to become more protective of their children and to allow them less independence in the aftermath of extrafamilial abuse, but over time they were generally able to allow the children increasing independence. Physical affection toward the children tended to increase in the first year after disclosure and to continue to be at higher levels than prior to the disclosure. However, fathers were significantly less comfortable with showing physical affection to their children in the first year after disclosure than they were either before the disclosure or at the 5-year follow-up. Mothers in the RSA group showed no changes in comfort with physical affection. The abuse disclosure tended to cause both parents to become more lenient in discipline in the first year after reported abuse; although mothers returned to their preabuse discipline style, fathers tended to remain more lenient than they had been previously.

All aspects of the marital relationship seemed to be affected in the first year after disclosure. Both the RSA and SA groups reported marital and sexual dissatisfaction, as well as poorer communication, in the aftermath of the abuse disclosure. Mothers tended to be more dissatisfied and to feel less close to their spouses than did fathers. At follow-up, however, parents in both groups reported higher levels of satisfaction and closeness in the marital relationship than they had had prior to the abuse disclosure.

Both mothers and fathers seem to agree that mothers were more certain about the reported abuse and were more preoccupied and distressed about it than were fathers; this appeared to be true in both the RSA and SA groups. At the 5-year follow-up, parents in the RSA group spent more time discussing the alleged abuse than parents in the SA group, probably as a consequence of legal and community differences in the outcome of the cases.

CHAPTER 15

IMPACT ON
THERAPISTS

Mary Kay Oliveri
Jill Waterman

You can exert no influence if you are not susceptible to influence . . . (Jung, 1931/1954)

IN OUR WORK with children reporting ritualistic and nonritualistic sexual abuse in preschools, the therapists who treated the children were an important resource. They were involved in data collection, and gave feedback on development of the parent interview. In our collaboration with them over time, we became aware that the therapists were experiencing a variety of stressors unlike any they had dealt with before.

First, although most of the therapists had experience with sexually abused children, they were dealing with uncharted territory—allegations of bizarre and horrible acts that had not previously been reported by young children. The therapists needed to make sense of allegations that were too terrible and strange to believe, coming from young children who were unlikely to be making them up. Moreover, there were few guidelines available to help therapists in treating the children reporting these experiences, who were often highly fearful and exhibited a variety of symptoms. Therefore, treatment techniques needed to evolve without the comfort of relying on earlier proven methods usually employed with child clients, or of going to the literature or other therapists to get help from those with previous experience in the field.

Second, the therapists found themselves in a whirlwind of media coverage, legal investigation, and public attention and scrutiny. For a period of time, articles appeared almost daily about new allegations that emerged; parents of the children (and occasionally the children themselves) were interviewed on television; and a few of the therapists and investigating clinicians also became involved with the mass media. Some of the therapists also had to testify, sometimes at several different points in time, in the long, acrimonious criminal trial in one of the RSA cases. Those testifying in the 18-month preliminary trial were subjected to cross-examination by each of the seven different defense attorneys.

As we became aware that the experience of providing psychotherapy to these groups of children was having profound effects on the therapists, we decided to develop a measure that would enable us to determine empirically just what the effects were. The questionnaire that we developed assessed the effects on the clinicians both professionally and personally, as well as the strategies that they utilized to cope with the events. The questionnaire was developed and administered approximately 5 years after the initial disclosures of abuse.

Because of the empathic connection believed to exist between therapist and client (Searles, 1955; Mattinson, 1975), we thought that clinicians would experience some of the overwhelming affective responses with which the children and families were struggling. We considered that the feelings associated with the clinical hour might intrude upon the clinicians' personal lives, and wondered whether the therapists might experience some symptoms of post-traumatic stress disorder (PTSD), paralleling McCann and Pearlman's (1990) work on "vicarious traumatization." We also investigated ways in which therapists coped, hoping to provide help for other therapists who might find themselves in similar traumatic situations.

THE THERAPISTS

Two groups of clinicians responded to the questionnaire: those who treated the children alleging ritualistic sexual abuse in southern California (the RSA group), and those who treated the children reporting nonritualistic sexual abuse in Reno, Nevada (the SA group). The questionnaire was sent to 28 clinicians, and 21 returned completed questionnaires; there were 16 female and 5 male respondents. The therapists included one with an MD, eight with PhDs in clinical psychology, eight with MSWs in clinical social work, two with MFCCs, and two respondents whose final degree status is unknown. There were 19 clinicians who treated RSA children, and 2 who treated SA children. (Sadly, one of the principal clinicians in the SA group died just prior to the completion of this phase of the study.) The vast majority of therapists indicated no significant professional change in status or in the emphasis of their work in the years since they began treatment with the preschool abuse clients.

Most of the clinicians reported spending slightly over 50% of their time in the provision of clinical service. Over 67% of the sample provided clinical supervision, about 50% were involved in training activities, and 40% had some research involvement. Of the 20 therapists who were working at the time of the survey (one had retired), 40% worked part-time and 60% worked full-time. Of the respondents, 33% were in full-time private practice, 14.3% were in full-time agency work, and the rest worked in more than one setting. All of the responding therapists indicated specific training experiences in child sexual abuse prior to their involvement with the RSA and SA children.

CLINICIANS' BELIEF IN ABUSE ALLEGATIONS

Because the perpetrator in the SA group admitted the abuse, only the responses of the 19 clinicians treating RSA children are included in the analyses of belief. As displayed in Table 15.1, the clinicians' level of belief in all aspects of the abuse allegations increased over the time of treatment. Although they were likely to believe allegations of sexual abuse and of threats during the early phases of treatment, clinicians appeared to move from relative disbelief about allegations of Satanic rites and ritualistic abuse during the early phases of treatment to a much higher degree of belief at the end of treatment. This move in belief seemed to parallel the later disclosures by the children of ritualistic abuse than of other forms of abuse (see Chapter 5).

We also asked the clinicians about what factors affected their belief in the children's disclosures. As shown in Table 15.2, the most important factors for the therapists were the children's affect in regard to the disclosure of abuse events and the disclosures themselves. The comments of several therapists are illuminating:

TABLE 15.1. RSA Therapists' Mean Level of Belief in Specific Abuse Events During the First Week of Treatment and at the Time of the Survey

Abusive event	First week	At time of survey	t
Sexual abuse	5.32	6.37	-3.04*
Verbal threat	5.24	6.58	-4.23*
Physical threat	5.00	6.59	-4.77**
Satanic rites	2.00	5.67	-7.17**
Terrorizing acts	3.94	6.28	-4.56**
Ritualistic abuse	2.17	5.89	-6.66**

Note. n = 16–19; 1 = "total disbelief"; 7 = "total belief."
*p < .001; **p < .0001.

TABLE 15.2. Importance of Factors Affecting Therapists' Beliefs: Rank Order of Mean Ratings, from Highest to Lowest

Rank-ordered factors	Mean score
Affect of child in regard to disclosure of abuse event	2.19
Content of child's disclosures	2.48
Parent's report of child's affect	3.81
Parent's report of child's behavior	4.14
Parent's report of child's disclosures	4.57
Collaboration with other therapists on case	6.24
Collaboration with clinical evaluation agency	6.90
Collaboration with therapists not on case	7.86
Collaboration with legal evaluation agency	7.91
Reports by the media	9.19

"The intense fear in the children I treated, including one child asking me to call the police to come to my office because he had just disclosed a serious experience (about being urinated and defecated upon and being forced to do this to others) and was certain that the abusers would come into the office and harm me."

"The repetition of themes in the disclosures by the preschool children in their play therapy sessions, despite the fact that the children did not know one another. . . . the themes were unique to this population, not like preschoolers in general."

"My own personal, emotional experience when I was listening to the children's disclosure—the dreams I had, the cold, chilly feeling that what I was hearing was very real and quite frightening."

CLINICIANS' AFFECTIVE RESPONSE TO CHILDREN AND PARENTS

Assuming that the clinicians would be empathic with their clients, we asked them about their own affective responses to the children and to the parents. In responding about the children, 81% of the therapists reported that they at least occasionally experienced feelings similar to those of their child clients. The most common affective responses that the therapists shared with the children were sadness, fear, and helplessness/powerlessness. As one therapist stated, "I felt a total overwhelming sense that I was being watched and would be punished [for my involvement], during some moments."

Similarly, 81% responded that they experienced feelings similar to those of the parents; here, the affective responses therapists most frequently shared with the parents were rage/anger and helplessness/powerlessness. Therapists were more bothered by intrusive affects about the children than about the parents; 76% of therapists reported that their affective response to the children often interfered with their attention to other tasks. For example, one clinician felt "horror and confusion about what happened and why, an inability to make sense of the things that happened to these children."

CLINICIANS' PERSONAL RESPONSES

Because of the intensity of the work with these young children and their families, we were interested in whether the clinicians experienced emotional distress or symptomatology during the period they were treating the children. Theoretically, we might expect that the enormity of a child's trauma would cause distress in a clinician, or that an individual clinician's own painful experiences with trauma or betrayal might be triggered through treatment of a child (McCann, Sakheim, & Abrahamson, 1988; McCann & Pearlman, 1990). We expected that both factors might operate to cause distress for the treating clinicians.

Therapists were asked to indicate whether they experienced a variety of symptoms and to what level they were experienced. As shown in Table 15.3, therapists did report experiencing distress at times. The most common symptoms were mood disturbances and inability to concentrate, both experienced sometimes or often by 71.4% of the therapists. These

TABLE 15.3. Clinicians' Symptoms during Professional Involvement, Rank-Ordered by Mean Ratings

Symptom	Mean score	Percentage experiencing symptom "sometimes" to "often"
Mood disturbance	4.43	71.4%
Attention disturbance	4.14	71.4%
Sense of alienation	4.05	61.9%
Unusual fears	3.91	61.9%
Sleep disturbance	3.48	42.9%
Work problems	3.33	42.9%
Relationship problems	3.10	42.9%
Eating disturbance	2.81	33.3%
Sexual intimacy problems	2.81	33.3%
Temper episodes	2.62	28.6%
Crying spells	1.91	14.3%

Note. n = 21; 1 = "never"; 4 = "sometimes"; 7 = "often."

mood and attention disturbances in some ways paralleled the disruptions that children and parents also reported. Two other symptoms were reported as occurring sometimes or more frequently by the majority of the clinicians, and both were perhaps linked to the nature of the trauma and abuses reported. A sense of alienation might be expected in light of the disbelief and community controversy generated by the more bizarre and frightening allegations of the children; in addition, unusual fears could easily follow from the children's reports of Satanic curses, killing of animals, and the like. Both these symptoms were reported as occurring at least sometimes by 61.9% of the therapists.

In general, the clinicians reported a mild to moderate level of distress. When asked to indicate in an open-ended fashion the most troubling symptom experienced, 32% listed fear or a general sense of suspiciousness. As one clinician put it, "Fear and alienation: no anchor of whom to trust, what to believe, or how to proceed." Others expressed the difficulty of feeling isolated from professional colleagues, as well as fear of others:

"Paranoid fears that cult members were 'everywhere.' Intense anger and frustration that the [alleged] perpetrators of the abuse were not charged or 'contained' by the justice system and could hurt others in the future. I still get teary-eyed when I think of the kids I saw."

"Profound sense of feeling different from, alienated from, reactive to colleagues not involved in the case who couldn't possibly under-stand . . ."

"Depression and lack of desire for an emotionally and sexually intimate relationship."

Difficulty in intimate relationships was noted as the most troubling symptom by 26%, while 16% reported they were most troubled by difficulty with their sense of adequacy as professionals as a result of their experiences on these cases.

Post-Traumatic Stress Disorder Symptoms

Given the nature of the reported trauma and the prevalence of symptoms of PTSD in the children treated, we anticipated that some of the clinicians might have experienced PTSD symptoms as well during the treatment process. We therefore calculated whether or not the therapists met the diagnostic criteria for PTSD (American Psychological Association, 1987, p. 250). The majority reported PTSD symptoms as present at least some of the time, and as frequently present during their most stressful period of interaction with the cases; fully 77.8% of the clinicians met criteria for a diagnosis of PTSD at this time. The most troubling PTSD symptoms were recurrent recollections of the abuse (81.5%), a sense of detachment or estrangement from others (75.0%), and hypervigilance (79.2%). It is clear that this group of therapists experienced PTSD at the height of their involvement with the children and families.

Impact on Relationships

Since the involvement of the therapists with these cases was so intense, we expected that it might have had effects on the significant professional and personal relationships in their lives. We therefore asked whether the therapists' relationships to a variety of types of people had become closer, had become more distant, or remained unaffected.

As shown in Table 15.4, the relationships that seemed to become significantly closer were those with other therapists treating the preschool cases, and to some extent those with administrators involved with the cases. Because of the unfamiliar territory in which therapists were operating, consultation with other therapists treating similar cases was seen as both therapeutically helpful and personally supportive. They may have felt that others involved in the cases could understand their intense and frightening feelings, and would be more accepting of the bizarre tales emerging from the children in treatment. In contrast, 50% of the clinicians reported feeling more distant from therapists who were not involved with the cases. Some of this distance appeared to result from isolation engendered by work with trauma victims, whereas part may have been attributable to a perceived lack of support or disbelief from other colleagues who were not involved.

TABLE 15.4. Profile of Effects on Clinicians' Relationships

Rank order of relationship	Mean rating	Percentage showing no change	Percentage becoming closer	Percentage becoming more distant
Therapists treating case	6.10	10	90	0
Own children	4.55	35	40	25
Administrators on case	4.30	40	40	20
Own siblings	4.05	63	21	16
Own parents	4.05	65	20	15
Friends	3.75	40	20	40
Significant other	3.76	38	19	43
Administrators not on case	3.71	76	5	19
Therapists not on case	3.35	45	5	50

Note. n's = 20–21; 1 = "more distant"; 4 = "no change"; 7 = "closer."

In terms of family relationships, many therapists reported feeling closer to their own children. This may have occurred as a result of the clinicians' empathic response to their child clients, or perhaps as a hypervigilance response focused on keeping their own children safe. Although relationships with parents and siblings were generally unaffected, it is striking that a sizable proportion of the clinicians (about 40%) felt more distant from their significant others, and from friends as well. This finding parallels results with parents; in general, dealing with the sexual abuse allegations placed a great strain on the marital relationship of the parents in the first year after disclosure (see Chapter 14).

Trust in Societal Institutions

Since therapists and families involved with these high-profile cases of reported abuse touched and were touched by a variety of societal institutions, we looked at how the experience had changed the trust of the clinicians in such institutions (the legal system, police, the mass media, doctors, etc.). As is evident in Table 15.5, this group of therapists became extremely disillusioned. Not only did they show significant decreases in trust of every institution besides religion queried, but in many instances they went from a generally trusting to an untrusting stance (e.g., teachers, babysitters, the legal system). Given that the abuse was reported in preschool settings, the decrease in trust toward teachers and babysitters are understandable. Experiences with police and medical doctors seem to

TABLE 15.5. Clinicians' Mean Ratings of Trust in Groups and Institutions before and after Involvement with High-Profile Cases of Reported Abuse

Institution	Before	After	t
Trust in legal system	4.14	1.76	6.84**
Trust in babysitters	4.81	2.86	6.25**
Trust in teachers	5.24	3.62	4.65**
Trust in media	3.29	2.00	4.05**
Trust in therapists	5.43	4.52	3.80**
Trust in medical doctors	4.95	4.38	2.55*
Trust in police	4.38	3.48	2.25*
Trust in religion	3.29	3.62	−0.94
Belief in satanic cults	2.67	6.52	10.33**
Belief in a fair and just world	4.15	2.55	−5.81**

Note. n's = 20–21; 1 = "total disbelief/much less trust-ing"; 7 = "total belief/much more trusting." *$p < .05$. **$p < .001$.

have been mixed; however, many of the RSA children's clinicians perceived that the legal system and the media mishandled the cases.

The therapists became believers in the existence of Satanic cults as a result of the children's disclosures. They also experienced a striking decrease in the belief that the world is a just and fair place; it seemed to us that this change in the therapists' cognitive schemas, perhaps more than any other change, might continue past involvement with the particular RSA and SA cases. Therapists seemed to feel that society had failed to protect its children, leaving them painfully exposed to attacks on their credibility and veracity as well as on their bodies and their minds.

CLINICIANS' COPING STRATEGIES

In addition to examining the emotional effects that work with the RSA and SA children had on the clinicians, we also surveyed them about what strategies they used to cope with the stress involved. Asking questions similar to those asked of parents about what they did to cope, we queried the clinicians about their use of a variety of possible coping strategies (e.g., seeking help from others, utilizing inner resources, engaging in social action, and using drugs and alcohol). We also asked them to rate whether the various strategies made things better, made things worse, or had no effect.

As shown in Table 15.6, the most frequently used strategies involved seeking help from professionals or others, and clinicians felt that these made things better. Over 90% sought individual consultation from another professional for help with their cases; 62% sought group consultation; and 38% utilized psychotherapy for themselves. As one therapist said, consultation with other involved professionals was helpful "to obtain information, to validate or to challenge my own assumptions, to draw mutual support against the backlash."

The most often utilized source of nonprofessional help was friends, a resource employed by over 95% of the therapists. In addition, two-thirds utilized help from their spouses or partners. The pattern of turning to friends more frequently than to significant others for help in coping with child sexual abuse was also found among the mothers of the children, and is discussed in detail in Chapter 16. Although relationships with friends and significant others may be placed under stress by the trauma of treating the children, as reported earlier, these people still provide important and positive sources of support for the clinicians.

Among the strategies involving social action, it is interesting to note that almost all of the clinicians became involved in educating others about sexual abuse, and over two-thirds felt that this was personally

TABLE 15.6. Coping Strategies Used by Clinicians

Strategy	Percentage utilizing strategy	Percentage for whom use made things better
Seeking help from professionals		
Individual consultation	90.5	76.2
Group consultation	61.9	66.7
Therapy for self	38.1	33.3
Seeking help from a lawyer	33.3	28.6
Seeking help from the police	33.3	19.0
Seeking help from the clergy	19.0	19.0
Seeking help from a physician	19.0	14.3
Family therapy	9.5	4.8
Seeking help from another professional	4.8	0.0
Seeking help from others		
Seeking help from friends	95.2	61.8
Seeking help from spouse or partner	76.2	57.1
Support groups	57.1	57.1
Seeking help from other relatives	52.4	28.6
Seeking help from other people	4.8	4.8
Seeking help from inner resources		
Thinking about other things	57.1	33.3
Withdrawing from others	57.1	9.5
Prayer	28.6	23.8
Attempting to forget	28.6	4.8
Other inner resources	28.6	4.8
Meditation or yoga	19.0	14.3
Social action		
Educating other professionals	90.5	76.2
Public education	81.0	66.7
Advocacy	57.1	38.1
Working for legislative change	52.4	23.8
Active role in investigation	28.6	4.8
Involvement with media	14.3	4.8
Other social action	4.8	0.0
Miscellaneous resources		
Educating self about sexual abuse	85.7	61.9
Using humor	81.0	76.2
Using alcohol	52.4	33.3
Using aggression in general	23.8	9.5
Using aggression with significant others	14.3	0.0
Other miscellaneous resources	4.8	4.8
Using drugs	0.0	0.0

Note. n = 21; 0 = "not applicable"; 1 = "worse"; 2 = "neither"; 3 = "better."

helpful to them. Educating others may have served both to give the therapists a mastery experience and to decrease their sense of isolation and alienation from their colleagues. Similarly, educating themselves about sexual abuse was seen as helpful by the majority of clinicians utilizing it. In contrast, being actively involved in the investigation of the cases made things worse for most of the clinicians who participated in investigatory activities.

Although none of the clinicians reported the use of drugs, slightly over half utilized alcohol; 33% reported that alcohol use made things better, and none reported that it made things worse. Although this finding is somewhat puzzling, it may reflect social drinking, possibly among groups of clinicians, where a glass or two of wine may have facilitated the relaxation of constraints against using humor or self-disclosure in dealing with their own discomfort and with their reactions to the clients' fear and pain.

When asked in open-ended fashion what strategies were most helpful, the therapists generally listed a range of very specific ones. Support groups were seen as most helpful by 19%, and group consultation or professional supervision was most useful for 14%. These findings support the pivotal role of educative and interactive activities in facilitating the clinicians' management of stressors.

When asked why coping strategies were helpful, 50% of the clinicians noted validation and support, and 22% pointed to emotional release or expression of feelings. Another 17% listed help with keeping their perspective, and 11% noted information learned. The therapists were also asked about what types of help they wished had been available. Strikingly, 22% responded that they would have liked more information on ritualistic abuse, while another 22% would have liked to turn to someone more expert than they. At the time, there were no therapists experienced in treating children reporting ritualistic sexual abuse who could provide treatment guidelines.

We also asked open-ended questions of the therapists about positive and negative outcomes of their participation in treatment of these cases. The principal positive outcome was the development of valuable professional contacts, endorsed by 38% of the clinicians. The sense of efficacy and of capacity to be helpful in a difficult circumstance was mentioned by another 24%, and 14% found that their own personal insight and growth were the primary positive results. Particularly encouraging was a hopefulness about future positive outcomes; 19% of the clinicians talked about anticipating continued healing for those involved, and 14% foresaw a general benefit from the information made available to others as a result of these experiences.

The most negative outcome, mentioned by 29% of the clinicians, was feeling professionally discredited as a result of their participation in these highly controversial cases. For another 24%, the loss of trust in one's surrounding world was the most negative result. Overwork, stress, or distress was listed by 20% of the group as the most detrimental outcome. Concerns related to negative legal experiences or outcomes were also expressed.

The therapists' responses about what they would tell others facing a similar set of circumstances were wide-ranging. Here is a sample:

"*Don't* [get involved], or at least be prepared for a loss of credibility, professional respectability, personal well-being, financial security, even hope for survival and recovery of your own and possibly your clients' premorbid strengths."

"You have to be 'brave' and able to consider the 'incredible.' Treatment requires a high level of empathy and an ability to listen to very painful experiences without losing your objectivity. Focus on the patient's experience. Concern for 'justice' is a lost cause when the victim is a child. These children in particular need to gain a sense of security and stability again. Even if you don't personally feel that way [secure], you have to convey it to the children."

"In part, I would want to say caution about involvement at all; however, watching and being with the children's healing was *very* worthwhile and did in the long run compensate for the professional, personal, and social stress faced. . . . MEET WITH OTHERS who can guide you or validate you through this experience!"

CONCLUSION

In summary, it is clear that work with child victims reporting sexual and ritualistic abuse had significant effects on their therapists. They struggled with issues of believing unbelievable stories of terror, abuse, and degradation. They shared affective states that the children and parents were experiencing. Fully 77.8% of the therapists met diagnostic criteria for PTSD at the peak of their involvement, with the most prominent features being recurrent recollections of the children's accounts of the abuse, detachment, alienation, and hypervigilance. They also experienced a variety of distressing mood and attention disruptions, as well as stress in their personal relationships. As a group, the clinicians involved fit very closely McCann and Pearlman's (1990) descriptions of "vicarious traumatization." Vicarious traumatization is seen as a normal reaction to the extremely stressful work with victims, just as PTSD is viewed as a normal reaction to an abnormal event.

The therapists in our sample coped by consulting with other professionals; meeting in support groups; finding out more information about sexual and ritualistic abuse and sharing it with others; and seeking help and support from important others in their lives. Many of the coping strategies noted by the therapists were also mentioned by McCann and Pearlman (1990), who encouraged support groups for therapists, and stressed the importance of balancing professional and personal lives.

Overall, the outcomes for the therapists were quite mixed. Although they felt that they had made valuable professional contacts, had helped children and families in very difficult circumstances, and had grown personally and professionally, there were also negative consequences. The most common negative outcomes were feeling professionally discredited and losing basic trust in the world as a safe and just place. The shifts in cognitive schemas about the world and the affective impact of their experiences are expected to have long-lasting consequences for the therapists.

PART V

Understanding the Effects: Coping Patterns and Mediators

CHAPTER 16

PARENTAL REACTIONS AND COPING PATTERNS

Jane McCord

T HE SEXUAL ABUSE OF A CHILD affects not only the child, but the family of that child as well. Parents, siblings, and extended family members are also traumatized by the discovery that a child has been victimized. Kelley (1990) found that parents of children who were sexually abused in preschools experienced psychological distress themselves, with elevations in depression, interpersonal sensitivity, hostility, paranoia, and anxiety. Many of these parents were themselves suffering from post-traumatic stress disorder. This chapter focuses on the reactions and coping strategies of a group of parents whose young children reported ritualistic sexual abuse in several different preschools (the RSA children). The RSA parents' reactions and strategies are compared with those of parents whose children reported sexual abuse, but not ritualistic abuse, in their preschool, (the SA children).

Two instruments that were created for this project assessed parents' responses to their children's abuse. The first instrument, the Therapist's Rating of Parental Reaction to Sexual Abuse (TRPRSA), was a 16-item questionnaire. Each item was rated by the therapist on a scale from 0 ("not at all") to 3 ("a great amount"). The scale was filled out on each child's mother and father separately; it was completed on 55 RSA couples and 11 SA couples. The items covered parental beliefs about the occurrence of abuse, attributions of blame, support for the child, negative reactions to the child, and personal distress and coping seen in the parents.

The second instrument, Coping with Sexual Abuse (CSA), was a 31-item questionnaire that was completed by each child's mother and father separately. These items assessed how the parents saw themselves as reacting to their child's report of molestation, and what resources they drew upon in their attempt to cope with the reported victimization. The parents were asked whether or not they utilized the resource listed, and if so to rate on a scale of 1 to 3 whether it made things worse, neither helped nor hurt, or made things better. Fifty-three mothers and 34 fathers from the RSA group, and 10 mothers and 3 fathers from the SA group, completed this instrument. Because of the small number of SA fathers who completed the CSA, this sample was not used in the analysis.

The findings from these two instruments are presented here in seven sections. The first one discusses parents' cognitive responses to the allegations that their children had been molested. In particular, beliefs about the occurrence of the abuse and attributions of responsibility are examined. Second, parents' reaction to the children in terms of support are assessed. The third section focuses on the personal reactions of the parents themselves upon being informed of the possible abuse of their children. The fourth section looks at various types of coping strategies used by these parents. The fifth section of the chapter looks at professional resources that these parents utilized in their attempt to cope with the reported victimization of their children. The sixth section examines utilization of and response to nonprofessional resources, and the final section looks at how these parents used prosocial action as a result of their children's reports of victimization.

COGNITIVE RESPONSES TO THE ALLEGED ABUSE OF THE CHILDREN

First, we looked at parents' reactions to the sexual abuse allegations in terms of their beliefs about what had happened and how they made sense of who was responsible. Tables 16.1 and 16.2 list the TRPRSA statements, the level at which each statement was characteristic of the parents, and whether any statistically significant differences between the mothers and the fathers. As shown in Tables 16.1 and 16.2, items 1 and 2, the therapists retrospectively rated the RSA mothers and fathers and the SA mothers and fathers in terms of their level of belief about the alleged abuse within the first few weeks of therapy. Both RSA and SA mothers and the RSA fathers from these two samples were seen as believing quite strongly that the abuse had indeed occurred, with very little denial of the occurrence of the abuse. The SA fathers were seen as somewhat more skeptical about what had happened to their children.

TABLE 16.1. TRPSA Results: RSA Full Sample (n = 55 Couples)

Item	Level characteristic of parents[a]	Significant differences between parents
1. Believed child was abused		
Mothers	High	Mothers > fathers
Fathers	High	
2. Believed child's report		
Mothers	High	Mothers > fathers
Fathers	High	
3. Denied abuse occurred		
Mothers	Low	Fathers > Mothers
Fathers	Low	
4. Blamed child for abuse		
Mothers	Low	No difference
Fathers	Low	
5. Blamed self for abuse		
Mothers	Moderate	Mothers > fathers
Fathers	Low	
6. Blamed offender for abuse		
Mothers	High	Mothers > fathers
Fathers	High	
7. Showed positive feelings for child		
Mothers	High	Mothers > fathers
Fathers	High	
8. Appropriately concerned for child's well-being		
Mothers	High	Mothers > fathers
Fathers	High	
9. Excessively interrogated child		
Mothers	Low	Mothers > fathers
Fathers	Low	
10. Overly protective of child		
Mothers	Moderate	Mothers > fathers
Fathers	Low	
11. Angry, hostile, or punitive toward child		
Mothers	Low	No difference
Fathers	Low	
12. Overly concerned for impact on own life		
Mothers	Low	No difference
Fathers	Low	
13. Depressed as a reaction to the abuse		
Mothers	High	Mothers > fathers
Fathers	Moderate	
14. Minimized significance of the event		
Mothers	Low	Fathers > Mothers
Fathers	Moderate	
15. Denied abuse-related feelings		
Mothers	Moderate	Fathers > Mothers
Fathers	Moderate	
16. Increased use of drugs or alcohol		
Mothers	Low	Fathers > Mothers
Fathers	Moderate	

[a]Scores ranged from 0 to 3. "Low" ranged from 0 to 0.9. "Moderate" ranged from 1.0 to 1.9. "High" ranged from 2.0 to 3.

TABLE 16.2. TRPRSA Results: SA Full Sample (n = 11 Couples)

Item	Level characteristic of parents[a]	Significant differences between parents
1. Believed child was abused		
Mothers	High	Mothers > fathers
Fathers	Moderate	
2. Believed child's report of abuse		
Mothers	High	Mothers > fathers
Fathers	Moderate	
3. Denied abuse occurred		
Mothers	Low	No difference
Fathers	Low	
4. Blamed child for abuse		
Mothers	Moderate	No difference
Fathers	Low	
5. Blamed self for abuse		
Mothers	High	Mothers > fathers
Fathers	Low	
6. Blamed offender for abuse		
Mothers	High	No difference
Fathers	High	
7. Showed positive feelings for child		
Mothers	High	Mothers > fathers
Fathers	Moderate	
8. Appropriately concerned for child's well-being		
Mothers	High	Mothers > fathers
Fathers	Moderate	
9. Excessively interrogated child		
Mothers	Low	No difference
Fathers	Low	
10. Overly protective of child		
Mothers	High	Mothers > fathers
Fathers	Low	
11. Angry, hostile, or punitive toward child		
Mothers	Low	No difference
Fathers	Low	
12. Overly concerned for impact of abuse on own life		
Mothers	Low	Mothers > fathers
Fathers	Low	
13. Depressed as a reaction to the abuse		
Mothers	High	Mothers > fathers
Fathers	Low	
14. Minimized significance of event		
Mothers	Low	Fathers > mothers
Fathers	High	
15. Denied abuse related feelings		
Mothers	Moderate	No difference
Fathers	High	
16. Increased use of drugs or alcohol		
Mothers	Low	No difference
Fathers	Low	

[a]Total scores ranged from 0 to 3. "Low ranged" from 0 to .9. "Moderate" ranged from 1.0 to 1.9. "High" ranged from 2.0 to 3.

However, there was a significant difference between the mothers and fathers on level of belief for both groups, with the mothers showing a higher degree of belief. This may indicate that fathers tend to be more skeptical and to expect a higher "burden of proof," and that mothers are more likely to take things at face value. Many of the parents acknowledged that this did happen in their families and that it became a cause of conflict between the parents when the allegations began to emerge.

Other parental reactions that have ramifications for children reporting abuse and their families are parental attributions of blame. These parents searched for reasons why this might have happened to their children, and, in an attempt to make sense of the tragedy, looked for explanations in terms of who was responsible and how the reported abuse could have been prevented. As indicated in Tables 16.1 and 16.2, items 4–6, the therapists thought that both parents attributed blame to the alleged offenders and almost never attributed any responsibility to the children. This, of course, seems understandable, since the reported perpetrators were teachers outside the family unit. Even though both parents attributed much blame to the alleged offenders, in the RSA sample the mothers were still significantly more likely to blame these individuals than were the fathers. Interestingly, mothers from both samples were significantly more likely to place part of the responsibility on themselves for the alleged abuse of their children than were the fathers. Mothers tended to place moderate levels of blame on themselves; whereas the fathers seldom felt any responsibility for what might have happened to their children.

These findings may have reflected the fact that the mothers in this sample were the parents primarily responsible for child care, as well as in general that mothers often see themselves as responsible for child rearing. Several of these mothers expressed concerns that they should have known that something was happening to their children; whereas the fathers seemed to feel less responsible for the children. As one mother stated, "I feel a lot of guilt. I think so much more than my husband, because he was working and it was my idea to put them in school." It would appear that gender stereotypes and expectations may play a role in how mothers and fathers react to trauma to their children.

PARENTAL SUPPORT FOR THE CHILDREN

A significant factor in the recovery of a victim of reported sexual abuse is the supportive reaction of the family. As can be seen in Tables 16.1 and 16.2, items 7 and 8, the therapists saw both mothers and fathers in the RSA sample as being highly supportive of their children. However, even within this high level of support, mothers were seen as significantly more supportive than were fathers. The SA mothers were also seen as supportive of their children, but the fathers were seen as less supportive. There was also a significant difference between mothers and fathers on level of support.

These findings may be indicative of the type of role that mothers have with their children. Mothers may tend to be more unconditional in their support for children than are fathers. Alternatively, it may be more difficult for men to accept the reported victimization of their children than it is for women.

As seen from item 10, the theme of more intense involvement of mothers with the children was also reflected in a wide difference between mothers and fathers in both samples on being overly protective of their children after the disclosure. Although fathers seldom reacted to the children in this way, mothers were rated as demonstrating low to moderate levels of such behavior in the RSA sample and moderate to high levels of such behavior in the SA sample. It may be that in their attempt to be supportive and protective, mothers may have a tendency to inhibit developmentally appropriate risk taking with their children who have reported abuse.

Neither mothers nor fathers were seen as acting in nonsupportive ways, such as blaming the child (item 4), excessively interrogating the child (item 9), or acting in angry ways toward the child (item 11). On these seldom-reported negative reactions, there were no significant differences between mothers and fathers except for RSA mothers, who were seen as more likely to question their children about what had happened at the preschool. This behavior on the part of the mothers seemed to be more closely related to their need to know what had happened to the children than to any disbelief that the abuse had occurred.

EMOTIONAL REACTIONS TO THE CHILDREN'S REPORTS OF ABUSE

Parents would certainly be expected to have strong emotional reactions to reports that their children have been abused. These emotions might run the gamut from fear, to despair, to rage. Both the TRPRSA and the CSA included items to assess some of these parental reactions.

We wondered to what extent the parents focused on themselves after their children disclosed abuse. As can be seen in item 12 in Tables 16.1 and 16.2, neither the RSA mothers nor any of the fathers were seen as demonstrating undue concern about the impact of their children's reported victimization on their own lives. The SA mothers, however, showed moderate levels of such concern and were significantly more concerned about the impact on themselves than were the SA fathers.

As indicated in item 13 in Tables 16.1 and 16.2, mothers in both samples were seen as experiencing moderate levels of depression, and their scores were significantly higher than were the fathers' scores. As one mother recalled, "I remember many times just throwing my arms around my husband and just crying because I can't think about it. You know, it's too hard to think about. And so we'd just sit there and hold each other." It appears that mothers may be particularly vulnerable to depression when children report abuse. This may also be related to the previously discussed issue of mothers' feeling more responsible for what happens to their children and thus more devastated in the aftermath of alleged abuse. In addition, women are more likely in general to react to stress with depression than are men.

As indicated in Tables 16.3 and 16.4, a set of items from the parent-endorsed instrument, the CSA, asked about the increased use of aggression by parents after their children's disclosures of abuse. A small percentage of the RSA mothers and fathers admitted that they had used aggression on a spouse or on others. This was also true of a few of the SA mothers. When asked whether they thought that such behavior had made things worse or better, they clearly indicated that aggression had made things worse.

In general, it would appear that depression and anger were experienced by these parents; of particular concern appears to be maternal risk of depression. From 10% to 21% of the parents admitted to the use of violence against others. When violence was resorted to, the aggressors felt that it certainly made things worse.

PARENTAL COPING STRATEGIES

Just as parents had different emotional responses to the abuse, they also dealt with the trauma in different ways. In this section, these various ways of coping with a child's abuse and the resources utilized by these parents will be examined.

Denial

Traditional ways of attempting to deal with reports of sexual abuse have included such defense mechanisms as denial and minimization. As indicated in Tables 16.1 and 16.2, items 14 and 15, the therapists were asked whether they thought the parents utilized such defenses. Very few

TABLE 16.3. CSA Results: RSA Full Sample (Mothers *n* = 53; Fathers *n* = 34)

Item	Percentage utilizing	Most frequent effect
1. Aggression on spouse		
Mothers	13	Made worse
Fathers	18	Made worse
2. Aggression on others		
Mothers	19	Made worse
Fathers	21	Made worse
3. Attempting to forget		
Mothers	21	No change
Fathers	35	No change
4. Thinking of other things		
Mothers	62	No change
Fathers	59	No change
5. Withdrawing from others		
Mothers	47	No change
Fathers	29	No change
6. Prayer		
Mothers	63	Made better
Fathers	52	Made better
7. Alcohol use		
Mothers	26	No change
Fathers	21	No change
8. Drug use		
Mothers	9	No change
Fathers	6	Made worse
9. Educating self about sexual abuse		
Mothers	85	Made better
Fathers	85	Made better
10. Use of humor		
Mothers	64	Made better
Fathers	44	No change
11. Diagnostic interview for child		
Mothers	95	Made better
Fathers	85	Made better
12. Psychotherapy for child		
Mothers	98	Made better
Fathers	97	Made better
13. Psychotherapy for self		
Mothers	68	Made better
Fathers	38	Made better
14. Family therapy		
Mothers	43	Made better
Fathers	55	Made better
15. Support groups		
Mothers	70	Made better
Fathers	65	Made better
16. Physicians		
Mothers	51	Made better
Fathers	85	Made better

TABLE 16.3. (*cont.*)

Item	Percentage utilizing	Most frequent effect
17. Lawyers		
Mothers	46	No change
Fathers	32	Slightly better
18. Police		
Mothers	70	No change
Fathers	59	No change
19. Clergy		
Mothers	39	Made better
Fathers	27	Made better
20. Seeking help from spouse/partner		
Mothers	82	Made better
Fathers	94	Made better
21. Seeking help from other relatives		
Mothers	74	Made better
Fathers	65	Made better
22. Seeking help from friends		
Mothers	91	Made better
Fathers	77	Made better
23. Active role in investigating abuse		
Mothers	50	Made better
Fathers	50	Made better
24. Involvement with media		
Mothers	37	No change
Fathers	38	No change
25. Advocacy programs		
Mothers	52	Made better
Fathers	53	Made better
26. Legislative change		
Mothers	52	Made better
Fathers	60	Made better
27. Public education		
Mothers	45	Made better
Fathers	35	Made better

mothers from either sample utilized these coping strategies, whereas fathers demonstrated moderate to high levels of denial and minimization. In both the RSA and the SA samples, fathers were seen as more likely to minimize the significance of the reported abuse than were mothers. As one of the fathers stated, "I don't know if it's normal or abnormal, but I just wanted to pretend that it didn't happen." This reaction also seemed characteristic of how mothers and fathers dealt with abuse-related feelings: Fathers were generally more likely than the mothers to put aside such feelings.

These same ideas were assessed on the parents' questionnaire, the CSA, in a somewhat different way. As indicated in Tables 16.3 and 16.4, items 3 and 4, parents were asked whether they attempted to forget about

TABLE 16.4. CSA Results: SA Mothers (n = 10)

Item	Percent utilized	Most frequent effect
1. Aggression on spouse	10	No change
2. Aggression on others	10	No change
3. Attempting to forget	60	No change
4. Thinking of other things	50	No change
5. Withdrawing from others	30	Made worse
6. Prayer	60	Made better
7. Alcohol use	10	No change
8. Drug use	10	Made worse
9. Educating self about sexual abuse	90	Made better
10. Use of humor	40	Made better
11. Diagnostic interview for child	90	Made better
12. Psychotherapy for child	100	Made better
13. Psychotherapy for self	80	Made better
14. Family therapy	70	Made better
15. Support groups	70	Made better
16. Physicians	20	Made better
17. Lawyers	80	Made better
18. Police	60	Made better
19. Clergy	10	Made better
20. Seeking help from spouse/partner	50	Made better
21. Seeking help from other relatives	70	Made better
22. Seeking help from friends	60	Made better
23. Active role in investigating abuse allegations	30	Made better
24. Involvement with media	20	Somewhat worse
25. Advocacy programs	40	Made better
26. Legislative change	0	Not utilized
27. Public education	30	Made better

the reported abuse and tried thinking of other things. From one-fourth to nearly two-thirds admitted that they had tried to get their minds off the abuse reports, but both mothers and fathers generally had not found this style particularly effective.

Withdrawing

We also asked these parents whether, in their attempt to cope with their children's reports of abuse, they had withdrawn from others. As seen in Tables 16.3 and 16.4, item 5, a moderate number of these parents stated that they had. All of the SA mothers felt that this had made things worse; the RSA parents had more mixed feelings about withdrawal, with some stating that it had not made things either better or worse. In general, it would appear that this was not an effective way of dealing with the trauma.

Prayer

We wanted to know whether religious practices had been helpful to the parents. As indicated in Tables 16.3 and 16.4, item 6, over half of all the parents had prayed during the time that they were dealing with their children's abuse disclosures. This was clearly seen as helpful with most of those who used prayer seeing it as making things better.

Substance Abuse

Substance abuse was also of concern to us in looking at how parents coped with this tragedy. As indicated in Tables 16.3 and 16.4, items 7 and 8, approximately one-fourth of the RSA parents admitted to using alcohol. This was true of 10% of the SA mothers. Those who drank generally felt that it made things worse or did not change things. Few individuals endorsed the use of other drugs. The therapists were also asked on the TRPRSA about the families' increased use of drugs or alcohol. As item 16 on Tables 16.1 and 16.2 indicates, the therapists did not see this as a major problem, but did indicate that this was more of a problem among the fathers than among the mothers. Certainly in times of crisis, families are at risk for alcohol or other substance abuse. It is difficult to determine from the data the extent to which this was actually a problem for these families. These may have been items that respondents were particularly hesitant to endorse on a questionnaire or to talk about with a therapist.

Miscellaneous Coping Strategies

Two other ways of getting through this difficult period in these parents' lives were their quest for more knowledge about child sexual abuse and their sense of humor. These two items were included on the CSA and are listed in Tables 16.3 and 16.4, items 9 and 10.

When asked about educating themselves on the subject of the abuse, 85% of the RSA parents and 90% of the SA mothers said that they had sought additional information on the subject and that it had helped them feel better. According to one father, "We pretty much stayed current on the reading, what's going on, the articles." It seemed that knowledge, even when unpleasant, gave them an increased sense of control. These findings on the significance of increasing a parent's understanding of sexual abuse are particularly significant for the treatment of families such as these.

On the second item, dealing with the use of humor, the differential response to the question between the men and women was somewhat surprising. About half of all of the parents stated that they had used humor as a way of coping. Of those who endorsed this item, over twice as many mothers as fathers felt that humor had made them feel better. Perhaps by injecting some levity into a tragic situation, these mothers were able to experience some relief.

RESPONSE TO PROFESSIONAL RESOURCES AND SERVICES

In their attempt to get through this traumatic situation, the families who were involved came into contact with and utilized a wide range of professional services. The initial data on this subject were collected by means of the CSA in 1986–1987. Tables 16.3 and 16.4 indicate which services were utilized by these families and how effective their contacts with professionals were in helping them cope with the reported abuse of their children.

Psychotherapy Services

Ninety-eight percent of the children participating in this project were involved in some type of psychotherapy as a result of the children's abuse disclosures. The parents overwhelmingly thought that therapy for the children had made things better. Two-thirds of the RSA mothers and 80% of the SA mothers had also sought individual therapy for themselves, with almost all of them feeling that it had helped. According to one mother, [Therapists] have really held the parents together. . . . They really helped in the healing process, for the kids and for the parents." The RSA fathers were less likely to seek therapy for themselves, with about one-third of the men being involved in individual therapy. They were also less likely to have experienced the therapy as beneficial for themselves, with most stating that it made things better but one-third stating that it did not change things either way. Some of the men seemed to put less faith in the therapeutic process. Here is how one father expressed his feelings:

> The therapists have been very nice people. I'm not a big believer in therapy to begin with. I'm even a little more skeptical of abuse situations because I think . . . there isn't a great deal of expertise. . . . I'm still very skeptical as to how effective it is.

Another form of therapy utilized by these families was conjoint family therapy, with more than half of the RSA sample and the SA mothers participating in this. About three-fourths of the parents felt that it had been helpful. Parent support groups also became a vital resource for some of parents. Some were facilitated by professionals and some were not. For some parents, these groups increased their anxiety; but for others, however, a sense of belonging and the feeling of being with others who truly understood them were available through these groups.

In addition to ongoing therapy, almost all of the participants in the project had obtained diagnostic interviews for their children during the early phases of the investigation of the molestation charges against the preschools. These interviews were generally seen as positive.

In general, the parents saw psychotherapy as a particularly beneficial form of help. Over half of these families participated in some form of therapy, and they generally felt that it had definitely helped them get through this difficult period in their lives. A trend emerged indicating that mothers were more likely than fathers to see psychotherapy as beneficial.

Physicians

These families also came into contact with physicians because many of the children had medical examinations. As indicated in Tables 16.3 and 16.4, item 16, the parents' utilization of physicians varied from a minority of the SA mothers to most of the RSA parents. They generally found this to be helpful, although many felt neutral about the benefits of these services.Frustration was frequently expressed over many physicians' lack of training in diagnosing genital trauma. Those who used physicians specializing in genital exams generally reported positive experiences.

Lawyers

Slightly under half of the RSA families and most of the SA mothers utilized the services of professionals in the legal field. Although some of the RSA parents had contacted attorneys regarding civil suits, most of these parents were probably referring to their contact with deputies from the district attorney's office who were investigating and/or prosecuting the cases. Their feelings about these professionals were quite mixed. Fewer than half stated that their involvement with lawyers had made things better. This was different for the SA mothers; almost all of them reported positive experiences with the legal profession. This probably stems from the fact that the SA case did not involve a trial and ended with the imprisonment of the sole perpetrator and a successful civil suit.

Police

The police were also involved with these families in the initial phases of the investigation. Tables 16.3 and 16.4, item 18, indicate the feelings of the two groups. Many of the RSA parents felt that the police did not have the necessary expertise to investigate such a case. This was one mother's experience:

> I had several contacts with [the police]. We sent to the police station and . . . they came over to our house because [child's name] was very young. And so he was afraid of them. The couple of times that we went to the police station, we had gone after school and he was very tired and he would just pass out. So they didn't get anything out of him, and when they came to our house he wouldn't talk with them either. So it wasn't a very good experience.

The SA experience was more positive and probably reflects the successful outcome (from the parents' point of view) of the case.

Clergy

The final group of professionals we asked about (listed in Tables 16.3 and 16.4, item 19) was the clergy. Turning to spiritual or religious resources would certainly be expected in trying times for these families. About a third of the RSA families stated that they had utilized the services of the clergy during this time in their lives. Over half of them felt that this contact had helped them get through, but there were almost as many of these parents who did not feel that they had been helped by their religious leader. According to one father, "A network of parents went to the 5 o'clock mass . . . and that was kind of the mass where the parents kind of huddled for support." Another mother reported a different experience: Her pastor advised her to switch therapists for her child, and the family ended up changing churches. Only one SA mother had sought the help of the clergy.

When we compared all of the professionals whose services these parents utilized, therapists were the most frequently used. Next in descending frequency of use were the police, physicians, lawyers, and the clergy. Both mothers and fathers believed that therapy was the most beneficial of the services that they received from professionals. Physicians and the clergy were seen as generally helpful. The police and lawyers were rated as the least helpful, especially by the RSA fathers.

RESPONSE TO NONPROFESSIONAL RESOURCES

Another form of parental coping investigated was the parents' seeking help from nonprofessional others. Items 20–21 from the CSA, listed in Tables 16.3 and 16.4, assessed some of these relationships.

Parents were very likely to turn to spouses or partners during this time, and this was generally seen as helpful. Many of the couples talked of how this crisis brought them closer together. Others, although a minority, found that existing problems were exacerbated by the experience.

Turning to friends was also seen as a major source of comfort for these families. But these friendships seemed to consist primarily of other families who were also involved in the allegations of abuse. As one mother stated,

> . . . Friends that I had before this happened . . . I have to say that I'm not very close with anymore. It's like there's a part of my life that I've not really been able to share totally with them, and it makes you feel isolated from them.

Another mother expressed the same experience:

> I can talk most about it with this core group of moms who have gone through it. Other friends have been, I think, as supportive as they know how to be. There have been times from each of them where I think they've seen things differently. And I've kind of felt a little sense of loss.

It would seem that for these parents, having friends who shared the same experience was particularly significant.

An interesting trend emerged between mothers and fathers on how they utilized friends and spouses. The mothers in both groups were slightly more likely to turn to friends than to spouses. This, however, may have reflected the fact that some of the mothers who participated in the study were single during this time. The fathers were more likely to turn to wives than to friends. The RSA fathers were more likely to find their wives helpful than the RSA mothers were able to find their husbands helpful. Both found friends equally helpful. This may reflect somewhat different relationships between men and women, in that wives may tend to have closer friendships outside the family than do husbands.

Other relatives were relied upon for support somewhat less often. These parents generally thought that their extended families were supportive, but they also reported mixed feelings and reactions from their relatives. Only the SA mothers reported that other relatives were almost always supportive. Reactions from these relatives such as discomfort, minimizing the significance of the reported victimization, or disbelief were reported by the RSA group. Some parents may have had preexisting conflictual relationships with certain relatives, and may thus have been more hesitant to confide in them. Others felt that grandparents or their siblings who did not live in the area would just not understand. One father described his feelings: "I mean, both my in-laws and my parents are probably shocked by it. And we did inform them. But I think that it's not something that's ever come up for discussion after that." A mother said,

... My mother and my stepfather ... they had a real hard time believing it. So it's really affected my relationship with them. ... I grew up in a home where you were not allowed to express a lot of your feelings. ... When it came to sharing it with my parents, they just have not wanted to hear it.

SOCIAL ACTION

Between one-third and one-half of the participants in this study became actively involved in social causes related to child sexual abuse. Tables 16.3 and 16.4 list items from the CSA related to social action (items 23–27). In the RSA sample, those who became involved with advocacy programs were the most satisfied with the results overall. These mothers and fathers differed on their satisfaction with becoming involved in promoting legislative change and public education about child abuse: Mothers found involvement in legislative change more productive, and fathers were more satisfied with their participation in public education. The RSA parents were particularly active in this area. According to one RSA mother, "I think becoming active, writing letters, doing speeches, stuff like that, I think gives you a sense of doingness that's real important."

A lesser percentage of the SA mothers participated in these activities, but public education, advocacy for abused children, and taking an active role in investigating the abuse were felt to be beneficial by those mothers who did participate.

In general, these activities seem to be a constructive way of working through feelings of helplessness and making a difference in the world. Parents frequently spoke of the sense of efficacy and control that came with active involvement in this cause.

Involvement with the mass media was generally seen as a less positive experience. These parents' participation generally consisted of granting interviews to television or newspapers or of writing letters. None of the SA mothers and only a third of the RSA parents found it helpful, but responses were mixed. One RSA mother stated, "Our experience with the media has been real good. CNN did a special with us before [the school] closed, and even though it was real hard to trust, it was handled very well." A different experience was recounted by another mother "[A relative] did [an interview that was shown on] 60 Minutes, and they [the interviewers] were just so bad. . . ." Many of these parents were also disillusioned by how their cases were reflected in the media and were left with negative feelings about their involvement.

SUMMARY

This chapter has examined the reactions of a group of parents whose children were allegedly abused at several preschools. The parents' responses to their children's reports of extrafamilial child sexual abuse differed from those often seen among parents in intrafamilial sexual abuse cases. The parents clearly believed what their children said about being abused and were highly supportive of them. They did not see their children as responsible in any way for what the children reported. However, mothers had a tendency to see themselves as responsible in some way for letting this happen to their children.

Trends emerged that indicated differences between mothers and fathers in terms of their emotional reactions and coping strategies with regard to their children's reported victimization. A small percentage of both mothers and fathers admitted to using aggression on their mates or others. Mothers tended to become more depressed than did fathers, whereas fathers were seen as more likely to deny feelings about the alleged abuse and to minimize its significance.

These parents also drew upon many different resources during this difficult period in their lives. Psychotherapy was seen as the most helpful professional service that the families received, although mothers tended to utilize it more often and to find it more beneficial than did fathers. Physicians and the clergy were also found to be helpful, and those who utilized spiritual resources within themselves such as prayer or meditation found these helpful as well.

Spouses and friends were extremely important during this time for both mothers and fathers. However, mothers found friends somewhat more supportive than their husbands, whereas fathers found their wives to be their best support. Other relatives were not found to be as helpful as were nuclear family members and close friends.

These families also participated in many social causes, in the interest of increasing awareness about child sexual abuse and bringing about changes to help child victims. These parents felt generally effective in their efforts with advocacy programs, involvement in legislative change, and public education, but were less satisfied with their efforts in obtaining the type of media coverage that they sought.

In conclusion, it appears that parents as well as children are affected by the children's victimization; that men and women may react differently to trauma; and that services and interventions may need to take these differences into account.

MEDIATORS OF EFFECTS ON CHILDREN
What Enhances Optimal Functioning and Promotes Healing?

Jill Waterman
Robert J. Kelly

GIVEN THE MANY SIGNIFICANT EFFECTS of reported ritualistic sexual abuse in preschools that the preceding chapters have documented, the questions of what factors mediate against the negative effects of such trauma and what processes help promote healing become paramount. Because of the small number of children in the group reporting sexual abuse only (SA), we concentrated on examining the group reporting ritualistic sexual abuse (RSA), where at least partial information was available for 82 children. Five categories of possible mediators were examined:

1. Demographic factors
2. Abuse characteristics
3. Treatment characteristics
4. Family factors (family life stressors, parental coping styles, and children's perceptions of their parents)
5. Parent action factors

Within each category, potential mediators were correlated with major outcome variables from parent, child, and therapist ratings. When many variables within a category were significantly correlated with the effects variables, multiple regression was conducted to pull out those mediators with the strongest effects in that category. These analyses were necessary mainly in sorting out the effects of various family variables. Then the strongest predictors in each category were put into overall multiple-regression equations to give the clearest picture of what contributed to a particular outcome measure. The effects measures examined were the following:

1. *Parent measures*: Child Behavior Checklist (CBCL), Louisville Fear Survey. (Maternal ratings were utilized because more questionnaires were obtained from mothers than from fathers.)
2. *Therapist measure*: Children's Global Assessment Scale (CGAS; rated at therapy termination, or currently if a child was still in therapy.)
3. *Child measures*: Age-appropriate Harter self-concept scales (mean self-worth scores), Draw-A-Person (DAP; significant emotional indicators score).

In addition, analyses of mediators were also carried out for the repeat CBCL for the 40 RSA children whose parents participated in follow-up 5 years after initial abuse disclosure. These results are discussed later in this chapter.

MEDIATORS OF SHORT-TERM OUTCOME

Demographic Factors

Because all families in the RSA group came from the same geographic area, the South Bay region of Los Angeles, there was not very much variability in some of the demographic characteristics examined. For example, parents were overwhelmingly white, generally upper-middle-class, and mostly married. The demographic factors examined were (1) child's sex; (2) socioeconomic status; (3) child's age; (4) child's religion; (5) parents' marital status at time of initial testing, 2 to 3 years after disclosure; (6) Full Scale deviation quotient (DQ, from the Wechsler Intelligence Scale for Children—Revised [WISC-R]); (7) Verbal DQ (from the WISC-R). The reader is referred to Chapters 3 and 8 for means and ranges for each of these factors in the RSA group.

Possibly partially because there was so little variation, few of the demographic variables were related to effects on the children. Socioeconomic status, child age, and developmental scores were unrelated to any of the effects variables studied. Girls tended to attain higher global functioning scores on the CGAS, as rated by therapists, than boys ($r = .24$, $p = .05$). Otherwise, boys and girls did not differ significantly on any of the outcome variables examined. Married mothers tended to rate their children as showing fewer behavior problems on the CBCL than did divorced or separated mothers ($r = .26$, $p = .03$).

Abuse Characteristics

Similar to what is reported above for demographic factors, there was little variability in the abuse experiences reported by the RSA children. The factors examined in this category were as follows:

1. Total Sexual Abuse Grid score—the sum of the five categories (listed below) rated by therapists from children's disclosures.
2. Category 1—less intrusive sexual acts.
3. Category 2—intrusive sexual acts.
4. Category 3—highly intrusive sexual acts.
5. Category 4—terrorizing acts.
6. Category 5—ritualistic acts.
7. Length of time since attendance at preschool where abuse was reported.
8. Number of months of attendance at preschool where abuse was reported.

Probably because of the lack of variability, the Sexual Abuse Grid scores were unrelated to most of the effects variables. The exception was for the Louisville Fear Survey, where children rated as more fearful by their parents had higher total Sexual Abuse Grid scores ($r = .35$, $p = .003$), and specifically reported more terrorizing acts ($r = .28$, $p = .03$) and more ritualistic acts ($r = .39$, $p = .001$). It makes sense that children who reported more terrorizing and more ritualistic acts would be more fearful, especially given the children's fears that they or their parents would be killed if they ever disclosed the abuse.

Treatment Characteristics

Although recruitment letters were initially sent to parents of all children who had initial diagnostic evaluations, whether or not they sought psychotherapy, the children in the final RSA sample had all participated in psychotherapy for at least some time. As a result, we were not able to compare the effects on children who received psychotherapy with those who did not. Therefore, the analyses on treatment variables also suffered from the lack of variability discussed above in connection with other factors. The variables we were able to examine were the following:

1. Total number of weeks child was in psychotherapy.
2. Number of family sessions.
3. Number of treatment modalities in which parents participated.

The findings that emerged seemed to reveal that children and parents who were experiencing more distress received longer psychotherapy and more types of psychotherapy—certainly not a startling conclusion. Children who were in psychotherapy longer showed more emotional distress indicators in their DAP drawings ($r = .27$, $p = .02$). Also, the higher the maternal rating of behavior problems on the CBCL, the more treatment modalities the parents had participated in. These findings seem to reflect that more severe symptomatology requires longer treatment.

Family Factors

The previous clinical and empirical literature (e.g., Summit, 1983; Browne & Finkelhor, 1986; Gomes-Schwartz, Horowitz, & Cardarelli, 1990) has shown that family response to sexual abuse of a child is extremely important in determining the outcome for the child. In the current study, family variables certainly mediated effects of the reported ritualistic sexual abuse to a much greater degree than any other category of variable scrutinized. The family factors examined were as follows:

1. *Family life stress.* Maternal and paternal ratings on the Family Inventory of Life Events (FILE) were examined.
2. *Parental coping styles.* Three different measures were utilized here, two obtained from parents and one from therapists. Maternal and paternal ratings on the Family Adaptability and Cohesion Evaluation Scales (FACES-III) and on the Family Crisis-Oriented Personal Evaluation Scales (F-COPES) were used. As another source of examining parental coping patterns, therapist ratings on a nonstandardized instrument developed for this project, Therapist Ratings of Parental Reaction to Sexual Abuse, was also used, with four factors examined: (a) parental belief of child (e.g., believed child's report of abuse, minimized significance of event); (b) support of child (e.g., showed positive feelings for child); (c) lack of support of child (e.g., blamed child, excessively interrogated child); (d) parental personal distress (e.g., depression, use of drugs or alcohol).

3. *Children's perceptions of their parents.* Children rated each parent on the Parent Perception Inventory (PPI), on which children can report the degree to which they perceive their mothers and their fathers as responding to them in a number of specific positive (e.g., comforting, praising, playing with them) and negative ways (e.g., nag, yell, criticize, hit them).

Because all of these family measures correlated significantly with many of the effects measures examined, we carried out multiple-regression analyses were carried out to further clarify the relationships.

Overall Behavior Problems

When we examined the effects of family factors on child symptomatology as rated by mothers on the CBCL, the most powerful predictors were therapist ratings of maternal supportiveness 'to the child in the aftermath of abuse disclosure and maternal ratings of total family life stress, as shown in Table 17.1. These two variables accounted for 39% of the variance in maternal Total Behavior Problems score on the CBCL. Specifically, mothers reported that children had more behavior problems if the mothers were relatively less supportive of the children in the aftermath of the abuse disclosure and if there were more family life stressors (e.g., parent–child conflict, tension between parents, etc.).

Fearfulness

Mothers' ratings of the children's fearfulness on the Louisville Fear Survey were related to therapists' ratings of fathers' supportiveness in the

TABLE 17.1. Family Mediators of Outcome: Parental Measures

Predictors	Percentage of variance accounted for
Significant predictors of children's behavior problems at time of most distress[a]	
Maternal support of child	28
Total life stressors (FILE)	11
Significant predictors of children's fears[b]	
Paternal support of child	23
Coping by mobilizing family to get help (F-COPES)	19

[a]Based on multiple-regression analyses of CBCL Total Behavior Problems score (n = 33).
[b]Based on multiple-regression analyses of Louisville Fear Survey ratings (n = 31).

aftermath of abuse and to paternal ratings of mobilizing the family to seek help, accounting for 42% of the variance. More fearful children had fathers who were relatively less likely to have been supportive in the aftermath of the abuse disclosure, and came from families that were less likely to seek out and utilize professional and community support.

Global Functioning

When we examined mediators of therapists' ratings of global functioning on the CGAS, 23% of the variance was accounted for by maternal ratings of mobilizing the family to seek support and by the children's perceptions of their mothers, as displayed in Table 17.2. Children whose families sought and utilized professional and community resources, and who perceived their mothers as responding less negatively to them (e.g., less yelling, nagging, physical punishment, threatening, criticism), were functioning more adaptively.

Self-Concept

We found that children's self-concept scores were most closely related to the child's relationship with the mother. As Table 17.3 shows, 44% of the variance was accounted for by the children's perception of the mothers and by the maternal ratings of family cohesion. Children who viewed their mothers as reacting more positively to them (e.g., spending time with them, praising, comforting), and who were part of highly cohesive families, had a more positive self-concept.

Emotional Indicators on Children's Drawings

Children with more indicators of emotional distress in their DAP drawings were more likely to come from families where the fathers

TABLE 17.2. Family Mediators of Outcome: Therapist Measure

Predictors	Percentage of variance accounted for
Significant predictors of children's global functioning[a,b]	
Coping by mobilizing family to get help (F-COPES)	16
Child's perception of mother (PPI)	7

[a]Based on multiple-regression analyses of CGAS ratings (n = 56).
[b]Rated for end of treatment (or currently, if still in therapy).

TABLE 17.3. Family Mediators of Outcome: Child Measures

Predictors	Percentage of variance accounted for
Significant predictors of children's self-concept scores[a]	
Child's overall perception of mother (PPI)	37
Family cohesion (FACES-III)	7
Significant predictors of emotional indicators in children's drawings[b]	
Coping by passive appraisal (F-COPES)	19
Family adaptability (FACES-III)	7
Family cohesion (FACES-III)	6

[a]Based on multiple-regression analyses of scores on age-appropriate Harter self-concept scale (n = 47).
[b]Based on multiple-regression analyses of DAP emotional indicators, according to Koppitz scoring system (n = 40).

reported coping by passive appraisal (e.g., watching television; feeling that given enough time, the problem would disappear). As shown in Table 17.3, there was also a trend for these children to have less adaptable, less cohesive families. These factors accounted for 32% of the variance in children's emotional indicators.

In summary, it appears that a variety of family factors influence how children function in the aftermath of reported ritualistic sexual abuse in preschools. In general, the RSA children experiencing fewer behavior problems and less emotional distress were those who (1) perceived their mothers as acting more positively (e.g., spending time with them, praising them, comforting them) and less negatively (e.g., less yelling, nagging, criticizing, physical punishment) toward them; (2) had fewer stressors in their families, and particularly less tension and conflict between family members; (3) experienced much family cohesion; and (4) had families that coped by mobilizing to get help from a variety of professional and community resources, rather than by taking a passive approach to problems.

Parent Action

As part of Coping with Sexual Abuse (CSA) a questionnaire assessing what coping styles parents utilized specifically in coping with their child's sexual abuse disclosures, parents noted whether they had been involved in various types of social and political action. Items included were (1) taking an active role in investigating the abuse, (2) involvement with the media, (3) involvement with advocacy programs and organizations, (4) involvement with legislative change, and (5) involvement with public education. When we looked at what types of social action on the parents' part might affect outcome for the children at the time of our main data collection, only a few relationships emerged. However, as we discuss later, this category also had an important impact on outcome at follow-up, 5 years after abuse disclosure.

When we examined the effects of social action on the mothers' part, it appeared that the only related type of action was involvement in public education: If the mothers were involved in public education about sexual abuse, the children were reported to have lower overall functioning by therapists on the CGAS ($r = -.29$, $p < .05$), and there was a trend for the children to have more indicators of emotional distress on the DAP ($r = .26$, $p < .08$). There are at least three possible explanations for these findings. First, if mothers were involved in public education about sexual abuse, their children would probably have been publicly identified as victims of ritualistic sexual abuse, and this might have increased feelings of stigmatization experienced by the children. Second, it may be that mothers whose children were most severely affected were more compelled to educate others about abuse issues. Third, if mothers were very involved in public education outside of the home, they may have had less time and/or emotional resources to give to their children in the aftermath of the abuse disclosure. As one mother stated in her follow-up interview,

After disclosure, there were times she seemed angry with me—I don't know if this is my own guilt. Around the time of disclosure, I was attending a lot of meetings, getting together with friends, a lot of phone calls. Looking back, I would have handled it different. I always tried to be there for her, but there were times I probably wasn't.

Involvement of fathers in social action, on the other hand, seemed to be associated with positive outcome. Most strikingly, fathers who were involved in working for legislative change were likely to have children with higher self-concept ($r = .51$, $p = .01$) and higher global functioning as rated by therapists on the CGAS ($r = .39$, $p = .03$). It is likely that fathers who worked for legislative change were attempting to attain court protections for testifying children (use of closed-circuit television, child-friendly courtrooms, etc.), which would be seen by the children as championing their cause. Fathers who were involved in political action on behalf of the children were rated as more supportive by therapists ($r = .70$, $p = .000$) and were part of families rated by mothers as more cohesive

($r = .37, p = .02$) and more adaptable ($r = .30, p = .08$). There was a strong relationship between fathers' working for legislative change and the children's perception of their fathers. Specifically, fathers who worked for legislative change were perceived by the children as reacting to them more positively ($r = .45, p = .009$) and less negatively ($r = -.41, p = .02$).

In summary, it appears that most maternal social action was unrelated to their children's functioning; however, mothers' involvement in public education was negatively related to some aspects of child outcome. In contrast, fathers' involvement in the legislative change process was related to positive child outcome, as well as to children's positive perceptions of their fathers.

Overall Mediators of Short-Term Outcome

To examine what mediated the outcome variables across all categories of factors investigated, overall regression equations were run, and discriminant-function analyses were also carried out. In general, all significantly correlating variables were included in the analyses; however, for family variables, only those significant in family regression equations were utilized, because there were so many significant correlations of the outcome variables with family factors. In some cases, variables with very low numbers of responses were dropped. For three of the outcome measures used—children's global functioning as rated on the CGAS, emotional indicators on children's DAP drawings, and self-concept—no factors other than family variables were significant predictors, and as a result the overall mediators regression analyses were essentially the same as those presented above in the "Family Factors" section. Therefore, those analyses are not detailed again here.

Behavior Problems

For maternal ratings on the CBCL, family life stress, marital status at time of data collection (2 to 3 years after abuse disclosure), and therapists' ratings of maternal support for the children accounted for 36% of the variance, as detailed in Table 17.4. The children rated as most distressed were more likely to have experienced divorce or separation in their families and to have endured many family stressors. It is difficult to know the direction of this effect; children from highly stressed families may simply have exhibited more behavior problems, or, alternatively, children who were highly distressed in the aftermath of their reported ritualistic sexual abuse may have become sources of major stress to their parents and families.

TABLE 17.4. Overall Mediators of Outcome

Predictors	Percentage of variance accounted for
Significant predictors of children's behavior problems[a]	
Total life stressors (FILE)	23
Marital status	8
Maternal support of child	5
Significant predictors of children's fears[b]	
Paternal support of child	23
Coping by mobilizing family to get help (F-COPES)	23
Total number of abusive acts reported	10

[a]Based on multiple-regression analyses of CBCL Total Behavior Problems score (n = 42).
[b]Based on multiple-regression analyses for Louisville Fear Survey ratings (n = 29).

Fearfulness

More fearful children, as rated by mothers, reported experiencing more abusive acts (particularly more terrorizing and ritualistic acts), had fathers who were less supportive after abuse disclosure, and were less likely to come from families that coped by mobilizing themselves to get help from professional and community resources. Together, these three factors accounted for 57% of the variance, as detailed in Table 17.4.

Discriminant-Function Analyses

In an attempt to examine what promotes *positive* outcome, high- and low-functioning groups were formed by creating an "outcome" variable. High-functioning children (n = 22) were those who were rated by therapists as exhibiting good functioning on the CGAS, *and* who scored above average on the age-appropriate Harter self-concept scale; low-functioning children (n = 15) showed at least some impairment in functioning on the CGAS, *and* were below average on self-concept. Discriminant-function analyses were then carried out to identify the mediating factors that provided the best prediction of the highest-functioning children and the lowest-functioning children. As shown in Table 17.5, the best predictors of positive outcome were low family life stress; the children's perception of their mothers as responding positively to them; high family cohesion; and a family coping style involving feeling empowered to solve major problems, facing problems head-on, and redefining family problems in a more positive way. These factors correctly classified 95.5% of the high-functioning children, but only 60% of the

TABLE 17.5. Discriminant-Function Analysis Predicting Highest- and Lowest-Functioning Children on "Outcome"

Variables	Correlation
Total family stressors (FILE)	–.64
Child's overall perception of mother (PPI)	.58
Family cohesion (FACES-III)	.55
Coping by reframing (F-COPES)	.33

$\chi^2 = 18.34$, $p = .001$

Percentage of high-functioning children correctly identified: 95.5%
Percent of low-functioning children correctly identified: 60.0%
Overall percentage of children correctly identified: 81.1%

Note. n = 22 for high-functioning children; n = 15 for low-functioning children. "Outcome" was defined as follows: high-functioning = CGAS > 70 and self-concept z score ≥ 0.05; low-functioning = CGAS ≤ 70 and self-concept z score ≤ 0.00.

low-functioning children, with the overall classification rate being 81%. Therefore, these family factors can be viewed more confidently as predictors of optimal outcome and healing than of negative outcome. In other words, the presence of these factors seemed to lead to positive outcome, although their absence did not necessarily lead to negative outcome.

MEDIATORS OF OUTCOME 5 YEARS AFTER DISCLOSURE

In our follow-up, 5 years after the initial disclosures of ritualistic sexual abuse in preschools, 40 mothers and 22 fathers filled out the CBCL on their children, assessing the children's behavior at the current time. These questionnaires were filled out approximately 2 to 3 years after the initial data collection. Because more mothers than fathers participated, our examination of the follow-up effects on children utilized the information gathered from the mothers. The main question we wanted to answer was this: What differentiated those children who were doing well 5 years later from those who were continuing to experience significant problems? There were no significant differences between those families who participated in the follow-up and those who did not on any measures of behavior problems, gender, age, socioeconomic status, or length of psychotherapy.

We examined a group of potential mediators similar to those described above for relationships with outcome at follow-up:

1. Demographic factors
2. Abuse characteristics
3. Previous symptomatology
4. Treatment characteristics
5. Family factors
6. Parent action factors

Demographic Factors

At follow-up, age, gender, marital status, religion, developmental level, and socioeconomic status were unrelated to outcome for any of the CBCL indices. As mentioned in discussion of the mediators above, lack of variability in some of the demographic indicators may have been partially responsible for the lack of positive findings.

Abuse Characteristics

None of the specific abuse categories, length of preschool attendance, or time since attendance at the preschool where abuse was reported were related to outcome on the CBCL at follow-up. Lack of variability here also may have played a part.

Previous Symptomatology

We were interested in examining how symptomatology as rated previously by parents, therapists, and the children themselves, some at the time of most distress and some at time of initial data collection 2 to 3 years after disclosure of abuse, would relate to measures of outcome at 5-year follow-up. Not surprisingly, multiple-regression analysis showed that the best predictor of the CBCL Total Behavior Problems score at follow-up was the CBCL Total Behavior Problems score at time of most distress, accounting for 27% of the variance. Fearfulness also was significantly related to Total Behavior Problems at follow-up, with 10% of the variance. Together, these two measures accounted for 37% of the variance. It does not seem surprising that the CBCL scores gathered 2 to 3 years earlier were the best predictors of follow-up scores. In general, maternal measures predicted CBCL scores at follow-up better than therapist or child measures, probably because the follow-up CBCLs were also filled out by the mothers.

Treatment Characteristics

In addition to the treatment variables examined earlier (length of psychotherapy, number of family sessions, and number of treatment modalities in which the child participated), two therapist variables were also scrutinized—number of years in practice, and number of abused children treated. None of the treatment characteristics were related to outcome at follow-up. Since almost all of the children participated in psychotherapy, these findings would be expected. It is important to note, however, that during the initial data collection, parents rated psychotherapy for the children as the type of help that benefited their children most. Similarly, during the in-depth parent interviews held 5 years after disclosure, parents again asserted that the children's psychotherapy was the most helpful step taken in ameliorating the effects of the reported ritualistic sexual abuse. ▪

Family Factors

In addition to the family measures whose results were examined in the previous analyses (the FILE, the FACES III, the F-COPES, and the PPI), several other family measures collected at the time of follow-up 5 years after abuse disclosure were also investigated. These included the Family Environment Scale (FES), a current measure of family stressors (FILE Time 2), and a companion measure to the PPI previously collected from the children that examined the parents' perception of their own parenting (PPI—Parent Version).

For the Total Behavior Problems score on the CBCL at time of follow-up, the significant family predictors accounted for 47% of the variance. High intrafamilial strains (11% of variance), family cohesion toward the enmeshed end of the continuum (13% of variance), and mothers' negative perception of themselves in relation to their children: such as taking away privileges, criticism, physical punishment, or yelling (23% of the variance) all predicted higher Total Behavior Problems at follow-up.

In general, children were seen as having more problems at follow-up when there was a great deal of strain and tension in the family; when there was a parenting style involving yelling, criticism, and physical punishment; and when their families were more enmeshed. It is difficult to know the direction of these relationships. Were these children harder to handle because of the behavior problems, so that more limit setting of all types was necessary? Or did negative family interaction lead to more problem behaviors? There is some minor evidence for the latter explanation, in that children were more likely to have Internalizing problems on the CBCL (e.g., withdrawal, somatic complaints, and depression) at follow-up than Externalizing problems (e.g., aggression or delinquency), which might require more limit setting.

Parent Action Factors

We examined parental action by looking at participation in a variety of political and advocacy activities related to the ritualistic sexual abuse reports. In addition to the items mentioned above—(1) taking an active role in investigating the abuse, (2) involvement with the media, (3) involvement with advocacy programs and organizations, (4) involvement with legislative change, and (5) involvement with public education—an Action Composite Score was computed by dividing parents into those who did not participate in any of the five parent action activities, and those who participated in one or more action activities.

Positive correlations with the CBCL Total Behavior Problems score at time of follow-up were obtained for both mothers' Action Composite Score ($r = .57$, $p = .004$) and fathers' Action Composite Score ($r = .55$, $p = .02$), indicating that children whose parents were involved in social and political action were showing more behavior problems and emotional distress at follow-up. For mothers, the relationship was strongest for the item involving taking an active role in investigating the abuse allegations ($r = .55$, $p = .006$). Children tended to perceive mothers who actively investigated the allegations as reacting significantly more negatively toward them ($r = .41$, $p < .003$), and viewed their mothers less positively in overall ratings ($r = -.31$, $p = .03$).

Similar results were found when examining the mothers' Action Composite Score. Highly active mothers were perceived by their children as reacting more negatively to them (e.g., yelling, nagging, criticizing, ignoring; $r = .36$, $p = .02$). Interestingly, children with activist mothers saw their fathers as reacting positively to them ($r = .30$, $p = .05$). Moreover, in contrast to the negatively perceived activist mothers, the activist fathers were more likely to be seen by their children as reacting to the children more positively (e.g., spending time together, comforting, saying nice things) ($r = .48$, $p < .005$) and less negatively ($r = -.33$, $p < .06$), and to be given a more positive total score ($r = .52$, $p < .002$).

In summary, parental participation in social action in the aftermath of ritualistic sexual abuse disclosure was associated with more behavior problems and emotional distress at time of follow-up. Moreover, it appears that mothers who were activists were seen more negatively by their children, whereas activist fathers were perceived more positively by their offspring. There are several possible interpretations for the surprising finding that parental participation in social action predicted increased behavior problems at time of follow-up. First, the highly activist mothers may have been less available to their children at the time of most distress, because they coped by being active in ways that took them away from home for significant periods of time. Second, the highly activist parents may have had trouble moving on in their lives when their children needed to, because they continued to be actively involved with the abuse allegations and court proceedings, which continued for many years. Third, it is possible that children may have been negatively affected by public exposure. For example, some children appeared on television with their parents, and several parents reported in follow-up interviews that their children were quite embarrassed by their parents' public role in media and legal proceedings, because then "everybody knew" that they were reported abuse victims; the children's need to conceal their "victim" status seemed to increase as time passed since disclosure.

The fact that activist mothers were viewed negatively and activist fathers positively is intriguing. It may reflect the children's expectations that their mothers should provide support to them at home, while any active support by fathers, inside or outside of the home, was viewed positively. Alternatively, the children's perception may have been related to the type of social action. The strongest findings that emerged were negative perceptions of mothers who actively investigated the abuse allegations (which may not have felt supportive to the children) and positive perceptions of fathers who were involved in working for legislative change (which is likely to have been viewed as very supportive, since most of this type of activism involved working to provide safeguards for children in the courtroom). Some support for this notion comes from the fact that children's negative perceptions of their mothers were associated with types of social action not specifically designed to protect or support the children (e.g., taking an active role in investigating the abuse allegations, involvement with the media); there was no relationship between children's perception of their mothers and types of social action designed to protect them (e.g., working for legislative change).

Overall Mediators of Outcome 5 Years after Disclosure

The factors contributing to positive or negative outcome 5 years after disclosure of ritualistic sexual abuse were examined in two ways. First, an overall multiple-regression equation was constructed, putting together factors that were significant in each category of mediator. Second, discriminant-function analyses were carried out to see what factors best predicted differences between the poorest-functioning 10 children and the best-functioning 10 children as indicated by Total Behavior Problems score at follow-up.

In the overall multiple-regression analysis, 68% of the variance was accounted for by a combination of previous symptomatology and family variables, as shown in Table 17.6. Children with more behavior problems

TABLE 17.6. Overall Mediators of Outcome Predicting CBCL Total Behavior Problems Score at Follow-Up

Significant predictors[a]	Percentage of variance accounted for
CBCL Total Behavior Problems at time of most distress	26
Maternal negative self-perception as parent (PPI—Parent Version)	20
Total fear score (Louisville Fear Survey)	8
Intrafamilial stressors (FILE)	7
Family cohesion (FACES-III)	7

[a]Based on multiple-regression analyses (n = 34).

at follow-up exhibited more behavior problems at time of most distress; had mothers who perceived themselves as reacting more negatively (e.g., yelling, criticizing) to their children; were relatively less fearful at time of initial data collection; experienced many family stressors; and came from enmeshed families.

Although many of these factors predicting overall outcome at follow-up are similar to those associated with outcome at initial data collection, 2 to 3 years after ritualistic sexual abuse disclosure, two findings are particularly striking. First, the children who showed more behavior problems at the 5-year follow-up were relatively *less* fearful several years earlier. This relationship is complicated, because fearfulness showed little correlation with behavior problems at follow-up ($r = -.03$), but added something unique after the variance due to behavior problems at time of most distress was removed. It is possible that children who reacted overtly earlier and expressed their fears were able to work through and resolve their abuse-related feelings through family support and in psychotherapy, whereas those who expressed fears less directly might still be dealing with unresolved feelings that were expressed through a variety of behavioral and emotional problems.

A second interesting but puzzling finding involves the relationship between family cohesion and outcome. At the time of initial data collection, very close-knit families had children who were functioning more adaptively and showing fewer problems than less cohesive families. In contrast, at follow-up, children from very close-knit families were experiencing more behavior problems.

Explanations for this discrepancy may be methodological or developmental. When we examined relationships of family cohesion with outcome at initial data collection, high family cohesion was correlated with higher self-esteem and global functioning (according to therapists' CGAS ratings) and with fewer emotional indicators on DAP human figure drawings. However, there was virtually no relationship between cohesion and maternal CBCL ratings at time of most distress ($r = -.02$), the parallel measure to that utilized in the analyses at time of follow-up. Perhaps different relationships with family cohesion would have emerged if measures from the children had been repeated at follow-up.

Alternatively, the role of high family cohesion in determining optimal child functioning may change with a child's developmental stage. At time of initial data collection, the average age of the children was about 8 years; at this stage, highly cohesive families (whose members like to spend most of their time together, feel very close to one another, and consult one another on decisions) might be functioning very adaptively in terms of the children's growth. In contrast, as children approach adolescence, a highly cohesive family style may be less functional. Children who need to reach out to peers and spend less time with the family as developmental tasks appropriate to their age may be hampered by parents who have difficulty letting go and push to continue the enmeshment.

In an attempt to assess what factors led to best and to worst outcomes, factors differentiating the 10 poorest-functioning children and the 10 best-functioning children on CBCL Total Behavior Problems score at follow-up were examined through use of discriminant-function analysis. The results, outlined in Table 17.7, showed that a combination of four factors could provide 100% correct classification: The 10 children functioning best at follow-up experienced fewer stressors in the family, exhibited fewer behavior problems at the time of most distress, had mothers who were less likely to perceive themselves as reacting negatively to their children, and experienced less overt family conflict than the 10 children whose functioning was most impaired at follow-up.

TABLE 17.7. Discriminant-Function Analysis Predicting Poorest-Functioning 10 and Best-Functioning 10 Children on CBCL Total Behavior Problems Score at Follow-Up

Variables	Correlation
Intrafamilial stressors (FILE)	.65
CBCL Total Behavior Problems score at time of most distress	.55
Maternal negative self-perception as parent (PPI—Parent Version)	.34
Family conflict (FES)	.29

$\chi^2 = 18.34$, $p = .003$

Percentage of children correctly identified: 100%

Note. Poorest-functioning 10 had Total Behavior Problems scores of 64 or above; best-functioning 10 had Total Behavior Problems scores of 47 or below.

CONCLUSIONS

In conclusion, it appears that several factors combine to promote healing in the aftermath of ritualistic sexual abuse disclosures: (1) warm, supportive families that are child-centered rather than punitive and critical; (2) lower numbers of family stressors, and especially less tension within the family; (3) coping styles that involve actively mobilizing resources and reframing situations to increase the sense of family power, rather than more passive approaches to problem solving; (4) families that are close but not enmeshed; and (5) families that resolve problems without a great deal of overt conflict and anger.

The importance of psychological treatment for families as well as for abused children, even in cases where the abuse takes place outside of the family context, cannot be underestimated, given the central role of family factors in promoting healing as discussed above. The focus should be on helping parents to develop supportive, nonpunitive interactions with their children, including positive involvement with both parents.

In addition, a therapeutic goal of empowering parents and supporting them in actively fighting for their children's safety and mental health seems very useful, in light of our findings. Consistently, we found that parents who utilized active coping styles—who sought to mobilize professional and community resources to help their children and families, and who felt that they could handle whatever problems arose, facing troubles head-on and trying to find solutions—had children who functioned more adaptively and experienced less distress than parents who coped by more passive means (e.g., relying exclusively on spiritual resources, watching television, and feeling that problems would go away if they waited long enough). An active stance can be especially useful when dealing with a trauma such as ritualistic sexual abuse, which engenders significant feelings of powerlessness in its victims and their families. Children *do* heal from the ordeal of ritualistic sexual abuse, and families can do much to help them.

CLINICAL IMPLICATIONS

Assault, Levels of Injury, and the Healing Process in Cases of Alleged Preschool Ritualistic Abuse

Mary Kay Oliveri
Martha Cockriel
Michele Dugan

T HERE IS NO ADEQUATE PREPARATION in life for something truly awful entering into our waking state, as it does when we are confronted with allegations made by children of assault and injury at the hands of trusted adults—reported experiences that leave the children with serious long-term problems. Our only rehearsals for such things are paler circumstances, such as frightening nightmares from which we awaken in terror, or childhood play at scaring ourselves and others. There are also less frequent events, such as the loss of some valued object, or a story from the newspaper that jumps out and grabs us about some stranger's horrible experience. And then there are the experiences of human tragedy that touch our own lives and the lives of others we know—serious illnesses, the loss of a loved one, the divorce of parents. Finally, there is that category of events labeled "Never in my lifetime" or "This just doesn't happen."

Early in life, the events we categorize as serious human tragedy seem improbable. As our experience grows, this category remains largely empty, with a naive assumption on our part that it may never be filled.

Occasionally, we allow for the possibility of betrayal in order to explain some unforeseen destructiveness that touches our personal world; however, in much of human experience there exists an illusion of safety, a sense that we are immune to loss, crisis, or change outside of our control. Whatever is based on illusion, no matter how useful, is itself vulnerable. With allegations of ritualistic abuse in a preschool setting, the category of "This never happens" pours out into a relatively safe world. Ideas and information about real people chronically sexually abusing, terrorizing, ritualistically using, and placing unusual or bizarre notions into the minds of real children becomes part of a reality we cannot quite comprehend.

The exposure of an unanticipated and hidden assault, with multiple levels of injury to the children involved, challenges our most basic assumptions about human experience. Those involved in such an uncovering are confronted with the sheer capacity of one human being to hurt, harm, or attempt to destroy another. This display of the base side of the human condition is not easy to look at in a direct manner. Those who are confronted with it encounter many levels of denial within themselves and others. Most will be faced with scaling a kind of wall of personal, professional, interpersonal, and community denial on the crudely constructed ladder made of young children's accusations and the exquisite quality of their emotional pain.

There is little else besides the child's anguish, revealed through emotional or behavioral reactivity, and the child's disclosures to guide any of us up the wall of denial that protects us from our own reactions of horror or distress to the child's experience. This chapter represents an attempt to explicate some of the basic clinical issues that emerge in the clinician's struggle with his or her own and others' denial, and in the overall treatment of individuals who experience and report the trauma associated with multiple and often sadistic abuses implied in their disclosures of ritualistic sexual abuse. These experiences are typically reported by children and vulnerable adults who, like other victims in the field of child sexual abuse, are very unlikely to find themselves in the courts for a variety of personal, clinical, and legal reasons. It has been indicated in the preface and it is reiterated here that allegations in the Manhattan Beach community were never legally proven. This is a clinical chapter that reflects the therapeutic experiences of the children in this project. When we illustrate basic clinical issues through the reports of these children, it needs to be understood that these are clinical vignettes and judgments rather than legally proven facts. The experiences of the author and her colleagues in consultation, readings, teaching, and being taught in the field as a whole, and in the treatment of still other children and adults reporting abuse associated with ritualistic activity have also contributed to the ideas reflected herein.

LEVELS OF INJURY

The process associated with disclosure does not occur all at once, although there are individual differences among children. The disclosures often come and go in bursts, which can be triggered by unusual or undistinguished experiences and, once triggered, are often subsequently denied or avoided. The events themselves in ritual abuse create a particularly poignant set of circumstances for a child. Both the work of uncovering and that of healing are often contraindicated by the child's need for the safety of secrecy. The therapeutic process is, realistically, a gentle assault on the accommodations that the child has made to a world where few things are as they seem and the power of the abusers is pervasive and magical. These accommodations form a matrix of defenses and incorporated levels of injury, which must be understood and approached respectfully, for the child perceives them as essential to survival.

The experience of a particular young boy comes to mind. This boy had disclosed some memories early in treatment, but had not disclosed for some time as he focused on mastery of events in his everyday life. However, on this particular day he had become quite agitated several hours before his session, shaking and crying in the car with his mother because of something he had seen on the street. As he calmed down, he asked her why a much younger child was being walked on a harness by an adult. She explained that some parents did this to keep their children from wandering away, and she was shocked by his belief that this was done to hurt and threaten the other child. He disclosed that in his own situation, he remembered being hung from such a contraption off a high place and told that he would be dropped if he did not do as he was instructed. His instructions included participation with others in degrading and sexual acts. By the time he got to his therapy session, he was calm and nonchalant, seeming to have forgotten the whole event. When his mother asked him to share his experience with the therapist, he acted as if he did not know what she was talking about. She sensitively challenged his lack of memory, but respected his decision not to tell. Within 15 minutes of the start of the session, while the boy was playing a game, the memory suddenly intruded—complete with fear, shaking, and a need to check thoroughly the safety of the room, the relationship with the therapist, and the relationship with his mother. The rest of the session was spent helping him to make sense of these memories, the attached emotion, and other associated times in his young life when he had felt tied up, trapped, and frightened. The therapist also reminded the boy of the resources he now had to deal with these experiences—resources that were not available to him when he was younger.

The levels of injury to this child and to other such children include the following:

1. *Emotional reactivity and hypervigilance to threats and harm.* It is difficult to overstate the fear that children experience as a result of reporting ritualistic abuse. There is a powerful impact on young children when they hear that to tell of their abuse experience will mean the loss of a parent, or that to refuse to participate in some ritualistic sacrifice will mean death before their sixth birthday. There is an impact to being kicked for kicking another child, only to be rewarded with candy for participating in more degrading acts. The impact is great when children experience firsthand the power of an abuser to destroy life, as when children witness acts of animal mutilation. The threats that children hear from abusive adults take on a frightening reality when juxtaposed with these acts of violence. The sexual abuse, degrading acts, terrifying experiences, and ritualistic activity combine to reinforce constructs and attributions about the self and others through an overwhelming combination of profoundly real, threatened, imagined, and magical consequences.

In addition, with each burst of disclosure comes all of the terror related to the abuse itself. The child fears that the threats related to all the acts he or she reports having experienced may now come true as the result of telling the secrets. The emergence of this specific incorporated fear intensifies all of the fears in the child's present life. Whether the perceived danger is potential or actual, the fears and thoughts about it are incorporated into the child's world view. And although the associated hypervigilance may be observed, the emotional reactivity is internal—often hidden and unexpressed, but of significant intensity.

The clinical issue here is to allow for the expression of hidden emotion and to facilitate containment of overwhelming emotion in the work with such a child. This is best done by entering into a kind of dialogue with the child's emotional response. This interaction can be spoken, written, or action-oriented. The purpose is to help the child learn to understand and use his or her affective world rather than to be ruled by it.

2. *The use of barriers and survival adaptations to form a matrix of protection around the hidden child.* The child seeks to protect some core of the self from harm, both by being vigilant for present or future danger and by protecting the self from the effects of past or present injury. Children utilize whatever is at their disposal to cushion and defend themselves. They may suppress or eventually repress both memory and affect for the

events. They may use fantasy escapes or imaginary powers to "pretend" that the events did not occur, that they were elsewhere, or that they somehow eluded their tormentors. They may deny aspects of the past events or present reality that threaten the intrusion of unwanted memory. They may seek power over others in identification with their aggressors to counteract the helplessness they feel. Or they may dive into an intense focus on something—developing an exceptional talent, skill, or an unusual fear or obsession—to manage their feelings of powerlessness. Whatever they choose, children develop layers of possible accommodations to past experience, associated phenomena in the present, and potential future danger that keeps them in a state of chronic readiness.

The clinician will need to respect the matrix, understand the purpose of the layers of defense, keep track of them, and map them for such a child. It can be useful both here and with emotional responsiveness to use lists, diaries, sequential stories, or plays that are kept track of by both the therapist and the child. These can be used to make the matrix visible to the child; they are also useful for reference in later stages of the work with the child.

3. *The presence of "encapsulated experiences" and confused realities, represented by multiple and at times paradoxical injunctions about what is expected in the world.* In ritual abuse, the disclosure process reveals experiences that may lie in direct opposition to the situations that other adults, particularly parents, in the children's world may provide for them. Children may make disclosures about experiences in which abusive adults dress in costumes of normally friendly figures (e.g., clowns, police officers, firefighters, or Santa Claus) and then abuse or frighten the children. These reported acts often involve the use of toys, further tainting the artifacts of the children's everyday experience. The disclosures reveal experiences that not only assault the children, but that undermine the other primary relationships in their lives. The children may also report experiences that lead them to believe that something bad has been placed inside of them (e.g., a monster, a poison, or a transmitter that guides their actions and may prevent them from being good). Finally, the children may come to believe the injunctions and threats they hear; for instance, one young boy was convinced that his grandfather's death, his parents' divorce, and his grandmother's hospitalization were all the direct result of his disclosures, because he had been told that such things would happen should he ever tell. A set of beliefs are associated with the rituals children describe and with the injunctions about right and wrong, good and evil, power and helplessness that the children hear and learn in the context of the reported abuse.

Deprived of the capacity to attack or flee in a physical sense, children are forced to make a series of accommodations to the abusive reality. They are also required to make an adaptation to the dual reality in which they live, one abusive and one nurturing. Given the duality of their experience, their ages at the time of the reported abuse, the severity and persistence of the abuse activities described, and the associated negative injunctions experienced, the children not only acquiesce; they also incorporate the abusive reality as a part of their personality structure. The traumatic experiences, along with other life experiences, form a set of competing expectations that organize and govern the children's reactions to and understandings about human interaction. The incorporation of these expectations and experiences within their personalities influences the children's developing sense of who they are and how they cope.

In essence, a child reporting ritualistic abuse learns a set of cognitive attributes that predict responses to an experiential world in which opposite or confused rules govern. Behavior is based upon the person(s) the child is with at any given time. It then becomes key in the clinical or healing alliance to provide the child with alternative understandings and predictions. Sometimes this may be done through the simple act of confirming for the child that the feared consequence did not occur. Other times it involves helping the child to mourn, heal from, and make sense of the loss that did occur.

4. *Disruptions to bonding, safety, ego formation, and the sense of the self.* Ritualistic abuse, because it occurs in one realm of a child's world in opposition to the relationships in another, attacks the child's sense of predictability in general and reliance on parents in particular. There is an assault on the developing child's sense of basic trust. At this critical time in a young child's life, the development of a sense of self as separate from others; vulnerability to shame; trust in relationships outside of the family; and issues of control, power, and mastery are paramount. The child is affected in each area by the ritualistic abuse, and two different versions of relatedness are spun. This creates a situation of duality for the child: in one sphere, he or she is cherished for competence, goodness, and a growing sense of self; in another, he or she is terrified into silence, compliance, and participation in powerfully destructive activities.

The impact of these activities is unlike that in any other form of child abuse, and the extent of potential damage to children's sense of self, relatedness with others, and rules governing the world in which they live is significant and pervasive. Children are assaulted on the physical, emotional, cognitive, and interpersonal planes of their developing reality.

The therapeutic goal here is to reconnect such a child with nurturing significant others by preparing those others and by helping the child to experience support. The "injured" hidden child must be aided in interacting on a symbolic and a real level with the "surviving" child self.

5. *Distorted, blurred, or blunted expression of a full range of emotion.*

Survival dictates that children experiencing ritualistic sexual abuse find some set of mechanisms for managing the overwhelming emotional reactivity that occurs, in order to prevent complete paralysis. All emotional states are potentially dangerous. First, there is the extreme discomfort manifested by the children. Then comes a subsequent exaggeration of the dynamic experience and the related expression of helplessness and powerlessness, which occur because of linkages with powerful and overwhelming affect. Finally, the possibility exists that emotional excitation will attract more attention to any given child in the abusive reality or give the secret away in the nonabusive one. All emotions become unacceptable in this paradigm, because of their potential to threaten the children's capacity to be safe and to keep their parents safe.

Rage is particularly terrifying, because it is so powerful and potentially destructive, and because it makes the children like their tormentors. One child was panic-stricken whenever he became angry, because he experienced it as an affirmation that he was like one of his principal alleged tormentors; as a result, the child could not own his own anger, but had to experience it as some foreign object inside of him.

Fear, like this child's panic, becomes the great mediator because of its critical role in alerting the human system to internal and external sources of danger. Fear predominates and governs decision making in the emotional and possibly the behavioral and cognitive domains. This emotion especially requires blunting, because of its potential to cause difficulty by threatening disorganization when danger is perceived in every direction. A child is emotionally flooded in response to the perceived danger, and the flooding creates more intensity then he or she is able to experience. Thus, what looks like no emotion is really too much emotion to be directly expressed or experienced.

It is in this arena that many clinical strategies already discussed are useful, most particularly the development of a "shared reality" that the child, parent(s), and therapist have been able to experience. This at least partially challenges the child's sense of danger and isolation. The suppression of some emotion, particularly at certain times, also needs to be supported.

6. *The presence of "anchors"—symbolic representations and aspects of experience—that trigger the reemergence of content or affect from the past into the present.* Anchors are incorporated symbols and experiences from the reported abuses that are disturbed or "triggered" by some present event or feeling associated with the past event in the mind of the child. Because of the particularly terrifying events reported by these children—events that have linked danger and powerlessness—there is a vulnerability to developing symbolic, emotional, and/or behavioral triggers that restimu-

late some aspect of the past events in the present. Triggers develop through the generalization of one event to another situation that a child perceives as similar, or through flashbacks, unusually strong affective responses to seemingly everyday events, and a myriad of other potential anchors of past experience to some trigger in the present situation. Generally the child and the child's caretakers are unaware of the connection between the present response and the past experience.

If the goal of a child's mastery of the self and of the traumatic experiences is to be met, then the uncovering of triggers and anchors that lie outside of conscious awareness is critical. These triggers are often subtle and difficult to discern, particularly as they relate to aspects of the abuse that are hard to imagine or believe. A kind of curiosity needs to be encouraged in the child, particularly an older child, to be interested in these phenomena. Again, the therapist's capacity to hold and keep track of information and patterns of response can be important here as a key to uncovering a trigger and its origin. There are many behavioral and cognitive–behavioral techniques of value to help in decreasing the power of a trigger and its anchor to the child's memory and experience.

7. *An illusion that, by choice, the children have engaged in destructive activities that bind them inextricably to a personal and group identity with their abusers, from which negative consequences flow.* These children are not allowed the luxury of being only victims; they are placed by the human need to survive into a role of active participation within the abusive situation. The harmful effects of this "forced" participation are intensified by the fact that the children are not allowed the expression of powerful emotions such as terror and rage. Through taking a part in the reported ritualistic experience, the children are provided with a bizarre but acceptable outlet for their "dangerous" feelings. This may happen as they watch others, as they act themselves, or as they are acted upon in orchestrated scenes of degradation, bondage, and destruction. The children's fear is used to keep terrible secrets and to push the children into ordinarily unacceptable activities, while pulling them away from the feelings and experiences that connect them to nonabusive others. The rage and accompanying excitation find vent through the abuse of others or participation in destructive acts, which are allowed by the alleged abusers.

These experiences teach the children directly and indirectly that by being part of the activity, they choose to be part of the destructive group. Children are supported and influenced in this belief by the supposed magic of the adults' power. The children are placed in an atmosphere in which they are encouraged to believe they have made a choice; in fact, this is an illusion, because there are no choices.

Whether a child acts within or outside of the group, there is an underlying assumption that the child is tied in some shameful and secretive way to the group. A therapeutic process that supports the child but not the secrets, and allows the child to come to terms with how he or she is like and unlike each of the powerful others in his or her life, allows the child to reconnect with the positive aspects of power.

Through successive experiences, powerful emotions are identified with the alleged abusers, while competing with the values and beliefs represented by others in these children's lives. For example:

As one child recounted his experiences about being forced to kill a rabbit, he struggled with his own shame at having enjoyed this release of anger and aggression while watching the rabbit's torment. While discounting his own pain and the victimization that led up to this event, he questioned, with a heavy sense of self-judgment, "But what if I enjoyed it?"

It was critical to the recovery process that he be allowed to ask this question and to seek his own resolution to the dilemma posed.

It is clear that the injuries experienced by these children occur on multiple levels and to varying degrees, and that they influence their cognitive, affective, and interpersonal development. These injuries occur as the result of the original series of reported assaults, which involved sexual, physical, and emotional abuse from multiple sources and left the children with a hidden core of trauma; the direct and the implied prevention of the children's natural tendency to flee or fight; the actual or intimated threats made to the child of harm that would befall them and their families if they did not comply; and the accompanying sense of absolute powerlessness this left the child to manage.

Injury is further accelerated by the children's emotional reactivity and vulnerability; by the shame, fear, and rage they experience in relation to the abuse; and by their own helplessness without the support of caring adults. Throughout this onslaught, children accommodate: They shut down their normal responsiveness, and become isolated by degrees from others.

In summary, children who have been subjected to ritual abuse incorporate experiences of assault and injury through a series of physical, emotional, and cognitive accommodations to the pragmatics of trauma. The powerlessness, isolation, disruption, distortion, illusion of free choice, and overwhelming but unexpressed emotion that these children experience in relation to their trauma leave them vulnerable to the events of daily living. Each dimension of their ordeal is reinforced by the other dimensions, and all are most strongly validated by the fear associated with the terrifying reported ritualistic events and abuses, which necessitates the suppression of rage or any other powerful response.

The only real choice that these children have is to do what they have to do in order to survive, in order to make it "home again."

As one youngster stated with a blank and incredulous expression, when attempting to make sense of his having followed instructions to kill an animal encountered while on a "field trip" rather than having used the instrument of destruction on his instructor, "I couldn't have killed him. I was too little. I don't think I was 4 yet. I didn't know my phone number. How would I have gotten home? I couldn't have gotten home . . . on my own."

During the abuse, children most often protect the core of the self by hiding or suppressing feelings, beliefs, and responses that are inconsistent with the purposes of survival at any moment in time. They are forced to encapsulate parts of themselves and of their trauma in order to go on with their lives. If these experiences enter the more ordinary spheres of the children's lives, they do so through dreams, symbols, or symbolic play, as well as through a vigilance for harm that reinforces the matrix of protection built to isolate the memories, feelings, and beliefs of the children's hidden ordeal.

ISSUES IN THE HEALING PROCESS

At the time of the trauma, children can only choose to survive by some series of accommodations to a reality that is on the one hand abusive, and on the other hand within the realm of normal childhood experience. Children, however, believe that these accommodations are a part of daily living. Because of their ages, the injunctions heard from the alleged abusers, and their parents' lack of knowledge, the children believe they have to handle these experiences alone. These circumstances juxtapose normal developmental egocentricity with a developmentally inappropriate set of relationships in such a way as to reinforce the extremes of omnipotence and helplessness. The children come to assume either that their parents know of the abuse and acquiesce to it, or that they are vulnerable to harm through the children's association with the more powerful others.

This leaves children to make a series of compromises that are possibly injurious, but that allow for continued development regarding their own capacity to influence, harm, and protect in the face of danger. Children make these compromises without the support and guidance of nurturing adults, because the traumatic experiences are not brought into their nonabusive relationships. The challenge of treatment is to help children learn to rely upon themselves and their parents in a new way in regard to the memories, recollections, and symptoms associated with the traumatic experiences.

The experience of a young boy and his parents comes to mind. He woke several nights a week screaming in terror, and he had done so for years. When asked about what had scared him in his bad dream, he would report about scenes of being chased, thrown into a car, sometimes tied up, and often made sleepy, and then of waking at another place with threatening men doing strange things that he could not describe because he was too frightened. He would scream, shake, and be unable to continue. He would generally become calm, stare blankly, and remember nothing, wondering why he was sitting with his parents on the sofa. These incidents increased dramatically within the time after assessment. During the course of treatment, the parents pieced together that this was their child's form of disclosure; for some time, he had been describing scenes and using names that were all too familiar to them. After ruling out other possibilities, the child and parents began to look to themselves for solutions. This child became the script writer in his own dreams, learning to write in escapes and eventually to create alternative endings for himself and the other children being tormented in his dreams. His parents were his backers, reminding him that he was now safe, that whatever had happened was over, and that he had the capacity to use himself and to use them to move beyond his nighttime terrors. The therapist facilitated this process by carefully attending to the dream fragments with the boy, and working with him to make emotional sense of his experience by helping him to make full stories of the bits and pieces with various resolutions. She also worked with the parents to learn brief but effective ways to reestablish safety for the boy when he woke afraid. This process had eluded them and had been damaged by the traumatic experiences outside of their control.

The disclosure of the previously hidden abuse threatens the accommodations made by children in very real ways, and they begin to display more overt distress. Simultaneously, their distress is observed and possibly understood by parents and others, who were previously prevented from seeing the children's pain and discomfort. The discovery of the children's pain by their parents is threatening to the established relationships between parents and children. The stress responses that are seen in children are based both on the present challenges to their matrix of defenses and on the emergence of previously hidden memories, thoughts, and feelings related to the abuse.

One young boy, not quite 5 years old at the time of treatment, repeatedly played a game with puppets in which the boy's kindly hound dog was made "mean" by a poison, and bit and poisoned the therapist's poodle, until a police dog came to the poodle's rescue. This led the "mean" and "poisoned" hound dog to fly into outer space. The play occurred over and over again as the boy tried to make sense of his overwhelming feelings. He feared his preschool, generalizing this to regular school and to the dark. The poisoning theme became more and more pronounced, even waking him from night dreams from which he could barely be comforted by his parents. Finally, he told his mother about a pink liquid he was forced to drink; this had made him sleepy, and all he could remember after drinking it was waking in a bad place with his preschool teachers doing bad things. In therapy this was expanded to include another "poison"—the one that followed swallowing in the course of a sexual act. Many trips to the moon later—after a long period of staying in space because it was safer than being with people; after doctors delivered antidotes to the puppet and to the therapist; after much nighttime comforting at home; after firm but gentle limit setting on angry, sometimes biting outbursts toward his sister; and after reminders to masturbate only in his room—the young boy and his dog puppet returned from space, resting on the moon before descending to earth. Through the puppet, the boy said, "It was very bad. The poison was all through me and through you, but I am well and you've had enough shots too. I'll go home, I'll play and laugh and only yell and stomp my feet when I'm angry. Today I'm not afraid." Shortly afterwards, he also stopped masturbating, and he began to sleep through the night.

In order to engage in a healing process with children, therapists and parents must understand and respect the enormity of the threat that the uncovering, reporting of the abuse, and being *seen* in a whole way represent to the children, to their sense of mastery over the self, to their relationships with others, and to their world view. Along with the threat that feared consequences will materialize, children must face the terror, shame, rage, loss, disorientation, and confusion that accompany discovery and trigger abuse-related feelings.

The healing relationship needs to provide the potential for some new or different set of experiences to be acquired. It may be useful to think of the healing process as similar to recovery from a puncture wound. This type of injury often heals over and appears to be fine, while underneath an injury exists that may be aggravated by a fragment or a foreign body, infection, or further trauma. When the trauma is discovered, the site of the wound must be reopened, drained, cleaned, explored, and dressed in such a way as to allow for further cycles of draining, cleaning, and exploration to occur without additional infection setting in. This type of wound needs to heal from the inside out, and access needs to be maintained to the site where injured tissue meets good or recently healed tissue. The healing process occurs in layers. Working within the layers is critical to help a traumatized child create and maintain a relationship to the hidden and injured self, which facilitates recovery.

Participation in the process of parenting or healing children injured in a manner that the adults find improbable, and that the children have hidden, requires of the adults not only the capacity to look sharply at the real and imagined securities with which they have surrounded themselves, but also to provide for themselves and for the children a core set of strengths and beliefs about the inherent ability to *survive*. This refers to the whole quality of life and human interaction, not just to physical survival.

Recovery from the significant effects of alleged ritualistic abuse requires an action stance and the ability to climb over or to dismantle barriers that children may have originally erected in order to provide some protection for themselves. The ability of the children to outlast the destructiveness of such abuse may have been aided by their capacity to make what for some is a sheltering enclosure and for others is a container that shields them from their experiences; the building blocks they use for this purpose may include denial, suppression, repression, or fantasy escape. However, this containment, through the creation of an internal safe place, is not sufficient to protect the children from the consequences of experiencing the unacceptable and the unbelievable. These same building blocks may come into play for the clinicians or parents involved. If the adults are to fully assist the children in their recovery, then the adults must first come to possess the capacities necessary to fully experience and integrate the events and feelings disclosed by the children about the ritualistic abuse ordeal, about its impact on their lives, and about their complete experience in the world.

Unique, at least in degree, to treating a child who reports ritualistic abuse experiences is the need for an adult to possess or to develop the ability to hear difficult and inconceivable accounts while staying focused on the child's needs, process, and perceptions. The adult may experience overwhelming emotional reactions, a need to prove the veracity of the child's reports, or a desire to understand the full implications of these events (including the motivations of the accused). These needs must be suspended while the adult is with the child if the child is to have a chance to tell the story, complete with his or her own thoughts, beliefs, feelings, and interpretations. The adult's belief that there is a story to be told and understood may be critical to the healing relationship, which requires belief in the unfinished quality of the child's story, as well as in the child's potential to move through and beyond the reported experiences and the associated trauma.

When children discuss ritualistic activity—blood sacrifice, bondage, and the degradation they experience while being used to satisfy the sexual, destructive, and perverse needs of the adults involved in bizarre ceremonial acts—it is important for helping adults not to get sidetracked by the need to uncover the absolute truthfulness of these events. All too often, the children involved are the only participants to speak of the events; it does them a disservice to place primary emphasis on the adults' need to know or to prove the accuracy of the children's reports, particularly within the context of a helping relationship. In the healing alliance, it is essential that the child's experience guide the process, for it is through the act of allowing the child to lead within the safeguards and limits of the therapeutic relationship that the possibility exists for the child to learn to trust, to control, to master, and in a whole way to grow beyond the trauma.

The therapist and parent(s) attempt to facilitate the healing through a delicate series of interchanges with the child. These include the following:

1. *Making contact with the full child, by placing an emphasis upon the visible and the hidden strengths and vulnerabilities of the child.* The challenge in cases of reported ritualistic abuse includes the adult's not flinching from the child's accounts or from his or her powerful, sometimes conflicting emotions of rage, pain, despair, terror, and excitation. At the same time, the adult will encounter the formidable barriers that the child has erected to prevent discovery and the associated threatened annihilation. The adult will need to follow the child's lead, provide support, remember the bits and pieces of things that the child has shared, and build a map from these experiences to return to the child when it is time for integration.

2. *Uncovering the nature of the injury and allowing it to come forward into the child's present relationship world.* This needs to be done with respect for the shame and fear the child experiences. Disclosure is an ongoing process, and the adult will need to work at being comfortable with his or her own and the child's hesitation and uncertainty.

3. *Allowing the child to express previously inhibited behavioral, emotional, and cognitive responses associated with the injury.* This expression threatens to recreate injury and destructiveness in the present, because of the power with which the memory of terrible aggressive and sexual ritualistic experiences returns. The adult must create a safe environment for this process to occur. This will mean focusing on the material while providing the child with a safe way to express and manipulate the associated action

and feeling. This can be done through symbolic play, drawing, storytelling, or puppet play, which is eventually linked by the child and therapist with the memories of abuse.

4. *Exploring with the child his or her past responses to the dual reality and the consequences that have occurred as a result of it, within the context of the child's current relationship experiences.* The adult will need to be ready to help the child distinguish the tendency to script and anticipate interpersonal relationships on the basis of the past, which does not account for present reality and the reaction of others. Ideally, the child will gain in skill and has available parents or other supportive figures with whom to interact in nonabusive ways.

5. *Validating the child's physical, affective, cognitive, and interpersonal responses then and now.* This means that the adult needs to tease out of the child's presentation the key patterns of response, take note of them, and allow their full complexity to emerge. The child may feel many feelings, may experience both helplessness and omnipotence, and may anticipate both success and failure within similar situations. Yet the child's tendency will be to cast these multiple possibilities aside and to allow only one controllable possibility to emerge, without the adults continued and gentle challenge of this stance.

6. *Helping the child to develop new emotional and cognitive experiences, language, and constructs that express and make sense of seemingly opposite experiences.* The adults will need to provide the child in an active way with new possibilities for understanding and accepting events and responses from the child's past experience that do not seem to go together.

7. *Providing the child with time, comfort, safety, and a relationship context in which exploration and integration of the abusive experiences can occur.* A key to this process is the creation of a relationship in which behavioral limits restrict the child's hurting or being hurt.

8. *Facilitating the child's ability to reconnect with external support systems, particularly emphasizing the development of safety anchors between the parent and the child, while encouraging the incorporation of the idea that the child now has choices that he or she did not previously have for managing internal reactions and interpersonal experiences.* Emphasis is placed upon balancing age-appropriate reliance on others with awareness and utilization of independent choices.

Each of these needs is present simultaneously for a child in the healing process. The child's process is the only guide to which experiences may need to take priority or assume principal importance at any one time. If a given child is not sleeping because of nightmares in which the abuse is relived, for example, facilitating the child's and parents' capacity to make night safe and sleep possible takes priority over other issues. Each significant player in the child's life will need to assist the child in finding the capacity to sleep safely. In therapy, the child and therapist may work to uncover the underpinnings of the nightmares and fears, using drawings, sand tray recreations, or puppets to allow the original memory to surface and to allow the appropriate emotion to attach itself to the memory. The child may assist in creating a feeling of safety at bedtime by helping to lock the house or to turn on the night light. The parent helps to create an atmosphere of safety for the child (which also allows the child to work on mastery of fear) by accepting and participating in the locking-up process, or by providing a pallet in the parents' own room to which the child can retreat for a brief time if the fear becomes overwhelming on a particular night.

The recovery process must be an interactive one among the child, the parent(s), and the therapist. Each plays a vital and unique role. There is a movement back and forth as the child's present needs and experiences and past trauma are revealed, enacted, and woven together into a fabric that provides cohesion and form in the context of the child's current life.

The helping adults must provide what the child was denied during the abusive experience and not given as the result of his or her hidden accommodations. This includes a critical role for the external validation of the child as a congruent being—as an individual with a core sense of self that is consistent in the face of relationship experiences, expectations, attributions about the world, and the positive and negative outcomes of human behavior. This means that within the healing relationship, the child needs to be experienced as possessing the capacity to be whole.

The child's ability to be both generative and destructive is embraced, with the belief in the child's capacity to act more often toward the preservation of what is good within himself or herself. Experiencing tolerance within the therapeutic and parental relationships for a range of behavior creates the seedbed in which the child's ability to perceive self and others more accurately and to integrate complex experiences can grow. The child has chosen before to preserve the self, and within the context of the healing relationship he or she can be allowed to experience this choice outright with a fuller complement of potential resolutions, rather than in the isolated, forgotten, or unacceptable shadows of the hidden experience.

Acceptance is at the core of treatment for these children, for it was denied them in the duality of their previous experience. They need to encounter their own capacity to take care of themselves, regardless of how primitive their attempts may have been or may continue to be. Simultaneously, they need to experience the protection afforded to them by others, particularly their parents. This realliance needs to occur while the children learn and experience that they can distinguish between those who are hurtful and those who are helpful, and between the harmful and beneficial aspects of themselves and others. Finally, the children need to come to an acceptance of their own and others' capacity to act in such incomprehensible and often paradoxical ways. The integration of their past experience with their present reality, and the incorporation of some new set of expectations about the human condition, require a kind of resignation to the human capacity to damage while other components of the self are utilized to repair and eventually move beyond the pain, rage, and despair associated with being injured or with the act of causing injury to another.

The therapeutic relationship is designed to provide a testing ground in which these children can experience new skills under controlled conditions, and in which they can be assisted toward reestablishing full contact with their capacity to trust, acquire, master, and enjoy relationships. The healing process for such a child requires a relationship in which an adult can be fully present alongside the child's injuries and the child's strengths, while providing the child with reasonable external safety, validation, and belief in the child's capacity to heal and grow from the inside out. Parents and therapists each provide this testing ground and relationship in different ways.

CONCLUDING THOUGHTS

In essence, the healing process involves a partnership between children and the adults who participate with them in the act of uncovering, discovering, and recovering from the trauma of severe and multiple abuses that are so overwhelming as to fall into the category of incomprehensible. These abuses leave the child with injuries on many levels, including the following: bodily or physical injuries; impairments of memory; cognitive beliefs about the destructive and powerless aspects of the self and others, which are based on the child's experience in the abusive reality; powerful, often destabilizing affective reactions, including unacceptable rage and incapacitating fear; behavioral manifestations of hypervigilance, particularly reactivity toward aggression or threat, and symptom formation; and finally, troubled and insecure relationships with parents and others. The adults involved in the children's healing process are faced with the need to provide a safe and effective environment for the exploration and mastery of the children's injurious experiences, and for the integration of these experiences with their more accomplished and capable selves. Simultaneously, these adults are reeling from the effects of the children's disclosures and reactions upon everyone's sense of the world as a fair, safe, and just place. The adults must also form or develop supportive partnerships with others, in order to fulfill their need to provide for the children's recovery while managing their own overwhelming experience.

The events of ritualistic abuse experiences and their disclosure are potentially overpowering for all involved. Something so powerful means that clinicians and parents must strike a clear alliance in support of the healing process. They will need to share their understandings and experiences of the children. Parents need to be made aware of their children's struggles, disclosures, and beliefs. Without such knowledge, the parents and the children will be limited in their capacity to challenge and to reframe the damage done to their relationship by the dual reality the children had to face alone at the time of the abuse. The parents will also be limited in their ability to provide an environment, outside of the relatively brief and limited therapeutic relationship, in which the children can safely learn about being with others in productive and nondamaging (although at times difficult) human interaction.

A partnership between the parents and therapists that allows for an exchange of information challenges some of the traditional concepts of confidentiality, even for children. The exchange is necessary for recovery and healing, and the children's participation in this process can accelerate their achievement of mastery rather than lead to an experience of betrayal. This is particularly true in terms of challenging the children's beliefs that to break the secret will mean dire consequences. If the children's fears are shared between responsive and responsible adults, then these consequences are more likely to be avoided. The children, even very young children, can work with a therapist to determine what and how to tell the parents about certain material shared in the therapy sessions. Some children will want to be a part of the telling. Others will want to be present but silent, needing to watch the parental reaction. Still others will want the therapist to tell in their absence, fearing what they might see or feel. And finally, some children will refuse to allow for material to be shared; in this case, their reasons need to be understood and validated. They may accurately fear how their parents might react to or use information about them in unhelpful ways, or they may accurately assess the parents' capacity to take in certain emotionally charged information. This reality may limit the flow of information between parents and therapists until such time as the children's roadblocks and the parents' own limitations can be transformed or removed. Parents may need their own therapeutic experience to be able to respond effectively to their children's needs.

Together, the children, parents, and therapists work toward the time when the children's emotional, cognitive, and behavioral experience will be sufficiently understood so that the past and present can be integrated and the children may resume a developmental course that includes all of their experiences, capabilities, and potential. Toward this end, the children need respect for their defenses and emotional reactivity, so that they do not reexperience debilitating helplessness. They need to be empowered to seek alternative resolutions in both their therapeutic and life experiences, thus countering their fears and beliefs acquired at a time of false choice in the abusive reality. They need to be held accountable for their false starts in a fair manner that allows them to harness their own rage. They need to be kept company, guided through, and kept safe without reactive rescue in the face of their full experience of injury, betrayal, guilt, shame, pleasure, magic, hate, forgiveness, and love in relationship to the past and present. They need focused attention to their symptoms that provides them with the cognitive and behavioral tools both to manage and to utilize their emotional reactions. This will allow them to connect emotion to past memory and present experience as it occurs, instead of suppressing or blocking feeling states and holding them in a kind of suspended animation until the cable snaps and they burst forth. The physical anchors and other triggers for memory and emotion deeply rooted in the child can then be explored and integrated.

PART VI

Final
Considerations

USES AND ABUSES OF RESEARCH
Cross-Currents of Community Exploitation

Roland C. Summit

INTRODUCTION: COMMUNITY PREJUDICE AND THE MISPERCEPTION OF RESEARCH

The present project fulfills an urgent need for sober, accurate information about an inflammatory, destructively controversial subject. The intrinsic value of this research is at risk of being obscured and overshadowed by those who will use it to advance predetermined beliefs and emotional arguments that serve legalistic, political, pecuniary, and even religious goals. Despite Robert Kelly's precautions in Chapter 4 against inappropriate generalizations, this study will be seized on to "prove" the prejudicial insistence that Satanists took control of southern California preschools. Even before such claims are attached, the project will be attacked by an equally opinionated argument that this study is just another piece of propaganda contrived by the same conspiracy of overzealous researchers, therapists, and parents who created the "ritualistic sexual abuse hoax" in 1983. Such divisive kindling overpowers the more reasonable human issues that beg for analysis. Is there really such a thing as ritualistic sexual abuse of tiny children? And if so, how can it be identified and contained? These issues remain deadlocked in polar dispute; *Behind the Playground Walls* should not be exploited to resolve them. Rather, the data address another question: What are the consequences for children and families who are involved in terrors that defy description? In view of the demonstrated consequences and the torment of community fragmentation, a disturbing and radical challenge should be addressed: Can existing community institutions address these unknowns, or do we need some kind of reorganization to develop more reasonable concepts and responses?

The data in this study imply that existing agencies are not only counterproductive but sometimes mutually antagonistic to the needs of children and families who speak out against unspeakable acts. The study identifies a number of characteristics and choices that families can mobilize in response to reported trauma, in order to minimize continuing damage. What is not obvious in the preceding chapters is that these best efforts of children and families can provoke community scorn and eventual disgrace within the very institutions that purport to insure a just and fair society.

The remarkable contrast in community response between the Nevada (SA group) and southern California (RSA group) allegations depended on the rapid, unequivocal resolution of the ultimate issue through the confession of the central suspect in the Nevada case. The words of an adult established that the reports of the children, delayed, inconsistent, and even self-contradictory as they were, could be and should be believed. The assurance of one nefarious adult gave the entire adult community permission to see the affected families as real victims, deserving of sympathy, therapy, healing, and financial reparation. The clinicians who helped identify and treat those adult-verified victims were seen as providing a community service, and were respected for the special expertise that enabled them to pry loose the reluctant disclosures and to sustain parental belief despite the transient retractions. If that one adult eyewitness had claimed innocence, any number of children could have been called liars, and any level of professional intervention could have been labeled not only incompetent but even dangerous to the well-being of the larger community.

The difference in Manhattan Beach, as well as with all but one of the so-called ritualistic sexual abuse cases reported throughout North America and in Europe, is that no adult has admitted eyewitness participation; this has thrown the credibility of the children, the character of the parents, and the methods of the clinicians into adversarial analysis. Complaints of terrorism, murder, and pornography were instrumental also to this divergent response. In the absence of physical evidence of such crimes, the alleged ritualistic acts served to invite logical disbelief and to justify the humiliation of those who chose to believe that such atrocities could really happen.

What resources can parents trust if they believe that their children are endangered within a community institution? How can families be empowered to protect themselves if their efforts to do so are condemned as irresponsible and libelous? What is a reasonable level of suspicion and a responsible level of belief? And what right has anyone to attempt to heal children of putative assaults that cannot be proven to exist? Does protection of children really depend on incrimination of adults? If a child's words lack credibility as a basis for imprisoning a trusted adult, are they then counterproductive as a cry for understanding and rescue? If adversarial argument is inconclusive in criminal courts, are there social and psychological data that can be spared forensic attacks for the purpose of child, family, and community reconstruction?

The purpose of this reflective chapter is to look at the merits of the present study, and to discuss some of the dynamics of community institutions, which can draw from this study either the objective, carefully defined potential for enlightenment or the presumption of inappropriate, deliberately misleading conclusions.

SPONSORS AND PRODUCTS: RESEARCH AS A TOOL FOR OPINION

Not all research is created equal. Academic research, clinical research, and commercial (product development) research are so far divergent as to be mutually exclusive and potentially contradictory. The present study brings academic rigor to clinical research, and it exists in brilliant contrast to research that has previously addressed the subject of ritualistic abuse. The project was all the more difficult to realize because the subject has been offensive to traditional scientists.

The academic researcher is charged to pursue basic truths according to traditional and carefully controlled constraints designed to guard against self-fulfilling bias. Basic research, which establishes theoretical models, is held in higher academic esteem than applied research, which might be commercially exploited and somehow self-serving for the researcher.

Clinical research covers a wide spectrum of observation, from anecdotal case reports by individual practitioners to double-blind studies of thousands of subjects and matched controls within rigorous protocols. It may be commercially sponsored for product development, as in testing a new drug, or it may be institutionally sponsored and even product-challenging, as in testing the impact of cigarettes on life expectancy. In any event, the researcher is expected to have no financial interest in the outcome. The most prestigious clinical journals, like their academic counterparts, tend to reject studies that are conspicuously commercial or socially controversial in favor of more pure and presumably more objective research.

Sophisticated research depends on substantial funding, and the choice to do research depends on its potential to reward the interests of a sponsor. Commercial research will be funded only if it will be a useful tool in developing a marketable product. Elaborate precautions and monitoring are required if public-interest research is conducted for the benefit of private-interest sponsors. Research disputing the hazards of smoking is questionably objective if it has been paid for by the cigarette industry. Similarly, a study of the credibility of complaining witnesses will fulfill a foregone conclusion if it has been commissioned by the defendant. But potentially exculpatory research is readily funded, freely conducted, and uncritically endorsed in the marketplace of the courts. Research that might endorse witness credibility or describe the effects of victimization is of limited value to prosecutors, so such research must compete for scarce governmental or philanthropic funding, with no exploitable product beyond the welfare of the victims as a class.

Ironically, if children complaining of sexual abuse constitute the class in question, the prevailing ethical mandate for child *subject* protection tends to eliminate research aimed at child *victim* protection. Any research involving the use of human subjects raises ethical issues about the impact of the research itself on the subjects. If human clinical research is to be at once meaningful, academic, and ethical, and if it proposes to examine children with procedures relevant to potentially hurtful, terrifying, and sexual experiences, then the methods and the motivations of the proposed researchers will be subjected to nearly prohibitive restrictions by both the sponsor and the academic institution authorizing the study.

If the projected outcome might be exploited for commercial or forensic purposes—as, for instance, an instrument of truthfulness concerning child victims of crime might be—it is likely to be vetoed by the academic research committee. Even the possibility that a study *might* be exploited for nonacademic purposes inhibits the generation of high-quality research that could help balance irresponsible exploitation. The willingness or reluctance of academic institutions to research divisive topics therefore becomes a critical factor in the resolution of current community disputes about sexual abuse allegations.

The preceding discussion is essential if the present study is to be viewed in accurate context and in comparison with other studies, especially when it is viewed in the courts of public opinion and in forensic argument. *Behind the Playground Walls* is a singular example of the successful marriage of the least congenial elements in scholarly endeavor. It presents academic-quality clinical research involving a field study of children who have reported each of two variations of sexual abuse, compared where possible with similar children who have made no such reports. The few references in the text to lawyers, the need for a federal Certificate of Confidentiality, and the UCLA Human Subjects Committee provide the tiniest hints of the immense problems and agonizing delays in accomplishing such a study. Anyone comparing the cautious, often nonstartling conclusions of this study with the authoritative claims and lurid proclamations of various clinical experts should be prepared to examine the origins and motivations behind such claims.

FOUNDATIONS OF
EXCULPATORY AUTHORITY

In view of the manifold impediments to producing ecologically relevant research to explore the coping mechanisms and the credibility of children subjected to extreme abuse, it should not be surprising that specifically relevant, academic-quality research still lags behind clinical opinion as the prevalent guide to explaining the vagaries of all child sexual abuse complaints, let alone the relatively fresh outrages of ritualistic reports. Child sexual abuse was barely acknowledged before 1975, and descriptions of ritualistic abuse have been recognized clinically only since 1983.

Some of the most telling opinion—certainly that which most incites controversy and which most paralyzes efforts toward more reasonable, more scientific study—is exculpatory court testimony that passes as clinical expertise. Such testimony is designed to explain abuse away, and its proponents can be predicted to challenge the validity of *Behind the Playground Walls*. The RSA cohort, they will say, was created not by real abuse but by a tragic hoax, as "proven" in court with the failure of criminal prosecution. They will name the parents and therapists who established the data as the perpetrators of unwarranted and abusive fears, which are not comparable with the "verified" sexual abuse in Reno. The authors of the study will be vilified in skeptical quarters for a bald and dogged attempt to legitimize the California hysteria by trying to link it to verifiable abuse. The boilerplate exculpatory theory, now promoted as gospel by many influential journalists (Bygrave, 1990; Nathan, 1987, 1989, 1990; Cockburn, 1990; Fischer, 1989; Allen, 1990; Rabinowitz, 1990), asserts that children who make outrageous complaints are not victims of sexual abuse but of interviewer indoctrination. This argument can dismiss any distress shown by the families in the Manhattan Beach sample as a measure not of external assault, but of their own self-serving and frustrated witch hunt.

Individuals who have made a career out of discrediting reports of child sexual abuse can qualify as experts on the basis of professional licensure alone, without demonstrated experience with abused children. They draw on clinical authority and irrelevant research to argue that children cannot resist parroting the subliminal cues of knowing interrogators, who elicit false allegations from nonabused children in their zeal to discover undisclosed abuse. These indoctrination theories are advanced not in scientific literature, but in trial lawyers' journals and entrepreneurial publications.

According to the indoctrination theory, the reports of ritualistic abuse that emerged in 1983 in Manhattan Beach, California, and in Jordan, Minnesota, and in the many other locations that followed, are aberrations that can be recognized as absurd by logical people, but that are seized upon or even implanted by self-styled experts in sexual abuse detection. When there is no conviction, as with all but one of the defendants in Jordan and with all of those implicated in the Manhattan Beach cases, the argument that improper questioning produced unwarranted accusations gains plausibility, along with the courtroom utility and income potential of designated experts for the defense.

The abrupt and sensationalistic eruption of bizarre, unprecedented complaints, coupled with the unique problems of bringing such anomalies to trial, marks 1984 as the turning point in what had been an orderly movement for child abuse recognition and child protection (Hechler, 1988). Before that, although only a small fraction of the thousands of newly discovered cases of child sexual abuse had been selected for prosecution, the predominance of convictions in those that went to court had threatened to upset the traditional balance of advocacy. The criminal defense of an accused adult, which had always relied on simply trivializing the competency of a complaining child, was now threatened by the emergence of social scientists and clinical specialists who believed in traditionally unbelievable complaints and who brought an informed empathy with children into courtroom discussions. Trial lawyers needed better strategies to discredit the emerging teamwork between clinical and forensic child advocates.

Allegations of ritualistic sexual abuse allegations left child protection teams bewildered, even divided (Marron, 1988). Teamwork that was lauded for intervention in single-victim incest could be impugned as conspiratorial when it claimed to flush out dozens of victims silently terrorized by groups of apparently upright adults. Any citizen, man and woman alike, could be a defenseless victim of such a witch hunt, which was exactly the fear that defense attorneys could now exploit.

The acquittal of the first and only attempt at prosecution in Jordan was a humiliation for the county attorney. She suspended further prosecutions in October 1984, citing the emerging allegations of ritualistic murder and the need to bring in the Minnesota Bureau of Criminal Apprehension and the Federal Bureau of Investigation (FBI). Children retracted their claims of ritual sacrifice when they were confronted with the inconsistencies in their stories by these outside investigators. The state attorney general mounted an investigation, and the ensuing report gave immunity from further prosecution, concluding that the interdependent alliance and blurring of roles among community investigators and clinicians had made it impossible to verify the complaints wrung out through such a profusion of interviews (Humphrey, 1985). Emancipated defendants sued the protective agencies for invasion of federal civil rights. Several formed what became the organization called Victims of Child Abuse Laws. An FBI conference on ritualistic abuse in February 1985 trained local police from around the nation to beware of the parental cross-germination and clinical contamination that supposedly generated shared beliefs in unholy ceremonies, despite the paucity of physical evidence. Los Angeles-area delegates to that conference came back suspicious of the alliance of clinicians, parents, and law enforcement officers that might have engendered an epidemic of paranoia in the South Bay area. Thus the RSA cohort in this study was affected by prejudicial disbelief and loss of interagency support as an immediate result of exculpatory testimony in Minnesota, years before facing those same humiliations in California courts.

Defense attorneys now had their much-needed wedge. Teams were divided and communities were confused. The indoctrination theory, which seemed so tenuous at the outset of the Jordan trials, took on such power that it could inculpate conspiracies of public servants in the defense of putative conspiracies of ritual sadists.

Despite similar cases with emphatic convictions, two high-visibility prosecution failures have been defined as turning the tide of reason against a passing wave of irrational zeal. Those two cases marked the simultaneous, coincidental outbreak of ritualistic abuse allegations in the late summer of 1983, and their defense triumphs bookended half a decade of suspended judgment. The McMartin investigation in Manhattan Beach is condemned as the seedbed of national hysteria, and the Jordan defense is recognized as the birthplace of the backlash (Hechler, 1988).

The impact of the defense victory in the Jordan cases and the ensuing demand for commercial research are illustrated by the destiny of the prevailing expert witness. Ralph Underwager, PhD, had virtually no experience as a criminal expert witness and had published nothing in the area of child sexual abuse prior to his Jordan testimony in 1984. Since then he has attacked the credibility of children in over 200 testimonies. He and his wife have written two books (Wakefield & Underwager, 1988, 1989). They also publish a journal, *Issues in Child Abuse Accusations*, under the auspices of their own Institute for Psychological Therapies (IPT). Dr. Underwager, Ms. Wakefield, and the five other editors write most of the articles, and there is no indication of an editorial board or other peer review process. Dr. Underwager's priorities for proper interrogations are emphatic: It is "more desirable that a thousand children in abuse situations are not discovered than for one innocent person to be convicted wrongly" (quoted in Crewdson, 1988, p. 195).

The cornerstone of research used by Dr. Underwager to challenge the disclosures of children is his Video and Audiotape Analysis Project (Wakefield & Underwager, 1988, 1989). This project analyzes recorded interviews for the prevalence of six categories of interviewer behaviors defined as error-producing: closed questions, modeling, pressure, rewards, aids (such as anatomically correct dolls), and paraphrase.

The origin of the research was the analysis of videotapes of clinical interviews given to Dr. Underwager as a consultant to attorneys defending clients against allegations of ritualistic abuse in a Reno preschool (not the one attended by the SA cohort in the present study). The children in these tapes became a research cohort by simple virtue of their referral for clinical evaluation in the wake of suspected abuse.

This research was commissioned April 26, 1985, by attorneys representing Farmers Insurance Company, which would bear the liability of the preschool if the children's complaints were not impeached. There was no written agreement, faculty review, or human use committee to encumber the process, which was designed, executed, and delivered in only 3 months. IPT charged $97,200 for establishing a comprehensive literature review and for the videotape tabulations performed by people hired from a temporary agency.

The information above is drawn from Dr. Underwager's sworn deposition, taken in the Country Walk Babysitting Service case in Miami, Florida (Underwager, 1985). John Hogan, the prosecutor taking the deposition, elicited the parameters and the conclusions of the study:

Q: How many different victims or children did you study in this? . . .

A: We had tapes from 15 children.

Q: All from Reno?

A: Yes.

Q: Were they all sexually abused?

A: That's the allegation. I don't believe that they were. (p. 123)

Q: What were the research conclusions? . . .

A: . . . [T]he interrogators caused the children to say the things that they said.

Q: How do you make that conclusion if you don't know whether or not what the children said was true or not?

A: That's [sic] whether or not it's true has no effect upon whether or not the interrogators elicited the statements. . . .

Q: Okay. So your study did not determine whether or not interviewing techniques would lead to fabrication of the truth, it simply dealt with whether interviewing techniques would cause responses from children?

A: Right. (pp. 127–129)

The Video and Audiotape Analysis Project continues to expand with the authors' testimonial caseloads. Using this "scientific" method, all of the interviews studied can be dismissed as error-producing, without any evidence that the questioning style was improper or that the questions elicited error instead of truth.

Several courts have rejected testimony based on the Analysis Project (Update, 1990), but those exclusions have little impact on the continuing demand for such expert testimony in other courtrooms, on the citation of the project by other defense experts, or on the growing popular and forensic credibility of the generic theory of interviewer indoctrination. Common sense demands such an explanation when children voice seemingly outrageous descriptions of unthinkable rituals. The indoctrination argument, once it was established in public consciousness by high-visibility ritual case acquittals (and somehow not diminished by high-visibility convictions such as that in the Country Walk case, or by careful academic research that refutes it—see Saywitz, Goodman, Nicholas, & Moan, 1991; Saywitz, 1990; Saywitz, Goodman, & Myers, 1990; Goodman, Rudy, Bottoms, & Aman, 1991), has moved to general utility in all disputed reports of any variety of sexual abuse.

The foregoing criticisms of clinical opinion as grist for adversarial dogma do not stand alone against defense testimony. An opposing diatribe can be promulgated for prosecution testimony, and I myself have been criticized for coining the basic follies (Coleman, 1986; Eberle & Eberle, 1986; Kendrick, 1988).

The polemic arguments underscore a common theme: Not enough is known clinically about child sexual abuse to supply a jury with proof beyond a reasonable doubt that a child has been victimized and that the named suspect can be held responsible for the specific crimes charged. It is arguably true that the early rush to identify victims was relatively naive to the risks of false incrimination, and that the now-familiar and here-documented process of sequential and self-contradictory disclosure shifts a burden of suspicion to those who elicit that process. But those tentative reflections call for sober, objective research, not for tools which further sharpen the ceremonial lances of attorneys. The jury of peers needed to explore the profound subtleties of children's reactions to trauma resides in the scientific community, not in a courthouse.

Research geared toward a court-exploitable product has something of a jump-start advantage, compared to that which qualifies for the halls of academe. It is generated not for the understanding of human behavior as much as for the exculpation of defendants. Our constitution makes no promises for education and research, but it guarantees to every criminal defendant the right to an attorney who must exhaust every opportunity to protect the presumption of innocence. This is a right we cannot abridge without undermining the foundations of our freedom. But this imperative, combined with various economic and power-vested interests, favors a quicker, more apparently decisive focus of opinion on the comfort of adults than on the discomfort of children. Whereas academic and clinical research is dependent on the vagaries of philanthropic or institutional funding, commercial research is fueled by the high stakes of criminal and civil contests, funded as needed by corporations intent on limiting massive financial liability.

The exculpation argument has worth, and the experts voicing it are valuable—not because the indoctrination theory is demonstrably true, but because it is needed to preserve adversarial balance in a court system suddenly faced with unprecedented numbers of sexual abuse reports supported by an impressive assortment of otherwise credible parents, police officers, and clinicians. This opposition is essential in adversarial arenas, both in courts of law and in the debates of the mass media. But verbal contests for the protection and reassurance of adults do not necessarily assure a fair hearing for the complaints of children. And rules that presume innocence for defendants impose the accusation of guilt on presumably innocent witnesses. What is missing in this equation is a more sober, genuinely truth-finding forum that can explore the dilemmas of the children and families. What is needed is a nonadversarial, child- and family-centered sanctuary for academic-quality clinical research.

DISCUSSION: IS THERE A SAFE HAVEN FOR MULTIVICTIM CASE RESEARCH?

A sanctuary such as the one described above requires a paradigm shift in public consciousness. In order to enter meaningfully into the domain of the abused child, we need to tolerate and adopt for ourselves the child victim's perception of a divided world. A victimized child learns to reconcile paradox by learning to assume that opposites coexist. Good and bad, love and contempt, fairness and outrage, trust and betrayal are so randomly and noncontingently imposed that the victim must contrive a third reality which offers shelter from the impossible tempests of adult betrayal. This dissociative sanctuary of the mind has been viewed in the past as bizarre and maladaptive—not because it does not work, but because we have refused to acknowledge the storms that our adult judgments have imposed on victimized children. At best, we have acknowledged that a dysfunctional family may be temporarily impossible for a child to live with, but we have promised the child and ourselves that as a community of enlightened, compassionate pseudoparents we will make it better. When parents are not the problem—when we must look at cherished institutions as a suspected source of destructive exploitation, we are bewildered by our inability to agree on a culprit. We find ourselves once more dividing against ourselves, attacking children, families, and the agents of child protection to conserve our own collective belief in a just and fair society.

Rather than holding to some naive, self-protective belief that adult society is just fine if we can only keep the kids from complaining, we must suspend our allegiance to dichotomy. The reality of complex human behavior, including the nature of interactive human institutions, is not "either–or" but "both–and." Adversarial assumptions are not mutually exclusive. We must not assume that either the defendants are guilty or the children are lying. Allegations of ritualistic abuse prove neither a massive conspiracy of evil nor mass hysteria. We must neither distrust all adults nor ignore all children, least of all those who have been invited to complain.

Although the extremes described above look fatuous on paper, they are played out in the thoughtless assumptions and unwarranted fears that we bring as a community to the unfamiliar challenges of child abuse. More reasonable realities are unsatisfying, inconclusive, even impotent; perhaps some of the allegations are real and some are reactive to some intermediate, still unrecognizable aspect of trauma. If some few adults are capable of unchallenged exploitation of innocence, everyone is not equally vulnerable to or eligible for that same misuse of authority. Children can be both a window to our greatest fears and a screen for our most fanciful projections. We can be wise and naive, guided and misguided, helpful and hurtful—all at once, but only rarely all or none.

Enlightenment reflects different colors in different lights. Diagnostic interviews that are appropriate for uncovering concealed abuse and identifying silent victims may be inappropriate for challenging authority and imprisoning suspects. A proud clinical achievement can be made to look humiliating in court.

Increased screening and maximum discovery of any malaise imposes the inevitability of both false positives and inexplicable outliers, which in turn lead both to more selective tests and to the discovery of still other, previously unsuspected disorders. What is first discarded as exotic and irrelevant may next be seen as prevalent and menacing, only to become eventually controllable and even beneficial. Diagnostic measures thought initially to be safe may become suddenly dangerous before unexpected risks are controlled.

X-rays, for example, were first unknown, then discovered and exploited carelessly. Early researchers actually died from chronic misuse before a more cautious and respectful view could emerge. The answer was not to ban experimentation or to imprison Thomas Edison (who subjected his assistant to fatal exposure), but to try harder to understand and harness an invisible energy.

When John Caffey used X-rays to discover the effects of physical child abuse in 1946, he was not allowed to publish his speculations that caretakers might have imposed such trauma or even that the bones had broken from external force, rather than from some still-unexplained internal weakness. X-rays eventually forced the more definitive exposition of child abuse in 1962 (Kempe, Silverman, Steele, Droegemuller, & Silver, 1962), but not before social workers and nurses had endured collegial censure and personal pain in wrenching descriptions of abuse from noncomplaining victims. Delayed, reluctant, extracted complaints were not enough. We had to have pictures. Pictures alone were misread. We also needed to learn the history that could not be volunteered by the patients themselves.

Diagnostic interviews for suspected sexual abuse are the equivalent of diagnostic X-ray surveys for physical abuse. Without some penetrating focus, abuse remains invisible. Although there is reason to attend to potential risks, there is no longer a conscionable argument for reverting to the tradition of not asking when circumstances or behavior suggest that a child may have been victimized. The risk of false positives must be balanced against the certainty of false negatives (Sorenson & Snow, 1991; Saywitz et al., 1991). Interviews have produced stories of ritualistic abuse; that much is certain. The challenge for society and for science is to find some better way than subjective debate to determine the meaning of those stories. Allegations of ritualistic abuse may be an artifact of diagnostic screening, or they may be a clue to some still-undefined and terrible malaise. Similar dilemmas in the public health domain have been resolved through research, not rhetoric.

The scattered, sequential process of disclosure is a clue to something worth knowing. The process is acknowledged as generic; yet two opposing arguments give opposite, self-nullifying reasons for its existence.

The challenge for readers of the present research study, like that for victims of continuing abuse, is to endure the uncertainty of two opposing views of the world without committing themselves to either position, all the while searching for the synthesis of clues that can allow for order and constructive resolution. We do not *know*, in the most satisfying sense of the word, what happened to the children in Nevada or to those in southern California, and this study does not presume to discover that elusive kernel of truth. We know that in both communities there was some smoldering, subliminal cause for concern that erupted through a series of interviews into epidemics of allegations. Was there something about the interviews or about the interviewers that led one cohort to a larger truth, as demonstrated by the even larger dimensions of an adult's confession, while the other exploded into exaggerations and hysterical chaos? Or does the improbable nature of ritualistic abuse allegations predicate an unprovable analysis?

An intriguing clue to the last question resides in the Reno community. Two groups of children complained of collective victimization in Reno preschools in 1985. Some of the same interviewers, using the same techniques, did the clinical screening in both cases. One cohort stayed within reason, complaining of less abuse than was ultimately revealed; this was the SA cohort examined in the present research. Interviews of the other group produced stories not only of sexual touching but also of ritualistic mayhem, and were therefore axiomatically false in the view of another researcher. These were the interviews that provided the foundation for exculpatory research. This other case resulted not in prosecution but in passionate, irresoluble debates, which eventually split the political and judicial communities of Nevada into warring factions (Editorial, 1988).

Did the questions and gestures of the interviewers in that monstrous case produce error, as asserted by Dr. Underwager and Farmers Insurance Company, or were the resulting allegations simply incredible? If interviews were error-producing in the second case, did they only accidentally point toward the truth in the first? In the primitive state of present dichotomies, the quality of the diagnostic interviews is determined by the face value of the outcome. It seems obvious that some of the most incredible allegations are distortions of something else, if not outright fantasies. But who will search for the meaning of the "something else"? Who will commission the research to find the truth, not just the presumptive error, in the allegations of children?

While we busy ourselves with not finding out the nature of whatever underlies allegations of ritualistic abuse, a very real and demonstrable psychological trauma continues for children, parents, and clinicians caught up in such allegations. The effects of that trauma are measured in the present study, which presages the immeasurable pain in similar epidemics that are still emerging throughout the Western world (Jonker & Jonker-Bakker, 1991; Campbell, 1990). There is little point in assuring these victims (children, parents, and therapists alike) that their view of ritualistic horrors is false; they know that it is subjectively real. It is all the more abusive to insist that the horrors are objectively false when there is no objective way to disprove them. Those who experience this trauma directly know that it brings genuine terror, whether or not it involves real pornography or real murders. Those of us who view these scenes from a distance cannot prove that the allegations are false merely because they are repulsively unfamiliar. Somehow, even before we can resolve the difficult truths of the ultimate answer, we must as a community find some way to stop punishing those who bring up the questions.

CONCLUSION: TOWARD THE EVOLUTION OF REASON OUT OF PREJUDICIAL DIALECTICS

For those who are already involved in whatever it is, the present study offers clear guidelines for healing. A child heals best in a climate of acceptance and demonstrated caring. Parents are most effective when they involve themselves in some level of advocacy for realizing and actively resolving the child's pain. Active measures include the search for a therapist who is not afraid of the unknown dimensions of bizarre disclosures, and who can also relieve the parents of the morbid necessity to probe for further details. Parents, therapists, and the extended community must provide all such children with acceptance and a model for comfort, security, and optimism in the face of continuing uncertainty and potential fear. Children, parents, and therapists benefit from peer support, as well as from the reassurance of open, unfettered catharsis and reframing of something that was once hidden and implosive.

The ultimate irony of ritualistic abuse allegations, demonstrated all too clearly in this study, is that all of the best that children, parents, and therapists can do has been forbidden, scapegoated, and punished by the community agencies that presume to provide security. The justice system is unbalanced by reports of trauma too strange to recognize, voiced by children too young to be really heard. The scientific community is stymied by the daunting irrelevance of these crime-and-punishment issues within the traditional schools of early childhood development and child psychiatry. Journalists are led and misled by dazzling opposites of authoritative opinion and common sense. Friends and neighbors, all of us, are torn with doubts and conflict of loyalty between institutions we cherish and conspiracy theories we distrust.

Such conceptual chaos is fueled by prejudice. We decide what we must believe according to traditions and opinions that buttress whatever we are determined to preserve. Those who insist on innovation are condemned as naive to the wisdom of the status quo. Those who respond to allegations of ritualistic abuse as if they could be real are seen as misguided and dangerous. Parents who endorse and share their children's stories can be said to abuse their children with unwarranted fears and to confound orderly investigation with cross-contamination. Parents who are hungry for more information and more relevant evidence are called vigilantes and accused of using their children as pawns in their own designs for attention and influence. Therapists who ask questions and who give respect to unexpected answers are blamed for inventing and implanting the terrors.

This study shows that parents and therapists become fearful and lose faith in themselves and in community institutions during such a process. How can therapists model serenity and optimism for children and parents if they are themselves assaulted by their peers and cross-disciplinary colleagues? How can researchers give appropriate foundation to clinicians if they are themselves bound by scholarly and economic sanctions that discourage such research?

The incredible dimensions of the southern California cases are explained away in the simplest theory by the assertion that improper interviews in one diagnostic agency implanted and confirmed the terrors of ritualistic abuse in all the children. Whatever the actual importance of the initial interviews to eventual extrapolation, it is clear in retrospect that the South Bay cases grew too large and too gruesome to be believed. Even prosecutors, who relied on the interviews initially, came to join with defense attorneys in condemning the interviews as leading and misleading.

But those same interviews had a powerful impact on parents, which created an unusual and universal turnaround from the predictable response. Although in most multichild allegations a certain number of parents refuse to hear the allegations and commit themselves to redeeming community confidence in a suspect institution, this was not the case in the South Bay. Although most parents approaching the interviews had been assured by their children that nothing had happened, and although many children retracted to their parents what they had acknowledged just before in interviews with strangers, parents viewing the disclosures on videotape came away stunned and grief-stricken in the steadfast belief that the reassurances from their children were false and the disclosures were real. The videotaped interviews created for the parents a paradigmatic shift, which united them around an agenda for confrontation and healing.

If abuse really happened, and if it is useful to identify victims and to endorse support and therapeutic follow-up for children, the interview process should be incisive and conclusive; emphatic validation should be provided for parents and children, who will otherwise grope for self-reassuring reversal. Whether or not abuse really happened, this process will come to be viewed as a witch hunt.

Whatever the forensic complications of the initial interviews of the South Bay children, the clinical implications were impressive. Parents trusted the interviewers and the allegations, despite prior misgivings and subsequent contradictions. Most parents followed through with recommended therapists. They came to accept the ensuing sequence of unbelievable allegations as credible, and they emerged believing that the therapy was helpful. It would appear that the same videotaped disclosures that McMartin jurors viewed as misleading were the articles of faith that freed parents from crippling ambivalence and allowed for collective endorsement of the worth of treatment.

So the smoke and mirrors persist. Interviews are neither good nor bad, but both. Disclosures are neither wholly credible nor definitively incredible. Monstrous rituals are hard to believe and impossible to ignore. Treatment requires belief—acceptance without assurance. Believers are overburdened by fear and bereft of support. Coalitions for support become labeled as conspiracies for attack. Collective belief is called hysteria. Dogmatic disbelief remains the voice of reason.

The shape of the illusion is defined not by what it is (if we could really see it) but by how we need to perceive it, and according to which of our senses and facilities and habitual resources we muster to resolve the taunting ambiguity.

Behind the Playground Walls does not tell us what really happened to the children. It cannot be used to prove whether ritualistic abuse is real, or whether a given interviewer can create an illusion of abuse in an impressionable child. This research base is not better or worse than the criminal trials in confirming the facts of abuse, and we must sustain a continuing, nagging uncertainty if the research is to provide other useful but less satisfying conclusions. If such research is to be exploited effectively, it must be sheltered from polarizing demands.

If such research is to be encouraged as a better basis for understanding than the more lucrative and authoritarian claims of forensic adversaries, the product will have to be at least as worthy of respect, and the producers must be seen as equally worthy of their hire. If insurance means security against assault as well as protection of institutional integrity, for little people as well as big, then it is the community at large, not the institutions of insurance, that must be invested in more accurate means of discovery and resolution.

Every individual, every family, and each agency of the community will suffer some disillusionment and loss of security, confidence, and trust if we are to understand fully why tiny children tell such horrible stories. It may mean that we cannot believe our children, that we cannot trust our memories, that we cannot trust each other, and even that we cannot trust ourselves. The world of early childhood looks less idyllic, less innocent, less trustworthy than it did in 1983. It is not up to the toddlers to set it straight for us again. They deserve for us to figure it out. We deserve to assure ourselves that we can develop the tools and muster the courage to accomplish that task. *Beyond the Playground Walls* gives us an important step in the right direction.

CHAPTER 20

EPILOGUE
The Research Perspective

David Finkelhor
Kathleen Kendall-Tackett

T HE STUDY DESCRIBED IN THIS BOOK is a rich compendium of findings and insights about the effect of reported sexual abuse on young children. Perhaps the most remarkable thing about it is that it was done at all.

Although the researchers are sparing in their description of the vicissitudes, the conditions for completing this study were tough. They might best be compared to trying to do research on a battlefield. It was undertaken at a time when an entire city—its legal and social service system, not to mention its mass media and the public at large—had become extremely polarized about the McMartin case. Nothing associated with the case, or with the concept of sexual abuse in day care, was free from controversy. Ordinary research problems, such as recruiting subjects or protecting confidentiality, were vastly complicated by this environment. Yet, in spite of these challenges, this study is noteworthy for its dispassionate tone, its comprehensiveness, and its adherence to scientific method.

This study breaks new ground in a number of areas that are worthy of note, making a major contribution to the already fairly extensive literature on the effects of reported sexual abuse. It is certainly the most comprehensive evaluation to date of the impact of alleged ritualistic sexual abuse. Although there are still many unanswered questions about the nature of this phenomenon, this study confirms the clinical impression that children who report such abuse are among those suffering the most devastating effects.

A comparison of this study with other studies on the effects of reported sexual abuse highlights this finding. For example, the impact of such abuse can be compared across studies by examining "effect sizes." This measure takes into account sample size and gives a standard coefficient of the strength of a relationship (Rosenthal & Rosnow, 1984). (Effect size gives an *r* statistic, so r^2 tells us the percentage of variance accounted for by the fact that the children reported abuse.) We selected Internalizing and Externalizing symptoms (as assessed with the Child Behavior Checklist), because several studies have examined these symptoms, and they cover a wide range of behaviors.

Table 20.1 shows how consistent the findings from the present study are with the results of past studies. Most studies show a healthy effect size for children reporting sexual abuse versus nonabused, nonclinical children. The results of this analysis give us an objective way to compare findings and see that, in particular, that children who report ritualistic abuse suffer serious effects. For Internalizing symptoms, the mean effect sizes across studies are .35 for reports of sexual abuse and .58 for reports of ritualistic abuse. For Externalizing symptoms, the mean effect sizes are .30

TABLE 20.1. Effect Sizes from Studies Comparing Children who Did and Did Not Report Sexual Abuse

Authors	Statistic	r^2
Internalizing		
SA *vs.* NA		
Shapiro, Leifer, Martone, & Kassem (1990)	$t(52) = 6.54$	.45
Lipovsky, Saunders, & Murphy (1989)	$F(107) = 12.66$	.11
Shapiro, Leifer, Martone, & Kassem (1992)	$t(52) = 6.11$	.42
Friedrich, Beilke, & Urguiza (1987)	$t(169) = 6.12$	.18
Kelley (1989)	$t(97) = 11.54$	.58
RSA *vs.* NA		
Kelley (1989)	$t(100) = 16.49$	.73
Present study (1991)	$F(99) = 71.6$	.42
Externalizing		
SA *vs.* NA		
Lipovsky et al. (1989)	$F(107) = 9.62$	.08
Shapiro et al. (1991)	$t(52) = 7.26$	.50
Friedrich et al. (1987)	$t(169) = 7.18$	.23
Kelley (1989)	$t(97) = 8.07$	.40
RSA *vs.* NA		
Kelley (1989)	$t(100) = 10.49$	.52
Present study (1991)	$F(99) = 38.3$	.28

Note. SA, children reporting sexual abuse only; RSA, children reporting ritualistic sexual abuse; NA, nonabused, nonclinical children.

and .40, respectively. Overall, there appears to be a stronger effect for reports of ritualistic abuse than there is for more typical reports of sexual abuse without ritualistic elements (although both create large effects). This gives a sense of how traumatized the children from the present samples were.

In addition, the present study, in its comprehensiveness, sets a model for future studies of impact, particularly studies of very young children. The combination of methods; the variety and scope of the instruments; the mixture of projective and nonprojective tests; the utilization of information from parents, therapists, and the children themselves—all of these elements go beyond the typical study in the field. The use of control groups broadens the application of this study beyond the highly publicized cases in Nevada and southern California. The use of multiple measures and of three reporting sources increases the validity of the findings and adds to the methodological literature on self-report versus other-report of symptoms of sexual abuse. Perhaps most impressive is the investigators' application of the traumagenic dynamics framework to these data. Not only is this a handy way to organize the findings, but it increases our understanding of how children are affected by both types of abuse. Researchers should study this approach carefully and adapt it in future studies.

Of particular note is the emphasis in this study on the family context of the victims. Other studies have noted that maternal response is an important (perhaps the most important) mediating factor in children's response to abuse. But this study looked at the response of both parents, and at family functioning, in a much more detailed way than has ever been done. Not surprisingly, the researchers found a more complex picture than has been found previously. Several characteristics were related to child functioning in the aftermath of reported abuse. Families who were cohesive (but not enmeshed), who reacted positively to their children, and who provided a supportive environment had children who functioned better and were less distressed. It also helped when parents mobilized community resources and sought therapy for their children. This active coping strategy was important because it countered the children's sense of powerlessness, which was a key dynamic in the alleged abuse. These results are consistent with several past studies indicating that lack of maternal support was significantly related to negative outcomes for child victims. The present study is much more detailed in this analysis and points to specific ways in which families can help.

But, in addition to looking at how the families' reaction affected the children, this study has been one of the first to look at how the reported abuse affected the families. Indeed, the study found that the abuse disclosures had a major impact on the parents, their marriages, their trust of the "outside world," and their parenting styles. Many parents were less likely to allow their children independence, more likely to display affection to them, and more likely to be lenient with them in the first year following the disclosures. The abuse reports also affected the parents' relationships with each other. Mothers in particular expressed more dissatisfaction with their marriages in the first year following disclosures than did fathers. Of course, this group of victims is unique in the literature on sexual abuse to date, because all the abuse occurred outside the family context. But the findings from this study suggest that studies in the future should devote more attention to looking at the effects of abuse disclosures and their aftermath on other family members as well.

Adding to a recent and growing trend, this study has also taken a longitudinal perspective on the impact of abuse disclosures. The literature now contains close to 10 studies with such a perspective. A longitudinal perspective is crucial for formulating policy conclusions about how to intervene and treat child victims. This study is noteworthy, in that the longitudinal period covered in the study is one of the longest in the sexual abuse literature.

The most important conclusion from this longitudinal perspective is that the majority of children who disclose abuse appear to heal, even children as initially traumatized as these children were. This is an extremely important conclusion, and one that has been lost in some of the extensive literature emphasizing the pathological effects of reported sexual abuse. Nonetheless, healing is not automatic. This study suggests that recovery is facilitated by a supportive family, by the use of community resources, and by psychotherapy.

Because of the new ground they have broken, the researchers in this study are able to offer some very useful recommendations. They should be commended for their ability to translate some of the science into policy and practice. Among their helpful recommendations are some specific suggestions for therapists who work with children reporting ritualistic abuse. For children, they recommend that treatment should focus specifically on concomitants of powerlessness, especially anxiety 'and fear. Betrayal and disillusionment are important issues for both children and parents in therapy. In addition, therapists need to address the entire marital and family system. These suggestions may help therapists focus on the most important treatment goals for children who report this type of abuse, without being swept away by bizarre or horrifying tales.

Where do we need to go from here? This study has pointed the field in a number of important directions.

1. We need information about the phenomenon of ritualistic abuse. We need to understand much more about the alleged perpetrators of such

abuse, the individual and group dynamics, and the nature of the experiences that the children report being subjected to.

2. We need research that tests specific theories about the impact of reported sexual abuse. Most research has simply added to this equation: Sexual abuse has negative consequences. What is most needed now is an understanding of why these consequences occur. This study made a conscious effort to use theory to structure its design. This must be done even more, with studies designed to test very specific aspects of trauma theory in regard to children.

3. We need research that looks at developmental issues in regard to reported sexual abuse. Past research has often lumped together children of a variety of ages and stages. We need a more systematic understanding of which symptoms occur at different developmental stages (e.g., sexual acting out is more common among preschoolers) and which symptoms occur at every stage. We also need to understand how victims process and resolve their experiences at each developmental stage. For example, how does being victimized as a child affect relationships with peers, authority figures, or future dating/sexual partners? The present study, looking at children in a relatively small age range, emerged with some very specific conclusions. We therefore join with the authors and urge follow-up of this sample as one fruitful way to gain information about the developmental aspects of reported sexual abuse.

4. Researchers need to document their findings more fully and to present them in systematic ways, to allow for comparisons among studies. The aggregation of conclusions about the effects of reported sexual abuse has been hampered by the presentation of findings in ways that new findings could not be compared with old findings. Authors need to present exact t, F or χ^2 values with degrees of freedom as these authors have done. In our analysis, the comprehensive presentation of findings from some studies allowed us to compare results, as we note above; however, most studies do not present all the necessary information.

5. We need studies of the process of recovery, rather than just the process of traumatization. Longitudinal studies of recovery have many policy implications. In these studies, we can look at the variables that can be changed and affected (e.g., participation in therapy and in court processes, support from professionals and family) rather than those that cannot (e.g., the seriousness of the disclosed abuse, the amount of force said to be used, etc.).

6. We need the development and refinement of measures to help in the study of effects. Too often researchers feel compelled to use the most conventional, well-established instruments. But we do not yet know whether these give us the full picture, or the best picture, of the effects of reported sexual abuse. It seems probable that at least some effects are not

tapped by currently available measures. Researchers must augment and experiment with current measures, and develop others. They must also look critically at the ones that are most often utilized, in order to understand their limitations. A study as comprehensive in its use of instruments as this one gives researchers a rich data base from which to look at some of these methodological issues.

In conclusion, the report from this study is a milestone in the literature on the effects of reported sexual abuse on children. Not only does it offer comprehensive information on the effects of alleged ritualistic sexual abuse, but it brings a message of hope. Most of the children in this study are recovering from the experiences they have disclosed, and therapists and families can do much to aid in this process.

CONCLUSIONS AND RECOMMENDATIONS

Jill Waterman
Robert J. Kelly
Jane McCord
Mary Kay Oliveri

CONCLUSIONS

From our extensive study of reported ritualistic and nonritualistic sexual abuse in preschool settings, several conclusions seem justified. First, ritualistic sexual abuse of young children has major effects on their functioning. As compared with nonabused children (the NA sample), children reporting ritualistic sexual abuse (the RSA sample) exhibited more behavior problems; had more negative attitudes in general and more negative attitudes toward school and family in particular; were highly fearful and suffered from post-traumatic stress disorder (PTSD); showed more sexualized behaviors; and exhibited a stance of hypervigilance toward the world. The majority of the effects listed were more severe in the RSA children than in the group of children who reported sexual abuse without ritualistic or terrorizing elements (the SA sample). However, it is difficult to distinguish the impact of the reported ritualistic sexual abuse from that of the ongoing community controversy and the apparently interminable (and ultimately indeterminate) legal proceedings that occurred in the RSA group and not in the SA group.

Follow-up 5 years after disclosure for the RSA group indicated that the children had made significant improvements in functioning and appeared quite socially competent. However, 17% of the children continued to exhibit significant residual problems, somewhat more of which were internalizing problems (e.g., somatic complaints, withdrawal) than externalizing problems.

The reported abuse had significant effects on families in both groups. Parents reported a variety of changes in their relationships with their children, as well as significantly impaired marital and sexual relationships in the wake of reported sexual abuse in preschools, whether ritualistic or nonritualistic. In the RSA group—which, as noted, experienced much community polarization and lengthy legal proceedings—parents had significantly less trust in the law, the mass media, teachers, babysitters, and the clergy after the abuse experience than before.

For the larger group of RSA children, variation in the impact of the experience on the children's functioning seemed to be mediated mostly by family factors. Families who were cohesive but not enmeshed (e.g., whose members felt very close to each other, asked each other for help, and consulted each other on decisions); parents who were perceived by their children as reacting more positively to them (e.g., spending time with them, comforting, giving physical affection, saying nice things to them) and less negatively (e.g., yelling, using physical punishment, criticizing); and families who provided a supportive rather than a hostile environment in the face of stress tended to have children who were functioning better and who were less distressed. Because of lack of variability on some factors that have been shown to mediate effects of abuse in previous studies (e.g., demographics, treatment variables, abuse variables), the minor contribution of these factors to child outcome cannot be taken as definitive. Parents overwhelmingly felt that the most helpful resource for healing was psychotherapy for their children.

RECOMMENDATIONS

A number of recommendations regarding investigation, assessment, and treatment of children and families reporting ritualistic sexual abuse in preschool or day care settings follow from our findings. These are delineated below.

1. *Treatment of children who report ritualistic sexual abuse must focus on concomitants of powerlessness, and specifically on anxiety and fear.* Some of the most pervasive effects on children's functioning found in this study were fearfulness, flashbacks, hypervigilance, and other symptoms of PTSD. These symptoms were also among the most likely to persist at follow-up, and must be addressed in the treatment of children reporting ritualistic sexual abuse. Perhaps anxiety symptoms can best be approached in terms of the dynamic of powerlessness. Through both talk and play, children's fears must be explored and understood, and then the children must be helped to feel empowered and able to be safe; some techniques that children and therapists in the present study found useful were role playing,

drawing of fears, "white magic" rituals (utilizing forces of good rather than evil), relaxation training, and structured fantasy play about powerful figures. In dealing with manifestations of PTSD, relaxation exercises and self-hypnosis tapes were useful in treating nightmares, flashbacks, and sleep disturbances, whereas hypervigilance and mistrust of others were often addressed by working directly within the child–therapist relationship.

Our data support the use of a similar strategy in helping parents to cope with the effects of reported ritualistic sexual abuse as well. Consistently, it appeared that parents who utilized active coping styles—who sought to mobilize professional, community and social resources to help their children and families, and who felt that they could handle whatever problems arose, facing troubles head-on and trying to get solutions—had children who were functioning more adaptively and experiencing less emotional distress than did parents who coped by more passive means (e.g., relying exclusively on spiritual resources, watching television, or feeling that problems would simply go away if they waited long enough). It therefore seems important to empower parents in taking a proactive stance, and to support them in fighting for their children's safety and mental health. Such active coping styles are certainly helpful in dealing with many types of adversity; they seem particularly important and necessary in ritualistic sexual abuse of children, because of the intensity of the powerlessness experienced, developed over an extended period of time by terrorization and ritual.

2. *Psychotherapy should address the disillusionment and betrayal that both parents and children experience in the aftermath of sexual abuse.* In our study, both parents and children in the RSA group felt a sense of disillusionment. Parents reported a significantly decreased sense of the world as a just and fair place, and children had significantly more negative, pessimistic attitudes than the control (NA) children. These attitudes must be identified and dealt with in psychotherapy. Both children and parents will be dealing with issues of betrayal and trust. Certainly the psychotherapeutic relationship is one avenue through which all parties involved can explore their mistrust and gradually work to redevelop the sense of trust in others. A therapeutic alliance with a child may be established quite slowly, as the child seeks to test whether the therapist is another supposedly trustworthy adult who may betray him or her. Issues of trust and betrayal may manifest themselves in the therapist's relationship with the parents as well, as they deal with their distress at inadvertently having placed their child in a damaging situation, and with their concern that future caretakers for their children keep the children's best interests as primary.

3. *Therapists should keep in mind that extrafamilial abuse has major ramifications for the marital and family systems.* Even though the reported

ritualistic and nonritualistic sexual abuse occurred outside the home, the families of the victims were highly affected. As the parent interviews revealed, parents became obsessed with the abuse allegations at times, and their functioning was impaired in a variety of areas. Sexual and marital relationships were dysfunctional, and there was a great deal of parent–child stress even though the alleged abusers were not family members. Reports from therapists of parental depression, dysfunction, and substance abuse during the postdisclosure period were highly predictive of child functioning in the aftermath of reported ritualistic sexual abuse. Therefore, it is vitally important to reach out with treatment resources to the families of children who report extrafamilial child sexual abuse, rather than to assume that since an alleged perpetrator is not a family member, the parents will not suffer the disruption and distress that follows disclosure of incest.

4. *Disclosure of sexual abuse must be seen as a process, and recantation is sometimes a part of the process.* Our findings that disclosures occur over time and may follow distinctive patterns, if replicated, would be useful for a variety of investigators, including police, therapists, social workers, and district attorneys. Particularly important is the finding that recantations may occur over time, and that these are almost always followed by redisclosure. Even in the SA group, where the perpetrator admitted abusing children and was sentenced to four life terms in prison, 23% of the children recanted their allegations at some time during the course of treatment. These findings broaden Summit's (1983) concept of the "child abuse accommodation syndrome"; they show that even children reporting molestation outside of the home experience pressures to recant their disclosures in the wake of family, community, and legal response.

5. *Long-term follow-up studies must be carried out to clarify issues for children at various developmental stages.* It is clear from follow-up interviews with the families that the needs and issues of children reporting sexual abuse are different at various developmental stages. For example, although children were exhibiting a great deal of sexualized behavior in the aftermath of abuse disclosure, these behaviors decreased significantly as the children reached their preteen years. It would be helpful to follow these children in midadolescence and again in early adulthood, to chart their sexuality and aggression as they progress through different developmental stages and their ability to form trusting relationships.

Whereas many have talked about the developmental hurdles that sexually abused children must negotiate, little empirical information exists on the patterns that particular children go through over time. Not only behaviors need to be examined, but also the sense of self, attitudes, fears, and expectations. The RSA group of children would be especially interesting to follow from a developmental viewpoint, since they all reported experiencing ritualistic sexual abuse during the same very early developmental stage (the preschool years—$2^1/2$ to 5 years of age).

6. *Families can take specific, effective steps to promote healing from reported ritualistic sexual abuse.* From the data obtained in this study, especially from parent interviews, four steps seem particularly vital in helping assure positive outcome. First, psychotherapy for the children was seen as the most helpful step, and the parents felt it was extremely important to obtain support for themselves too—from professionals, family, and friends. Second, a child who reports abuse requires a great deal of support, and parents should keep in mind the perspective of the child. He or she will not feel supported by extensive questioning about the abuse, or by advocacy activities that take a parent away from home a great deal, even though these actions are meant to be supportive. Third, overt and hostile family conflict should be minimized whenever possible. There will be increased strains and tensions, and if the family members can focus on supporting one another and weathering this crisis together, the outcome will be more positive. Fourth, parents should empower themselves and their children as much as possible. Parents who mobilize themselves to get needed resources, reframe problems to maximize finding positive solutions, and remain optimistic about getting through the trauma will help their children get through it optimally as well.

7. *Children do heal.* Although 17% of the children in the RSA group remained in the clinical range on total behavior problems at the 5-year follow-up, 83% were not exhibiting clinically significant symptoms. The children had all received psychotherapy and been part of generally healthy, resourceful families. It is important to keep in mind that most children recover and should not be subjected to the stigmatization associated with the label "sexual abuse victims." Many of these children had been thus labeled in a very public fashion, because of the controversy and publicity that dogged them for years. Follow-up interviews with parents 5 years after initial disclosure revealed that most children were getting on with their lives successfully. Families, however, need to be aware that abuse-related issues may reemerge at various developmental stages for their children (e.g., adolescence, as sexuality is explored; young adulthood, as issues of intimacy and development of love relationships arise). It is important to convey a message of hope, justified by our findings, that despite the overwhelming nature of reports of terrorizing and ritualistic activities and highly intrusive sexual abuse, children and parents often show great courage in confronting the adversity. As they heal, they may emerge from their traumas more self-aware and closer to their families.

REFERENCES

Abel, G. G., Becker, J. V., Mittelman, M., Cunningham-Rathner, J., Rouleau, J. L., & Murphy, W. D. (1987). Self-reported sex crimes of nonincarcerated paraphiliacs. *Journal of Interpersonal Violence*, 2(1), 3–25.

Achenbach, T. M., & Edelbrock, C. S. (1983). *Manual for the Child Behavior Checklist and Child Behavior Profile*. Burlington: University of Vermont, Department of Psychiatry.

Achenbach, T. M., & Edelbrock, C. S. (1986). *Manual for the Teacher Report Form of the Child Behavior Checklist and Teacher Version of the Child Behavior Profile*. Burlington: University of Vermont, Department of Psychiatry.

Adams-Tucker, C. (1981). A sociological overview of 28 sex-abused children. *Child Abuse and Neglect*, 5, 361–367.

Adams-Tucker, C. (1982). Proximate effects of sexual abuse in childhood: A report on 28 children. *American Journal of Psychiatry*, 139, 1252–1256.

Allen, C. L. (1990, February 26). Children's veracity cross-examined. *Insight*, pp. 50–53.

Alter–Reid, K., Gibbs, M. S., Lachenmeyer, J. R., Sigal, J., & Massoth, N. A. (1986). Sexual abuse of children: A review of the empirical findings. *Clinical Psychology Review*, 6, 249–266.

American Psychiatric Association. (1980). *Diagnostic and statistical manual of mental disorders* (3rd ed.). Washington, DC: Author.

American Psychiatric Association. (1987). *Diagnostic and statistical manual of mental disorders* (3rd ed., rev.). Washington, DC: Author.

Anderson, S. C., Bach, C. M., & Griffith, S. (1981, April). *Psychosocial sequelae in intrafamilial victims of sexual assault and abuse*. Paper presented at the Third International Conference on Child Abuse and Neglect, Amsterdam, the Netherlands.

Bagley, C., & Ramsay, R. (1985, February). *Disrupted childhood and vulnerability to sexual assault: Long term sequelae with implications for counseling*. Paper presented at the conference on Counseling the Sexual Abuse Survivor, Winnipeg, Manitoba, Canada.

Bagley, C., & Ramsay, R. (1986). Sexual abuse in childhood: Psychosocial outcomes and implications for social work practice. *Journal of Social Work and Human Sexuality*, 4, 33–47.

Basta, S. M. (1986). *Personality characteristics of molested children*. Unpublished doctoral dissertation, University of Nevada at Reno.

Basta, S. M., & Peterson, R. F. (1990). Perpetrator status and the personality characteristics of molested children. *Child Abuse and Neglect, 14*, 555–566.

Beery, K. E. (1982). *Revised administration, scoring and teaching manual for the Developmental Test of Visual–Motor Integration*. Cleveland, OH: Modern Curriculum Press.

Bell, A., Weinberg, M., & Hammersmith, S. (1981). *Sexual preference: Its development in men and women*. Bloomington: Indiana University Press.

Ben-Meir, S. (1989). *Emotional functioning in children alleging ritualistic sexual abuse in preschool*. Unpublished doctoral dissertation, University of California at Los Angeles.

Berliner, L., & Wheeler, J. R. (1987). Treating the effects of sexual abuse on children. *Journal of Interpersonal Violence, 2*, 415–434.

Blake-White, J., & Kline, C. M. (1985). Treating the dissociative process in adult victims of childhood incest. *Social Casework: The Journal of Contemporary Social Work, 66*, 394–402.

Bolton, F. G., Morris, L. A., & MacEachron, A. E. (1989). *Males at risk: The other side of child sexual abuse*. Newbury Park, CA: Sage.

Brandt, R., & Tisza, V. B. (1978). The sexually misused child. *American Journal of Orthopsychiatry, 48*, 80–90.

Brassard, M. R., Tyler, A., & Kehle, T. J. (1983). Sexually abused children: Identification and suggestions for intervention. *School Psychology Review, 12*, 93–97.

Brenner, A. (1984). *Helping children cope with stress*. Lexington, MA: Lexington Books.

Briere, J. (1984, April). *The effects of childhood sexual abuse on later psychological functioning: Defining a post-sexual abuse syndrome*. Paper presented at the Third National Conference on Sexual Victimization of Children, Washington, DC

Briere, J. (1988). The long-term clinical correlates of childhood sexual victimization. *Annals of the New York Academy of Sciences, 528*, 327–334.

Briere, J., & Runtz, M. (1985, August). *Symptomatology associated with prior sexual abuse in a nonclinical sample*. Paper presented at the 93rd Annual Convention of the American Psychological Association, Los Angeles.

Briere, J., & Runtz, M. (1986). Suicidal thoughts and behaviors in former sexual abuse victims. *Canadian Journal of Behavioral Science, 18*, 413–423.

Briere, J., & Runtz, M. (1987). Post-sexual abuse trauma: Data and implications for clinical practice. *Journal of Interpersonal Violence, 2*, 367–379.

Browne, A., & Finkelhor, D. (1986). Initial and long term effects: A review of the research. In D. Finkelhor (Ed.), *A sourcebook on child sexual abuse* (pp. 143–179). Beverly Hills, CA: Sage.

Burgess, A. W., & Grant, C. A. (1988). *Children traumatized in sex rings*. Washington, DC: National Center for Missing and Exploited Children.

Burgess, A. W., Groth, A. N., & McCausland, M. P. (1981). Child sex initiation rings. *American Journal of Orthopsychiatry, 51*, 129–133.

Burgess, A. W., Hartman, C. R., McCausland, M. P., & Powers, P. (1984). Response patterns in children and adolescents exploited through sex rings and pornography. *American Journal of Psychiatry, 141*, 656–662.

Burgess, A. W., & Holmstrom, L. (1978). Sexual trauma of children and adolescents. *Nursing Clinics of North America, 10*, 551–563.

Burns, R. C. and Kaufman, S. H. (1972). *Actions, Styles and Symbols in Kinetic-Family-Drawings (KFD): An Interpretive Manual.* New York: Brunner-Mazel.

Bygrave, M. (1990, February 11). McMartin: California's Cleveland. *The Sunday Correspondent* (London, England), pp. 38–46.

Caffey, J. (1946). Multiple fractures in long bones of infants suffering from chronic subdural hematoma. *American Journal of Roentgenology, 56*, 163–173.

Campbell, B. (1990, October 5). Ritual abuse: Vortex of evil. *The New Statesman and Society* (London, England), pp. 12–15.

Christensen, A., & Shenk, J. (1988). *Parent Perception Inventory—Parent Version.* Unpublished manuscript, University of California at Los Angeles.

Cockburn, A. (1990, February 12). Out of the mouths of babes: Child abuse and the abuse of adults. *The Nation*, pp. 190–191.

Cohen, J. A., & Mannarino, A. P. (1988). Psychological symptoms in sexually abused girls. *Child Abuse and Neglect, 12*, 571–577.

Coleman, L. (1986, January–February). False allegations of child sexual abuse: Have the experts been caught with their pants down? *Forum: Journal of the California Attorneys for Criminal Justice*, pp. 12–22.

Connell, J. P. (1985). A new multi-dimensional measure of children's perceptions of control. *Child Development, 56*, 1018–1041.

Conte, J. (1985). The effects of sexual abuse on children: A critique and suggestions for future research. *Victimology: An International Journal, 10*, 110–130.

Conte, J., & Schuerman, J. (1987). The effects of sexual abuse on children: A multidimensional view. *Journal of Interpersonal Violence, 2*, 380–390.

Courtois, C. A. (1986, May). *Treatment of serious mental health sequelae of child sexual abuse: Post-traumatic stress disorder in children and adults.* Paper presented at the Fourth National Conference on Sexual Victimization of Children, New Orleans.

Courtois, C. A., & Watts, D. L. (1982). Counseling adult women who experienced incest in childhood or adolescence. *Personnel and Guidance Journal, 60*, 275–279.

Crewdson, J. (1988). *By silence betrayed: Sexual abuse of children in America.* Boston: Little, Brown.

Damon, L., Todd, J., & MacFarlane, K. (1987). Treatment issues with sexually abused young children. *Child Welfare, 66*(2), 125–137.

DeFrancis, V. (1969). *Protecting the child victim of sex crimes committed by adults.* Denver, CO: American Humane Association.

DeJong, A. R., Hervada, A. R., & Emmett, G. A. (1983). Epidemiological variation in childhood sexual abuse. *Child Abuse and Neglect, 7*, 155–162.

deYoung, M. (1982). Innocent seducer or innocently seduced? The role of the child incest victim. *Journal of Clinical Child Psychology, 11*, 56–60.

DiPietro, S. B. (1987). The effects of intrafamilial child sexual abuse on the adjustment and attitudes of adolescents. *Violence and Victims, 2*, 59–78.

Dixen, J. & Jenkins, J. O. (1981). Incestuous child sexual abuse: A review of treatment stategies. *Clinical Psychology Review, 1,* 211–222.

Dunn, L. M., & Markwardt, F. C. (1970). *Peabody Individual Achievement Test.* Circle Pines, MN: American Guidance Service.

Eberle, P., & Eberle, S. (1986). *The politics of child abuse.* Secaucus, NJ: Lyle Stuart.

Editorial. (1988, February 26). Judge–DA dispute must be resolved for public good. *Reno Gazette-Journal.*

Elizur, A. (1949). Content analysis of the Rorschach with regard to anxiety and hostility. *Rorschach Research Exchange and Journal of Projective Techniques, 13,* 247–284.

Eme, R. F. (1979). Sex differences in childhood psychopathology: A review. *Psychological Bulletin, 86,* 574–595.

Erickson, M. F. (1986, August). *Young sexually abused children: Socio-emotional development and family interaction.* Paper presented at the 94th Annual Convention of the American Psychological Association, Washington, DC.

Eth, S., & Pynoos, R. S. (1985). Developmental perspective on psychic trauma in childhood. In C. R. Figley (Ed.), *Trauma and its wake* (pp. 36–52). New York: Brunner/Mazel.

Exner, J. E. (1986). *The Rorschach: A Comprehensive System. Vol. 1: Basic Foundations (2nd ed.).* New York: Wiley.

Exner, J. E., & Weiner, I. B. (1982). *The Rorschach: A Comprehensive System. Vol. 3. Assessment of children and adolescents.* New York: Wiley.

Faller, K. C. (1987). *Child sexual abuse: An interdisciplinary manual for diagnosis, case management, and treatment.* New York: Columbia University Press.

Finkelhor, D. (1984). *Child sexual abuse: New theory and research.* New York: Free Press.

Finkelhor, D. (Ed.). (1986). *A sourcebook on child sexual abuse.* Beverly Hills, CA: Sage.

Finkelhor, D. (1987). The trauma of child sexual abuse: Two models. *Journal of Interpersonal Violence, 2,* 348–366.

Finkelhor, D., & Browne, A. (1985). The traumatic impact of child sexual abuse: A conceptualization. *American Journal of Orthopsychiatry, 55*(4), 530–541.

Finkelhor, D., & Browne, A. (1986). Initial and long-term effects: A conceptual framework. In D. Finkelhor (Ed.), *A sourcebook on child sexual abuse.* Beverly Hills, CA: Sage.

Finkelhor, D., Williams, L., & Burns, N. (1988). *Nursery crimes: Sexual abuse in daycare.* Newbury Park, CA: Sage.

Fischer, M. A. (1989, October). McMartin: A case of dominoes? *California,* pp. 126–135.

Frederick, C. J. (1986). Post-traumatic stress disorder and child molestation. In A. W. Burgess & C. Hartman (Eds.), *Sexual exploitation of clients by mental health professionals* (pp. 133–144). New York: Praeger.

Friedrich, W. N., Beilke, R. L., & Urquiza, A. J. (1987). Children from sexually abusive families: A behavioral comparison. *Journal of Interpersonal Violence, 2,* 391–402.

Friedrich, W. N., Beilke, R. L., & Urquiza, A. J. (1988). Behavior problems in young sexually abused boys. *Journal of Interpersonal Violence, 3,* 21–28.

Friedrich, W. N., Grambsch, P., Broughton, D., Kuiper, J., & Beilke, R. L. (1991). Normative sexual behavior in children. *Pediatrics*, 88, 456–464.

Friedrich, W. N., & Reams, R. A. (1987). The course of psychological symptoms in sexually abused young children. *Psychotherapy: Theory, Research, and Practice*, 24, 160–170.

Friedrich, W. N., Urquiza, A. J., & Beilke, R. L. (1986). Behavior problems in sexually abused young children. *Journal of Pediatric Psychology*, 11, 47–57.

Gelinas, D. J. (1983). The persisting negative effects of incest. *Psychiatry*, 46, 312–332.

Gislason, I. L., & Call, J. D. (1982). Dog bite in infancy: Trauma and personality development. *Journal of the American Academy of Child Psychiatry*, 21, 203–207.

Gold, E. R. (1986). Long-term effects of sexual victimization in childhood: An attributional approach. *Journal of Consulting and Clinical Psychology*, 54, 471–475.

Gomes-Schwartz, B., Horowitz, J. M., & Cardarelli, A. P. (1990). *Child sexual abuse: The initial effects*. Newbury Park, CA: Sage.

Gomes-Schwartz, B., Horowitz, J. M., & Sauzier, M. (1985). Severity of emotional distress among sexually abused preschool, school-age, and adolescent children. *Hospital and Community Psychiatry*, 36, 503–508.

Goodman, G. S., Aman, C., & Hirschman, J. (1987). Child sexual and physical abuse: Children's testimony. In M. Toglia, D. F. Ross, & S. Ceci (Eds.), *Children's eyewitness memory*. New York: Springer-Verlag, pp. 1–23.

Goodman, G. S., Rudy, L., Bottoms, B. L., & Aman, C. (1991). Children's concerns and memory: Issues of ecological validity in children's testimony. In R. Fivush & J. Hudson (Eds.), *What young children remember and know* (pp. 249–284). New York: Cambridge University Press.

Goodwin, J. (1984). Incest victims exhibit post-traumatic stress disorder. *Clinical Psychiatry News*, 12, 13.

Gould, C. (1987). Satanic ritual abuse: Child victims, adult survivors, system response. *California Psychologist*, 22, 1.

Gross, M. (1979). Incestuous rape: A cause for hysterical seizures in four adolescent girls. *American Journal of Orthopsychiatry*, 49, 704–708.

Harter, S. (1985). *Manual for the Self-Perception Profile for Children*. Denver, CO: University of Denver.

Harter, S., & Pike, R. (1984). The Pictorial Scale of Perceived Competence and Social Acceptance for Young Children. *Child Development*, 55, 1969–1982.

Haugaard, J. (1988, April). *Children who do and do not reveal sexual abuse experiences*. Paper presented at the National Symposium on Child Victimization, Anaheim, CA.

Hazzard, A., Christensen, A., & Margolin, G. (1983). Children's perceptions of parental behaviors. *Journal of Abnormal Child Psychology*, 11, 49–60.

Hechler, D. (1988). *The battle and the backlash: The child sexual abuse war*. Lexington, MA: Lexington Books.

Heims, L., & Kaufman, I. (1963). Variations on a theme of incest. *American Journal of Orthopsychiatry*, 33, 311–312.

Herman, J. (1981). Father–daughter incest. *Professional Psychologist*, 12, 76–80.

Herman, J., & Hirschman, L. (1977). Father–daughter incest. *Signs, 2*, 735–756.

Herman, J., & Hirschman, L. (1981). *Father–daughter incest*. Cambridge, MA: Harvard University Press.

Hobbs, C. J, & Wynne, J. M. (1989). Sexual abuse of English boys and girls: The importance of the anal examination. *Child Abuse and Neglect, 13*, 195–210.

Hollingshead, A. B. (1975, June). *Four factor index of social status*. Working paper.

Horowitz, M. (1974). Stress response syndrome. *Archives of General Psychiatry, 31*, 768–781.

Humphrey, H. H., III. (1985, February 12). *Report of the Scott County investigations*. St. Paul: Minnesota Attorney General's Office.

Hunt, P. (1988, April). *Children of sex rings*. Paper presented at the National Symposium on Child Victimization, Anaheim, CA.

Jiles, D. (1981). Problems in the assessment of sexual abuse referrals. In W. Holder (Ed.), *Sexual Abuse of Children*. New York: Pergamon Press.

Johnston, M. S. K. (1979). The sexually mistreated child: Diagnostic evaluation. *Child Abuse and Neglect, 3*, 943–951.

Jones, D. (1986). Individual psychotherapy for the sexually abused child. *Child Abuse and Neglect, 10*, 377–385.

Jones, D., & McGraw, J. M. (1987). Reliable and fictitious accounts of sexual abuse in children. *Journal of Interpersonal Violence, 2*, 27–45.

Jonker, F., & Jonker-Bakker, P. (1991). Experiences with ritualistic child sexual abuse: A case study from The Netherlands. *Child Abuse and Neglect, 15*(3), 191–196.

Jung, C. G. (1954). Problems of modern psychotherapy. In *The collected works of C. G. Jung (Vol. 16)*. London: Routledge & Kegan Paul. (Original work published 1931)

Kagy, L. (1986). Ritualized abuse of children. *RECAP: Newsletter of the National Child Assault Prevention Project, 1–2*.

Katan, A. (1973). Children who were raped. *Psychoanalytic Study of the Child, 28*, 208–224.

Kelley, S. J. (1989). Stress responses of children to sexual abuse and ritualistic abuse in day care centers. *Journal of Interpersonal Violence, 4*, 502–513.

Kelley, S. J. (1990). Parental stress response to sexual abuse and ritualistic abuse of children in day-care centers. *Nursing Research, 39*, 25–29.

Kelly, R. J., Waterman, J., Oliveri, M. K., & McCord, J. (1988, September). *Powerlessness and subsequent fears in victims of alleged ritualistic child sexual abuse*. Paper presented at the Seventh International Congress on Child Abuse and Neglect, Rio de Janeiro.

Kempe, C. H., Silverman, F. N., Steele, B. F., Droegermuller, W., & Silver, H. (1962). The battered child syndrome. *Journal of the American Medical Association, 181*, 17–24.

Kendrick, M. (1988). *Anatomy of a nightmare: The failure of society in dealing with child sexual abuse*. Toronto: Macmillan.

Kent, C. (1988, April). *Presenting symptoms and three year follow-up data of children alleging abuse during the preschool years in multi-victim, multiperpetrator circumstances*. Paper presented at the National Symposium on Child Victimization, Anaheim, CA.

Kercher, G., & McShane, M. (1984). The prevalence of child sexual abuse victimization in an adult sample of Texas residents. *Child Abuse and Neglect, 8*, 495–502.

Kluft, R. P. (1987). An update on multiple personality disorder. *Hospital and Community Psychiatry, 38*, 363–373.

Knittle, B., & Tuana, S. (1980). Group therapy as primary treatment for adolescent victims of intrafamilial sexual abuse. *Clinical Social Work Journal, 4*, 236–242.

Koppitz, E. M. (1968). *Psychological evaluation of human figure drawings.* New York: Grune & Stratton.

Koppitz, E. M. (1984). *Psychological evaluation of human figure drawings by middle school pupils.* New York: Grune & Stratton.

Krentz-Johnston, M. S. (1979). *Non-incestuous sexual abuse of children and its relationship to family dysfunction.* Paper presented at the Fourth National Conference on Child Abuse and Neglect, Los Angeles.

Laird, M., Eckenrode, J., & Doris, J. (1988). *Maltreatment and the academic and social adjustment of school children.* Unpublished manuscript, Cornell University.

Leaman, K. M. (1980). Sexual abuse: The reactions of child and family. In U. S. Department of Health and Human Services (Ed.), *Sexual abuse of children: Selected readings* (DHHS Publication No. OHDS 78-30161, pp. 21–24). Washington, DC: U. S. Government Printing Office.

Lew, M. (1988). *Victims no longer.* New York: Nevraumont.

Lewis, M., & Sarrel, P. M. (1969). Some psychological aspects of seduction, incest, and rape in childhood. *Journal of the American Academy of Child Psychiatry, 8*, 606–619.

Lindberg, F. H., & Distad, L. J. (1985a). Post-traumatic stress disorder in women who experienced childhood incest. *Child Abuse and Neglect, 9*, 329–334.

Lindberg, F. H., & Distad, L. J. (1985b). Survival responses to incest: Adolescents in crisis. *Child Abuse and Neglect, 9*, 521–526.

Lipovsky, J. A., Saunders, B. E., & Murphy, S. M. (1989). Depression, anxiety, and behavior problems among victims of father–child sexual assault and nonabused siblings. *Journal of Interpersonal Violence, 4*, 452–468.

MacFarlane, K. (1986). Helping parents cope with extrafamilial molestation. In K. MacFarlane, J. Waterman, & Associates, *Sexual abuse of young children: Evaluation and treatment* (pp. 299–311). New York: Guilford Press.

Mannarino, A. P., & Cohen, J. A. (1986). A clinical–demographic study of sexually abused children. *Child Abuse and Neglect, 10*, 17–23.

Mannarino, A. P., Cohen, J. A., & Gregor, M. (1989). Emotional and behavioral difficulties in sexually abused girls. *Journal of Interpersonal Violence, 4*, 437–451.

Marron, K. (1988). *Ritual abuse: Canada's most infamous trial on child abuse.* Toronto: Seal Books.

Mattinson, J. (1975). *The reflection process in casework supervision.* London: Institute of Marital Studies, Tavistock Institute of Human Relations.

McArthur, D. S., & Roberts, G. E. (1982). *Roberts Apperception Test for Children.* Los Angeles: Western Psychological Services.

McCann, I. L., & Pearlman, L. A. (1990). Vicarious traumatization: A framework for understanding the psychological effects of working with victims. *Journal of Traumatic Stress, 3,* 131–149.

McCann, I. L., Sakheim, D. K., & Abrahamson, D. J. (1988). Trauma and victimization: a model of psychological adaptation. *The Counseling Psychologist, 16,* 531–594.

McCann, J., Voris, J., Simon, M., & Wells, R. (1989). Perianal findings in prepubertal children selected for nonabuse: A descriptive study. *Child Abuse and Neglect, 13,* 179–194.

McCubbin, H. I., Larsen, A. S., & Olson, D. H. (1982). *F-COPES: Family Coping Strategies.* St. Paul: Department of Family Social Science, University of Minnesota.

McCubbin, H. I., Patterson, J. M., & Wilson, L. R. (1981). *FILE: Family Inventory of Life Events.* St. Paul: Department of Family Social Science, University of Minnesota.

Meiselman, K. C. (1978). *Incest: A psychological study of causes and effects with treatment recommendations.* San Francisco: Jossey-Bass.

Mian, M., Wehrspann, W., Klajner-Diamond, H., LeBaron, D., & Winder, C. (1986). Review of 125 children 6 years of age and under who were sexually abused. *Child Abuse and Neglect, 10,* 223–229.

Miller, L. C. (1974). Phobias of childhood in a prescientific era. In A. Davids (Ed.), *Child personality and psychopathology: Current topics.* New York: Wiley.

Miller, L. C. (1976). Method factors associated with assessment of child behavior: Factor artifact? *Journal of Abnormal Child Psychology, 4,* 209–219.

Miller, L. C., Barrett, C. L., Hampe, E., & Noble, H. (1972). Factor structure of childhood fears. *Journal of Consulting and Clinical Psychology, 2,* 264–268.

Money, J. (1988). Sin, sickness, or status: Homosexual gender identity and psychoneuroendocrinology. *American Psychologist, 42,* 384–399.

Moos, R. H., & Moos, B. A. (1981). *Manual for the Family Environment Scale.* Palo Alto, CA: Consulting Psychologist Press.

Muram, D. (1989). Child sexual abuse: Relationship between sexual acts and genital findings. *Child Abuse and Neglect, 13,* 211–216.

Murphy, S. M., Kilpatrick, D. G., Amick-McMullen, A., Paduhovich, J., Best, C. L., Villeponteaux, L. A., & Saunders, B. E. (1988). Current psychological functioning of child sexual assault survivors: A community survey. *Journal of Interpersonal Violence, 3,* 55–79.

Naglieri, J. A. (1988). *Draw-A-Person: A quantitative scoring system.* San Diego: Psychological Corporation.

Nathan, D. (1987, September 29). Are these women child molesters? The making of a modern witch trial. *The Village Voice* (New York), pp. 19–23, 26–32.

Nathan, D. (1989, April 7–13). False evidence: How bad science fueled the hysteria over child abuse. *L. A. Weekly,* pp. 15–18.

Nathan, D. (1990, June 12). What McMartin started: The ritual sex abuse hoax. *The Village Voice* (New York), pp. 36–42.

Nowicki, S., & Duke, M. F. (1974). A preschool and primary locus of control scale. *Developmental Psychology, 10,* 874–880.

Olson, D. H., & Killorin, E. (1985). *Clinical Rating Scale for the Circumplex Model* of Marital and Family Systems. St. Paul: Department of Family Social Science, University of Minnesota.

Olson, D. H., Portner, J., & Lavee, Y. (1985). FACES-III: Family Adaptability and Cohesion Evaluation Scales. St. Paul: Department of Family Social Science, University of Minnesota.

Overall, J. E., & Pfefferbaum, B. (1982). The Brief Psychiatric Rating Scale for Children. Psychopharmacology Bulletin, 18, 107–109.

Paradise, J. E. (1989). Predictive accuracy and the diagnosis of sexual abuse: A big issue about a little tissue. Child Abuse and Neglect, 13, 169–176.

Pascoe, D. J., & Duterte, B. O. (1981). The medical diagnosis of sexual abuse in the premenarcheal child. Pediatric Annals, 10, 40–45.

Perlmutter, L. H., Engel, T., & Sager, C. J. (1982). The incest taboo: loosened sexual boundaries in remarried families. Journal of Sex and Marital Therapy, 8, 83–96.

Peters, J. J. (1976). Children who are victoms of sexual assault and the psychology of offenders. American Journal of Psychotherapy, 30, 398–421.

Peters, S. D. (1985, August). Child sexual abuse and later psychological problems. Paper presented at the 93rd Annual Convention of the American Psychological Association, Los Angeles.

Putnam, F. W., Guroff, J. J., & Silberman, E. K. (1986). The clinical phenomenology of multiple personality disorder: Review of 100 recent cases. Journal of Clinical Psychiatry, 47, 285–293.

Pynoos, R. S., & Eth, S. (1985). Children traumatized by witnessing acts of personal violence: Homicide, rape, or suicide behavior. In S. Eth & R. S. Pynoos (Eds.), Post-traumatic stress disorder in children (pp. 19–43). Washington, DC: American Psychiatric Press.

Rabinowitz, D. (1990, May). From the mouths of babes to a jail cell. Harpers, pp. 52–63.

Rorty, M., Waterman, J. M., Kelly, R. J., Oliveri, M. K., & McCord, J. (1990, April). Kinetic family drawings of abused and non-abused children, and relationship to family functioning. Paper presented at the National Symposium on Child Victimization, Atlanta.

Rosenbaum, P. R., & Rubin, D. B. (1985). Constructing a control group using multivariate matched sampling methods that incorporate the propensity score. American Statistician, 39, 33–38.

Rosenfeld, A. A., Nadelson, C. C., & Krieger, M. (1979). Fantasy and reality in patients' reports of incest. Journal of Clinical Psychiatry, 40, 159–164.

Rosenfeld, A. A., Nadelson, C. C., Krieger, M., & Backman, J. J. (1977). Incest and sexual abuse of children. Journal of the American Academy of Child Psychiatry, 16, 327–339.

Rosenthal, R., & Rosnow, R. L. (1984). Essentials of behavioral research: Methods and data analysis. New York: McGraw-Hill.

Russell, D. E. H. (1983). The incidence and prevalence of intrafamilial and extrafamilial sexual abuse of female children. Child Abuse and Neglect, 7, 133–146.

Russell, D. E. H. (1986). The secret trauma: Incest in the lives of girls and women. New York: Basic Books.

Sattler, J. M. (1988). Assessment of children (3rd ed.). San Diego: Author.

Saywitz, K. J. (1990). The child as witness: Experimental and clinical considerations. In A. LaGreca (Ed.), Through the eyes of the child (pp. 329–367). Boston: Allyn & Bacon.

Saywitz, K. J., Goodman, G. S., & Myers, J. E. B. (1990, September). Can children provide accurate eyewitness reports? Violence Update, 1, 8–11.

Saywitz, K. J., Goodman, G. S., Nicholas, E., & Moan, S. (1991). Children's memories of a physical examination involving genital touch: Implications for reports of child sexual abuse. Journal of Consulting and Clinical Psychology, 59, 682–691.

Schetky, D. H. (1978). Preschoolers' response to murder of their mothers by their fathers: A study of four cases. Bulletin of the American Academy of Psychiatry and Law, 6, 45–47.

Searles, H. F. (1965). The informational value of the supervisor's emotional experience. Collected Papers on Schizophrenia and Related Subjects. Hogarth Press.

Sedney, M. A., & Brooks, B. (1984). Factors associated with a history of childhood sexual experience in a nonclinical female population. Journal of the American Academy of Child Psychiatry, 23, 215–218.

Sgroi, S. M. (1982). Handbook of clinical intervention in child sexual abuse. Lexington, MA: Lexington Books.

Shaffer, D., Gould, M. S., Brasic, J., Ambrosini, P., Fisher, P., Bird, H., & Aluwahlia, S. (1985). A Children's Global Assessment Scale (CGAS). Psychopharmacology Bulletin, 21, 747–748.

Shapiro, J. P., Leifer, M., Martone, M. W., & Kassem, L. (1990). Multimethod assessment of depression in sexually abused girls. Journal of Personality Assessment, 55, 234–248.

Shapiro, J. P., Leifer, M., Martone, M. W., & Kassem, L. (1992). Cognitive functioning and social competence as predictors of maladjustment in sexually abused girls. Journal of Interpersonal Violence, 7, 156–165.

Shaw, V. L., & Meier, J. H. (1983). The effect of type of abuse and neglect on children's psychosocial development. Unpublished manuscript, Children's Village, U. S. A., Beaumont, California.

Siegel, J. M., Sorenson, S. B., Golding, J. M., Burnam, M. A., & Stein, J. A. (1987). The prevalence of childhood sexual assault: The Los Angeles Epidemiologic Catchment Area Project. American Journal of Epidemiology, 126, 1141–1153.

Sorenson, T., & Snow, B. (1991). How children tell: The process of disclosure in child sexual abuse. Child Welfare, 70(1), 3–15.

Steele, B. F., & Alexander, H. (1981). Long term effects of sexual abuse in childhood. In P. B. Mrazek & C. H. Kempe (Eds.), Sexually abused children and their families (pp. 223–234). Elmsford, NY: Pergamon Press.

Strieff, S. (1988, April). Ritualistic abuse: Its victims and the professional's response. Paper presented at the National Symposium on Child Victimization, Anaheim, CA.

Summit, R. (1983). The child sexual abuse accommodation syndrome. Child Abuse and Neglect, 7, 177–193.

Terr, L. (1979). Children of Chowchilla: A study of psychic trauma. *Psychoanalytic Study of the Child*, 34, 547–623.

Terr, L. (1981). "Forbidden games": Post-traumatic child's play. *Journal of the American Academy of Child Psychiatry*, 20, 741–760.

Terr, L. (1983a). Chowchilla revisited: The effects of psychic trauma four years after a school bus kidnapping. *American Journal of Psychiatry*, 140, 1543–1550.

Terr, L. (1983b). Life attitudes, dreams, and psychic trauma in a group of "normal" children. *Journal of the American Academy of Child Psychiatry*, 22, 221–230.

Terr, L. (1983c). Time sense following psychic trauma: A clinical study of 10 adults and 20 children. *American Journal of Orthopsychiatry*, 53, 244–261.

Terr, L. (1984). Time and trauma. *Psychoanalytic Study of the Child*, 39, 633–665.

Terr, L. (1985). Children traumatized in small groups. In S. Eth & R. S. Pynoos (Eds.), *Post-traumatic stress disorder in children* (pp. 45–70). Washington, DC: American Psychiatric Press.

Terry, W. (1990, January). *Victim minimization or exaggeration: A comparison of victim and perpetrator accounts*. Paper presented at the Health Science Response to Child Maltreatment Conference (with American Professional Society on Abuse of Children), San Diego.

Timnick, L. (1985a, August 25). 22% in survey were child abuse victims. *Los Angeles Times*, p. 1.

Timnick, L. (1985b, August 26). Children's abuse reports reliable, most believe. *Los Angeles Times*, p. 1.

Tong, L., Oates, K., & McDowell, M. (1987). Personality development following sexual abuse. *Child Abuse and Neglect*, 11, 371–383.

Tsai, M., & Wagner, N. (1978). Therapy groups for women sexually molested as children. *Archives of Sexual Behavior*, 7, 417–429.

Underwager, R. C. (1985, July 30). Deposition in the case of the State of Florida vs. Francisco Fuster Escalona. Circuit Court of the Eleventh Judicial Circuit in and for Dade County, Criminal Division, Case No. 84-19728, A and B.

Update. (1990, July). Defense expert excluded. *National Center for the Prosecution of Child Abuse*, p. 1.

Urquiza, A. J., & Crowley, C. (1986, May). *Sex differences in the survivors of childhood sexual abuse*. Paper presented at the Fourth National Conference on the Sexual Victimization of Children, New Orleans.

Valliere, P. M., Bybee, D., & Mowbray, C. T. (1988, April). *Using the Achenbach Child Behavior Checklist in child sexual abuse research: Longitudinal and comparative analyses*. Paper presented at the National Symposium on Child Victimization, Anaheim, CA.

Van Gijseghem, H. (1978). Father–daughter incest. *Vie Médicale au Canada Francais*, 4, 263–271.

Wakefield, H., & Underwager, R. C. (1988). *Accusations of Child Sexual Abuse*. Springfield, IL: Charles C Thomas.

Wakefield, H., & Underwager, R. C. (1989). *The real world of child interrogations*. Springfield, IL: Charles C Thomas.

Waterman, J. M., Kelly, R. J., Erhardt, D., McCord, J., & Oliveri, M. K. (1988, September). *Human figure drawings of allegedly sexually abused and nonabused children.* Paper presented at the Seventh International Congress on Child Abuse and Neglect, Rio de Janeiro.

Waterman, J. M., Kelly, R. J., McCord, J., & Oliveri, M. K. (1988, April). *Therapists' descriptions of alleged molestations in Manhattan Beach preschools.* Paper presented at the National Symposium on Child Victimization, Anaheim, CA

Waterman, J. M., & Lusk, R. (1993). Psychological testing in evaluation of child sexual abuse. *Child Abuse and Neglect, 17,* 145–159.

Waterman, J. M., & Lusk, R. (1986). Scope of the problem. In K. MacFarlane, J. Waterman, & Associates, *Sexual abuse of young children: Evaluation and Treatment.* (pp. 3–12). New York: Guilford Press.

Wechsler, D. (1974). *Wechsler Intelligence Scale for Children—Revised.* New York: Psychological Corporation.

Weinberg, S. K. (1955). *Incest Behavior.* New York: Citadel.

Weiss, J., Rogers, E., Darwin, M. R., & Dutton, D. E. (1955). A study of girl sex victims. *Psychiatric Quarterly, 29,* 1–26.

White, S., Halpin, B., Strom, G., & Santilli, G. (1986, May). *Behavioral characteristics of young sexually abused, neglected, and nonreferred children.* Paper presented to the Fourth National Conference on the Sexual Victimization of Children, New Orleans.

White, S. T., Ingram, D. L., & Lyna, P. R. (1989). Vaginal introital diameter in the evaluation of sexual abuse. *Child Abuse and Neglect, 13,* 217–224.

Yates, A. (1982). Children eroticized by incest. *American Journal of Psychiatry, 139,* 482–485.

Zivney, O. A., Nash, M. R., & Hulsey, T. (1988). Sexual abuse in early versus late childhood: Differing patterns of pathology as revealed on the Rorschach. *Psychotherapy, 25*(1), 99–106.

INDEX